Women Take Charge

Asserting Your Rights in the Marketplace

By Nina Easton

Preface by Ralph Nader

Research by Debbie Smolover
Heidi Halleck
Evelyn Pursley

Edited by Ronald Brownstein

Cover by Chuck Myers

Center for Study of Responsive Law
Washington, D.C.

Published by:

Center for Study of Responsive Law
P.O. Box 19367
Washington, D.C. 20036   Price: $6.50

ISBN #0-936758-09-0

Special thanks to the following for materials reprinted: Federal Trade Commission, National Women's Health Center, Pension Rights Center, National
Insurance Consumer's Organization, Estelle Ramey, E. C. Publications, Inc.,
1980 President's Advisory Committee on Women.

TABLE OF CONTENTS

PREFACE

—A woman declares that her doctor treats her in a very condescending manner, prescribes tranquilizers and says her problems are mostly emotional.

—A federal judge's wife relates that she never brings in her own car to the repair shop without her husband.

—A woman applying for a loan to start a cosmetics business is told by the banker that she should file a joint application with her husband because the bank would not "loan money to a woman to sell cosmetics."

—A department store shopper complains that women's jeans, blouses and shoes are more poorly constructed, have less material, but cost more than comparable men's wear.

—A woman walks into a department store and tells the salesman that she wants to buy comfortable shoes; the salesman asks her: "What's wrong with your feet?"

—A venerable medical school so-called joke: "What are the symptoms for a hysterectomy? Answer: A Blue Shield card and $200."

—Podiatrists report women—their major customers—complain that their feet hurt, that they have developed bunions and lower back problems, yet they continue to wear cramped, pointed-toe shoes perched on three- or four-inch stiletto heels.

—Men's voices in television advertisements advise women on everything from how to become 'beautiful' to household cleaning materials. In most ads men are shown as assertive, intelligent, powerful individuals, while women are shown as sex objects, dependent, ornamental beings for men's pleasure or appraisal.

—A family was travelling across the country in their station-wagon and stopped at a service station. The father went to the restroom. An attendant came out, saw only the mother and children in the car, and began telling her that the car had a serious engine problem that had to be fixed promptly. When the father returned, the attendant immediately retracted his analysis.

It is not surprising if these episodes bring to mind familiar recollections. Many of the durable cultural stereotypes of female flightiness, hysteria, insecurity, ignorance, hypochondria, and inexperience still endure, notwithstanding the recent expansion of women's rights and roles. Progress against sexism has been grossly exaggerated when reality, rather than rhetoric, is measured. In no place is this ingrained sexism more widespread and less publicized than in the marketplace. The stereotypes themselves have become full-blown merchandising strategies supported by billions of dollars of design and promotion to turn them into profits for the sellers, or to exclude women from a comparable right to services such as credit and insurance.

Women Take Charge by Nina Easton invites the reader to explore in economic sector after sector—clothing, advertising, health, credit, and many consumer services from auto repair to legal counseling—the ways women are being harmed, cheated and manipulated because they are women.

Attention to the area of gender and markets has not been as broad and deep as desirable due to glib obfuscations of the real problems. Obfuscations wrapped up in phrases such as: "Well, women like fashion and style"; "Women will pay a lot more than men"; "Women are just more emotional, you know, it's just part of being feminine"; "Women just don't know about technical things like cars or plumbing or the law."

Over the years I have received letters from women who recite these words in order to denounce them, in order to declare their resentment at continually being treated as a lower order of intelligence. They want to tell the stores, the offices, the companies, and the rest of the male world that this cruel, wasteful, destructive and unjust nonsense has got to stop.

There has been some response over the past decade. Laws such as the Equal Credit Opportunity Act of 1975 have been passed. Women moving into the legal and medical professions, as well as other trades, in greater numbers have helped chip away at long-held biases. The quest for sensible and comfortable clothes is certainly more widespread than the bygone years of the 19th century when Victorian women wore corsets so tight their lungs sometimes collapsed and the ribs were fractured or deformed.

But gender-based selling, where none is called for, has a way of bouncing back at the Main Street level, regardless of what laws are on the books or what liberationist attitudes are on display by both buyers and sellers. Laws to curb such damaging discrimination are ideals which never run as deeply as the debilitating cultural roles and attitudes they are meant to change. All societies are witness to that phenomenon. The purposes of such laws are best achieved through awareness, arousal and action by the victims—in this case by sharper shopping and questioning and acting toward a new daily routing of challenging bias in the marketplace. If more women individually reject the notion that to have taste means you can be taken, or that vulnerabilities are fair game for a targeted marketing campaign ("You've come a long way, baby," says Virginia Slims, playing on women's desires to be both slim and "liberated") then the practice of change becomes widely emulated. Little girls begin to learn these wiser ways from their mothers. Ever less gradually, the billions of dollars of wasteful promotion, poor quality merchandise, unnecessary surgery and drugs, together with much spending to repair or counter the "gender-gouging" built into the economy, would be squeezed out. Health, safety, efficiency and more proactive (rather than reactive) buying behavior would be advanced.

As this book demonstrates, sellers time and time again will choose to exploit women's vulnerabilities, anxieties and passive self-images as long as they can profitably get away with it. If such marketing approaches come up against the rugged terrain of women taking charge, then sellers will have to win their sales by concentrating more on quality, durability, price competition, safety, truth, competent service and useful product information. Whether it is the making of shoes, cosmetics, and clothing for women, or in the provision of medical, financial, repair or other services, the result on the overall economy would be a superior quality of living and labor standards. Which, after all, is what the economy should be producing, especially at a time of high unemployment and recession.

The Center for Study of Responsive Law is publishing *Women Take Charge* in support of equity in the marketplace. Nina Easton's introductory suggestions are meant as guides for readers to obtain the greatest use from this volume. We welcome reports of your own experiences and observations.

Ralph Nader
Washington, D.C.
December, 1982

HOW TO USE THIS BOOK

Women Take Charge is designed to shed some light on common problems that women face as consumers: how you are treated by your doctor, your lawyer, your auto repair shop, your bank, the local department stores, and advertisers. Sometimes that treatment may be merely annoying; other times it can cause serious financial, even physical, harm.

This book does not assert that *all* women face these kinds of discrimination in *all* aspects of their daily life. (Indeed, some women insist they are untouched.) Rather, it is an overview of many of the problems about which women complain; it is the story of the millions of women who do fall victim to discriminatory practices. Neither is this report based on broad statistical surveys of women as consumers; unfortunately there is little academic work in this important field. Instead, *Women Take Charge* draws upon studies and writings aimed specifically at certain areas such as healthcare and legal services, and on our own discussions with experts on women's issues in each of the sections covered, as well as letter interviews with dozens of women around the country.

The volume is also designed to awaken women to forms of discrimination they never considered. Ask yourself these questions: When you take your car or home appliance in for repair, do you bring along your boyfriend or husband as back-up? Many women do, realizing through experience that they are vulnerable to attempts at fraud. Have you ever been told by a doctor that your real physical pains are just "emotional" or "psychological"? Sometimes doctors, trained by textbooks and instructors that perpetuate myths about women's physiology, will mistakenly accuse their female patients of exaggerating or imagining their symptoms. Have you ever asked yourself, or a salesperson, why the selection of women's shoes is limited to poor quality, often dangerous styles? Is it really just because we are more "fashionable" than men?

This volume is divided into six chapters. The first, *Advertising,* and the second, *Fashion,* should be carefully reviewed by all readers as they pertain to the everyday-life of each of us. Through this discussion, we hope you will better understand why women are still typecast throughout the marketplace as frivolous, decorative beings who are intellectually inferior to men.

The subsequent four chapters pinpoint common problems in specific areas: *Finance* (credit, pensions, insurance); *Consumer Services* (auto, home and appliance repairs); *Health* (doctor-patient relationships, the phenomenon of overdrugging and overoperating on women); and *Legal* (access to the legal system and lawyer-client relationships). You will probably find that only one or two of these areas apply to your immediate needs. But you will want to keep the book on hand as a reference tool, in case you or a friend encounter difficulties in another area.

But *Women Take Charge* is more than an enumeration of forms of discrimination. It is also an action guide, with which women can begin taking control of situations as consumers. Therefore, at the end of each chapter is a section called "Taking Charge" which gives some specific recommendations to women.

Interested readers should glance through each of the "Taking Charge" sections, whether or not they seem immediately applicable, since they contain some pertinent information. For example, if married do you know whether or not you have established your own credit history? Many widowed and divorced women have found themselves unable to obtain loans or credit cards, despite the good credit record of their former husbands. Do you know whether and how much you are covered by your husband's pension in the event of his death? Too often widowed women are shocked to learn that they are ineligible for pension benefits.

The "Taking Charge" sections also include some suggestions that could protect you from unpleasant situations in the future. For example, you may want to start a referral network of competent and trustworthy doctors and lawyers, or repair shops, at your local club, church group or other organization.

In the appendix of the book I have included resource materials, such as lists of helpful organizations, publications, and articles to further an understanding of the problem. Many of the publications listed are free of charge from the government or are available for a modest fee from nonprofit organizations. The materials in the appendix are divided into the same categories as the chapters.

It has been said that the most potent educational force is one that can teach a woman to identify, analyze and thereby resist those conditions that keep her in a second-class position. I hope that this volume will contribute to that educational process, heightening the awareness and understanding of the problem, and providing some means of resistance. I hope also that this will not be the only word on discrimination in the marketplace, but rather the beginning of more inquiry and discussion toward taking charge.

Nina Easton
Washington, D.C.

ADVERTISING

"The most valuable educational experience a woman can have is one which teaches her to identify and analyze—and resist—the conditions in which she lives, the morality she has been taught, the false images of herself received from high art as well as cheap pornography, classic poetry as well as TV commercials."

—Adrienne Rich

Ever since the emergence of mass advertising encouraging people to consume—and to keep consuming—Madison Avenue has instilled in women insecurities and anxiety about their looks, their housekeeping, their relationships, even their natural body processes. In return, the ad makers have offered products that promise to relieve those very feelings of inadequacy it nurtured in the first place.

Advertising has taught men contempt for women and women contempt for themselves. It steals a woman's "love of herself as she is and offers it back to her for the price of a product," writes critic and novelist John Berger.[1]

*How many women feared dishpan hands before Madge warned them about it?

*Who worried about "ring-around-the-collar" until the makers of Wisk told them to? (TV commercial: Woman at a square dance, looking at man's shirt exclaims—"Ring around the collar!" Woman with man winces; later she's seen scrubbing wildly.)[2]

*Were "panty lines" a vital issue for women before Underalls?

*What about feminine odor, of which we all now live in deathly fear? (Ad in *TV Guide:* A couple embracing next to the words, "Female Odor is Everyone's Problem.")

*Who was concerned about how their clothes smelled until Downy Fabric Softener warned women they risked losing the respect of their loved ones if they did not?

*Who ever heard of "split ends" before makers of hair conditioners found them to be an effective means of selling their product? And what ever happened to "split ends"? Now, they have been replaced by the quest for "PH balance."

*Who feared pervasive household germs before the 1920s, when Lysol began warning mothers that even "the doorknobs threaten [children] . . . with disease"?[3]

Advertising has manufactured these concerns in two ways. First it has sharply defined the role of a woman based on old-fashioned stereotypes; then it has defined a woman's success by her achievement in those roles. She is depicted, principally, as a homebody. Anyone who watches daytime television is familiar with the frequency with which women are shown as happy housewives, and the rarity of men depicted doing household chores or caring for children.

Advertising, of course, did not create these stereotypes. But it plays a large role in perpetuating them and encouraging women to fulfill them. "Advertising is the worst offender in perpetuating the image of women as sex symbols and an inferior class of human being," concluded the United Nations Commission on the Status of Women.

TV commercials, according to many studies, portray women most often in family roles, while men are shown in a wide variety of roles, mostly outside the house. "The most common role for a woman is that of family member—wife, mother, grandmother, or daughter," write Matilda Butler and William Paisley in their study, *Women and Mass Media*.[4]

In addition, advertisements generally show women doing only household-related activities—washing dishes, doing laundry, serving dinner—and men as the beneficiaries of these activities.[5] The woman is, in effect, subservient to her husband, and even her children. "Great Scott, Marge!" hollars Harry Cromley from the shower. "We're out of Dial!" The magazine copy continues:

> There are some people who wouldn't dream of starting the day without Dial. Harry Cromley is one of them. After all, Dial does have twice the deodorant ingredient as the #2 brand. To help you face the world. And keep you feeling confident. All day long. *Which is why Mrs. Cromley, bless her heart, tries to make sure Harry doesn't run out of Dial . . .*" (Emphasis added.)

Not only is Marge Harry's maid, she is referred to in a patronizing tone—"bless her heart"—just as one would talk to a child.

A Woman's Place

Since the industrial revolution, women have been trained as the purchasing agents and managers of their households. "While women were cultivated as general purchasing managers for the household, the basic definition of *men* in the ads was as bread-winners, wage earners," writes Stuart Ewen.[6]

During the early part of the 20th century, advertisers offered housewives thousands of new products and machines that promised to free them from household drudgery—vacuum cleaners, toasters, electric blenders, can openers, washing machines. But housework remained a full-time job, as women were exhorted to pay attention to minute details in their household. At the end of the day she would still be exhausted. "Rather than viewing the transformation as labor-saving, it is perhaps more useful to view them as labor changing," writes Ewen.

Walk in any department store and you will be bombarded by women's products—perfumes, cosmetics, handbags, shoes and blouses. But you usually have to search for the men's departments. Department stores are designed for women. (See Fashion chapter.) Household products are pushed on women. Grocery stores are also designed with women in mind. Vance Packard, author of *The Hidden Persuaders,* reports on one research facility that determines which packaging colors most attract women. "According to some psychologists," Packard writes, "a woman's eye is most quickly attracted to items wrapped in red; a man's eye to items wrapped in blue."[7] One package designer insists that women leave their eyeglasses at home when they go shopping so packages should stand out from "the blurred confusion."[8]

A psychiatrist hired by food markets, Gerald Stahl, reported in a 1956 interview with the *New York Times* it takes the average woman 20 seconds to cover an aisle in a supermarket; so a good package design should hypnotize her, with colors like red and yellow or images with a dreamlike quality, like mouthwatering frosted cakes, or sizzling steaks.[9]

"Most of the modern supermarkets by the mid-fifties," Packard notes, "were laid out in a carefully calculated manner so that the high-profit impulse items would be most surely noticed." The problem with designing stores principally for women is that, as he notes, "the only people who are more prone to splurging when they get in a supermarket than housewives are the wives' husbands and children." So products to attract them are strategically placed. The result is that people spend 35 percent more than they intend to in the supermarket, says Packard.

Despite the influx of women into the job market over the past two decades most advertisers have continued to assume that the home is still only a woman's domain. And despite the rise of single men living alone, advertisers still insisted that only women are interested in such things as bathroom cleaners. "I assume that most kitchen products are used by women and that men don't give a damn about them, even bachelors," said one advertising executive. "Since women are the major consumers, the main purpose of such an advertisement is to present a product in an average situation, usually the kitchen, being used by an average type person—the middle class housewife."[10]

He of course neglected to add that advertising has not instilled in men the kinds of fears and anxieties over household cleaning that it has instilled in women. Clean floors and germ free bathrooms have become an obsession for the American housewife.

Advertising has defined the successful housewife in this way. To be an accomplished homemaker, she must have polished floors and furniture—no waxy buildup—bright and sweet-smelling laundry, and shining silver. To be a good mother, her cake has to be moist and the family's toilet paper soft.

It is not any one ad, or even a pool of ads, that is damaging to women's image. As a 1977 study by the Canadian Advertising Advisory Board explained, "it is the cumulative impact of a whole series of commercials showing household products in use, with women demonstrating the products—often with enthusiasm bordering on ecstasy . . . [that viewers] find incredible, hilarious or insulting."

Though household cleanliness is certainly an admirable goal, the study's authors note wryly, "when cleanliness becomes an obsession . . . it reflects a strange set of priorities bordering on emotional ill health."

Women in advertising are commonly depicted as intellectually inferior to men—either dumb blondes or happy housewives. A 1971 study by Alice Courtney and Sarah Lockeretz published in the *Journal of Marketing Research* concluded that in addition to asserting that a woman's place is in the home, advertising in magazines implies that women do not make important decisions, men do; and that women depend on men and need their protection.[11]

Thus, commercials generally use a male voice-over—by one count fully 96 percent of all commercials have male voice-overs[12]—and male authority figures, even for women's products. Everyone is familiar with the Man from Glad zooming in to assist the helpless housewife; or the man who takes away the woman's Clorox, leaving her in a state of helpless anxiety; or the little man on the raft helping the homemaker clean her toilet bowl.

A rugged-looking farmer walks from his work outside into the kitchen where his dutiful wife is baking a pie. She silently spoons LaCreme whipped topping onto a piece of pie and hands it to her husband, who remarks on the product's "real cream taste." Though the commercial is clearly aimed at homemakers, the wife does not say a word. She defers, dutifully.

Authoritative professionals are almost always men: the dentist telling the young woman about "new triple protection Aqua-fresh"; to the oral surgeon explaining impacted wisdom teeth to two young girls, and a female nurse, who beams up at him.

Women are also often depicted as a meddler in men's affairs; the nagging housewife or persnickety mother-in-law is a common sight.

"Fly Me: I'm Barbara"

The second role of a woman in advertising is that of sex-object. In ads aimed at men, sexy young models in skimpy gowns are used as decorative commercial props—for cars, office equipment, stereos, alcohol. *MS*. magazine regularly chastises the worst offenders in its "No Comment" column: the Viking Leisure Products ad with a naked woman stepping into a sauna and copy that reads "Just what you need around the office;" or the scantily clad nymph straddling a man's leg, pulling off his boot, underneath the words, "treat 'em good and they'll treat you good." Are they advertising the boot or the woman?

The 1971 Courtney and Lockeretz study found that advertising teaches the public that men regard women primarily as sex objects and are not interested in them as people. With the prevalence of alluring young blonds saying, "take it off, take it all off," and attractive young stewardesses saying, "Fly me, I'm Barbara," in those days, the study's findings are not surprising. Those types of ads, said media analyst Dr. Jean Kilbourne, have a "cumulative unconscious impact" on the public, preaching that "a woman's body is just another piece of merchandise."[13]

Women, of course, are offered products to enhance their roles as sex objects. "The first duty of a woman is to attract," said a perfume ad from the 1920s.[14] "It does not matter how clever or independent you may be, if you fail to influence the men you meet, consciously or unconsciously, you are not fulfilling your fundamental duty as a woman . . ." Advertisements since then have been more subtle but the message is the same.

John Berger, who has studied images of women everywhere from high art to television commercials, tells how these messages affect men and women:[15] "Men *act* and women *appear*. Women watch themselves being looked at. This determines not only most relations between men and women but also the relation of women to themselves. The surveyor of women in herself is male: the surveyed female. Thus she turns herself into an object—and most particularly an objection of vision: a sight."

Erving Goffman in his 1976 study *Gender Advertisements,* offers some more insights into the differences between the portrayals of men and women in advertisements:

*"Children and women are pictured on floors and beds more often than men." Symbolically they are lower in stature than those in the scene sitting in a chair or standing.

*"In contrived scenes in advertisements, men tend to be located higher than women," symbolizing a higher social place.

*"Women smile more, and more expansively, than men."

*"Men are displayed in formal business and informal gear . . . each guise seems to afford him something he is totally serious about . . . Women in ads seem to have a different relationship to their clothing . . . as though life were a series of costume balls . . . female garb in advertisements locates women as less seriously present in social situations than men."

*"Women are shown mentally drifting away from the physical scene around them while in close physical touch with a male, as though his aliveness to the surroundings and ability to cope are enough for both of them."

*"Women nuzzle children but men apparently do not. Indeed, sometimes, women are pictured nuzzling objects. And, of course, women are pictured nuzzling men."[16]

Changing Times?

Are not these roles that advertising defined for women losing credibility as more women move into the workforce—many taking on professional careers—and more middle-aged homemakers go back to school? Yes and no.

Advertising executive Rena Bartos recently wrote a book, *The Moving Target,* that her colleagues on Madison Avenue have greeted with much interest. Bartos's message is that women *are* becoming more independent and that traditional images in advertising will not appeal to them anymore. "The dramatic increase in the number of working women is one symptom of a more fundamental change in women's self-perceptions," she writes. "Traditionally women have been identified in terms of derived status. Their lives were defined in terms of whose daughter they were and whom they married. It is only in recent years that even the happiest of wives and mothers has also yearned for a sense of self-identity that goes beyond her family role . . . These days wives of some of the most affluent, achieving men are distinctly uncomfortable in social situations when someone asks them: 'And what do you do?' "

Whereas 65 percent of women were housewives and 35 percent worked in 1948, now 41 percent are housewives and 59 percent work. Put simply, the moral of Bartos's work is that very few female business executives will suffer anxiety attacks over waxy buildup.

Bartos's premise that most housewives in the industrial age were *ever* happy just staying home would certainly meet argument from other experts on women's issues (i.e. Betty Friedan, author of *The Feminine Mystique*), but there is no doubt that Bartos's work has had some impact on Madison Avenue. That reassessment, combined with the rise of women as a potent political force, has chipped away at some of the worst biases in advertising.

Convinced by female colleagues like Bartos that they were missing out on a potentially lucrative market, many advertisers are starting to portray women in professional roles and outside the home, while men now change diapers and clean bathrooms and clothes. But have things changed much?

"No" is the emphatic answer of Jean Kilbourne. "I've done content analysis [of ads] and it has not changed to the extent we think. Women are still overwhelmingly shown in the home and as sex objects."

Today, though, more women are trying to change the images they see in advertising. *MS.* magazine's "No Comment" column, for example, is a powerful forum for making the producers of overtly sexist ads look foolish, out of step with contemporary society.

But just as dangerous—yet largely overlooked—are the ads *inside MS.* and almost every other magazine in America, as well as on TV. Those are the advertisements that portray women as sex objects, but are aimed *at* women, the ads that hold out the elusive hope that you, too, can and *should,* look like the sexy model in the picture. They propose to each one of us that we are not yet enviable (as Berger phrased it) yet could be. If we buy.

"The sex object," said Jean Kilbourne, "is a mannequin, a shell. Conventional beauty is her only attribute. She has no lines or wrinkles (which are, after all, signs of maturity, of expression and experience), no scars or blemishes—indeed, she has no pores. She is thin, generally tall and long-legged, and, above all, she is young. All 'beautiful' women in advertising (including minority women) regardless of product or audience, comform to that norm."

For years women have aspired to be the glamorous beauties in the Revlon ads; teens aspired to be the pretty young women pushing Maybelline. They have bought moisture whip to remove wrinkles, gloves for dish-pan hands, tummy control top panty hose for bulge. They have covered their gray hairs with Clairol and whittled their waists with diet aids. They religiously followed all five steps of Estee Lauder's face plan. Still, with very, very few exceptions they did not come out looking like Cheryl Tiegs or Lynda Carter or Lauren Hutton.

"Those ads play right on women's sensibilities," complained a frustrated 29-year-old woman. "Madison Avenue has told them once you get a wrinkle, you're ugly. They put these examples up to women, and it's basically impossible for 99 percent of women to reach that level of great physical beauty."

"Women are constantly exhorted to emulate this ideal, to feel ashamed and guilty if they fail, and to feel that their desirability and lovability are contingent upon physical perfection," says Kilbourne.

Madison Avenue has spent lots of time and money to find out our points of vulnerability. Advertisers "are systematically feeling out our hidden weaknesses and frailties in the hope they can more efficiently influence our behavior," writes Vance Packard.[17]

What are the images the ad makers push?

Youth is peddled as compulsory: A man looks distinguished with a little gray around the temples, women look haggard. According to one study only 16 percent of the women shown in television commercials are over 40, while 44 percent of the men shown are over 40.[18] If one were exposed only to the 1,500 advertisements that bombard us each day, one would assume women in America die or go into hiding shortly after age 35.

So is thin. Diet soda, diet pills, diet sweeteners, are all directed principally at women. Drink one-calorie Tab, and look like the pert young blonde with colt-like legs in minishorts who trots by men as their heads turn. Now even vitamins are peddled as the perfect complement to a rigorous diet. Often women receive mixed signals: an ad for luscious Sara Lee cake will run into an ad for diet pills or diet soda. This obsession with body weight has produced in women serious inferiority complexes—since few of us can reach that ideal body—and severe eating disorders. At college campuses about 20 percent of the women suffer from serious eating disorders, either anorexia—a neurotic fear of food that leaves women looking like skeletons—or bulemia—the binge-vomit syndrome.[19]

The advertising industry has cashed in on all these anxieties. One Milwaukee ad executive, says Packard,[20] wrote to his colleagues that women will pay $2.50 for skin cream but only 25 cents for soap. Why? Soap, he explained, only promises to make them clean. The cream promises to make them beautiful. "The women are buying a promise. The cosmetic manufacturers are not selling lanolin, they are selling hope . . . We no longer buy oranges, we buy vitality. We do not buy just an auto, we buy prestige," said the ad executive.

TV consumer reporter Betty Furness demonstrated the profitability of playing on women's anxieties when she displayed an array of skin lotions ranging from 45 cents to $35. A dermatologist had found the ingredients in the products were essentially oil and water, with a bit of various chemicals. The main difference between the 45-cent product and the $35 product was that in the latter the water was purified.[21]

"Females concerned about how they look to men still, in 1980, waste hundreds of millions of dollars on overpriced products of the Hope merchants. The image created by design works and a big ad budget can create fantastic profitability," writes Packard.

The women's political movement has made some inroads into other aspects of sexist advertising, encouraging advertisers to show more working women and women as authority figures. But no one has made a dent in the selling of women as sex objects. The percent of alluring women in advertising has actually *increased* over the last two decades, according to Butler and Paisley.[22]

Advertisers continue to skillfully prey on women's insecurities. But now they show a sexy business executive instead of a secretary. The Charlie girl is free, independent—and beautiful. The attractive Virginia Slims women flaunt their "liberation."

Maidenform in its latest campaign shows that even professional women are sex objects—even a doctor or lawyer is reduced to that role, stripped to their underwear in a courtroom or a hospital room, surrounded by men. "It is unthinkable that there would be a reversal of that," showing professional men in professional forums wearing only underwear, says Kilbourne.

Today women are told how to attract men—not at home but in the business world. Women are taught to use Oil of Olay not only to attract their husbands, but to rise up the corporate ladder. "Would looking younger make you feel more confident at work?" asks the new magazine ads for Oil of Olay (a way of telling women reentering the workforce that they *should* feel insecure about their age.) "You know you're good at your job," the ad continues. "Running a household and raising a family gave you the inventiveness and organizational expertise that are necessary in the business world. You're already preparing for the next step, going to adult education classes or maybe a company training program to acquire additional skills. But sometimes, when they hire a new co-worker fresh out of school, with a bright young face and bright ideas, you wonder if you're moving ahead as rapidly as you should. That's when looking young could well give your confidence a welcome boost."

Attractiveness, ironically, also works against women. They find themselves in a double bind; advertising tells women to be attractive, yet studies show that physical attractiveness handicaps women in the business world because they are more likely to be considered mindless by their male colleagues.[23]

The superwoman image now pushed by advertisers is a good example of how the situation is not really improving, just changing. "You know the superwoman," said marketing research manager Laurie Ashcraft in a recent speech. "She's the one wearing Enjoli who 'brings home the bacon and fries it up in the pan' and waltzes off to an Aviance night . . . The superwoman puts in a full day on the job, she's a model mother, serves three course dinners and hot breakfasts and has time and energy for romance while the children are asleep."[24]

As Ashcraft adds, "trying to live up to this myth has led to frustration, resentment and exhaustion." However, she insists the image is a temporary one, an attempt by advertisers to appeal to a broad segment of women.

The Power of Suggestion

Suggestiveness, alluring images, rather than claims on the merits of the products itself, are commonly used in selling to women. John Berger writes that advertising "proposes to each one of us that we transform ourselves and our lives by buying something more . . . [it] persuades us of such transformation by showing us people who have apparently been transformed and are, as a result, enviable . . . [ads] are about social relations, not objects; promises not of pleasure but of happiness."[25]

That is especially true for advertising aimed at women. Through images advertisers promise women a new life if they buy their products: "Revlon celebrates '83: New Year, New You."

Perfume ads are a good example of how images are used to sell the product: they boldly create images of romantic fantasy worlds—riding a white horse bareback through a field of flowers, warm autumn nights in France, Sophia Loren, tropical islands in the sun. Some are more adventurous. "Her life was more daring than most people's fantasies," says an ad for Isadora perfume. In a Paco Rabanne ad, a photo of a woman, looking like a glamorous James Bond, and a handsome man at her side is clipped with the note: "Robert: I caught up with them at Verfour. The man is definitely Max, her bodyguard. The woman may be Danielle . . . or it may be her damn double again. One of the few things anyone knows about her is that she always wears Calandre." Daring, adventure, romance, all yours for the price of perfume.

By relying on images like these, advertisements can be purposely misleading. "More" cigarettes often does not show the female in its ad smoking a cigarette. Instead she is pursuing a lively and fun single's life, feeding her dog, shopping for houseplants, talking on the phone. Not only is it "More You" but "It's beige"—the implication being that the cigarette simply fits in with the lively decor. The reality of someone smoking a cancer-causing cigarette is entirely omitted.

8

Words can also create images. "Salem *Slim* Lights" ("one beautiful menthol") and Maybelline slim eye shadow stick both play on women's obsession with being slender.

Certainly advertising takes advantage of men's vulnerabilities, too—questioning their masculinity and then selling them products to bolster it. But, as Kilbourne points out, there are some key differences. First, the emphasis on attractiveness in men's ads is not nearly as extensive as in women's. "Men are not exhorted to spend enormous time and money to achieve attractiveness. It is artificially achieved for women, but not for men," says Kilbourne. However, as she also notes, advertisers are beginning to use the same tactic for men—selling hair spray, perfume/cologne and skin care products by promising sexual attraction.

Second, men are usually depicted as invulnerable, powerful, authoritative. Though that can put a lot of weight on men's shoulders—just as the emphasis on beauty hurts women—it also tells men that their proper place in society is on top. It bolsters their self-confidence, and tells them they are superior to women. Sometimes, men are shown as idiots or buffoons, but is generally when they are doing "woman's work" (such as household chores), according to Kilbourne's research.

Goffman notes that generally in domestic scenes the male is "In no way contributing [to the housework] at all, in this way avoiding either subordination or contamination with a 'female' task . . . Another answer is to present the man [doing housework] as ludicrous or childlike—unrealistically so—as if perhaps in making him candidly unreal the competency image of real males could be preserved . . . A subtler technique is to allow the male to pursue the alien activity under the direct appraising scrutiny [of a woman]."[26]

Generally, single men are shown as powerful—tall and handsome—while married men are often hen-pecked fools—short and bald. "That," says Kilbourne, "is contempt for women."

Men are deeply affected by the negative images of women in advertising, the way in which they are trivialized as sex objects and homebodies, unable to make important decisions, concerned only by their appearance and that of their home, Kilbourne argues. Such advertising teaches "contempt for every quality that is considered female," says Kilbourne. "It affects us deeply, from our sexual behavior to our foreign policy,"

So what? many women ask. Ads don't affect me, I just ignore them.

Unfortunately, they do affect us, subtly but powerfully because we are taught these ways of seeing ourselves.

For women consumers, the messages sent by advertising can be debilitating. Bombarded by hundreds of these messages each day—that women are nice to look at but should not be taken seriously—merchants and manufacturers, doctors and lawyers, continue to treat women according to old-fashioned stereotypes: the message is not only that such treatment is okay but that women expect it. As a woman you may find yourself the butt of jokes by auto repairmen, your body sized up by a male loan officer, your questions ignored by your doctor.

"As a consumer what you most want is to be taken seriously," says Kilbourne. "And that is exactly what women are not." And that is exactly what advertising reinforces.

That treatment is compounded by the way in which women are taught by advertising to view themselves. Unable to measure up to the beautiful women

9

or the happy housewives in the ads we see everyday, women begin to feel like failures. "It makes us feel incredibly insecure," says Kilbourne.

Because women are told everyday that they cannot think for themselves, that they are dependent on men, many women themselves fall into the stereotypical role of the helpless female.

As a result of not only advertising, but also the way women have been trained, they are often less assertive in situations that require a take charge attitude, less likely to challenge an unscrupulous repairmen, less likely to ask questions of a lawyer or doctor. There is something "unfeminine" about asserting our rights in the marketplace, about making a fuss about a defective product. So many of us shy away from confrontation, instead letting the people we pay for goods and services bowl us over. We slowly begin to lose control over our own lives.

Today's advertising hurts women as consumers in another way: it impedes our ability to make rational decisions about what we buy. Certainly that is the advertisers' aim. As one ad executive told Vance Packard about the type of research marketers conduct on consumers: "Motivation research is the type of research that seeks to learn what motivates people in making choices. It employs techniques designed to reach the unconscious or subconscious mind because preferences generally are determined by factors of which the individual is not conscious ... Actually in the buying situation the consumer generally acts emotionally and compulsively, unconsciously reacting to the images and designs which in the subconscious are associated with products."

That technique is particularly effective with women, so they continue to buy and buy, seeking as Berger said, not pleasure but happiness. To advertisers that is perfectly acceptable. Advertising executive Howard Goldstein, producer of advertisements for Jordache jeans (where 10-year-olds are portrayed as sex symbols), says that if a woman or man is sitting at home feeling lousy and wants to buy a certain cologne or wear certain jeans to make them feel better "that's a positive force."[27]

Experts contacted by Packard disagreed. Said Bernice Allen of Ohio University: "We have no proof that more material goods such as more cars or gadgets have made anyone happier—in fact the evidence seems to point in the opposite direction."[28]

TAKING CHARGE

The first step toward getting out from under the thumb of advertisers is developing a critical eye, knowing what weaknesses the advertiser is attempting to reach in you. When you look at an ad, ask yourself some of these questions, based on guidelines developed by both the National Advertising Review Board and the National Association of Broadcasters, and expanded:

√ Are sexual stereotypes perpetuated in the ad?

√ Are the women portrayed as stupid, or incapable of making important decisions?

√ Does the ad use belittling language toward women (i.e. "bless her heart . . .")?

√ Does the ad show a woman waiting on her husband and children?

√ Does the ad portray women as more neurotic than men?

√ Is there suggestive sexual language about women's role or bodies? (i.e. "turn 'em on with frost and tip . . .")

√ Is the woman shown in an alluring, suggestive position?

√ Does the ad portray women in a situation that tends to confirm the view that women are the property of men?

√ Do I really want and need this product or am I reacting to suggestive images?

√ Is the ad suggesting that I can look like the beautiful model in it?

√ Does the ad promote the idea that all women have to be slender and "young-looking?"

√ Does the ad show working or professional women as sex objects?

If you find an ad particularly offensive, write to the advertiser stating so and telling them that you intend not to buy their product *because* of the ad. Get your friends to write letters too. If an ad on television has been offensive, ask the local television station if you or a friend could respond with a guest editorial about women in advertising.

If you and your friends want to learn more about the hazards of advertising for women, you may want to have Dr. Jean Kilbourne present her slide/lecture discussion to your club or other organization. Information about her presentation can be found in the appendix of this book.

"A man-pleaser dinner you know will please your man."

—Man Pleaser Dinners

"He touched me and suddenly nothing is the same."

—Chantilly

"I know where my wife learned all that good cooking—perfect mother-in-law, perfect rice!"

—Minute Rice

"There's a kind of warmth that's uniquely a woman's."

—Correctol

FOOTNOTES

1. Berger, John *Ways of Seeing* (Penguin, BBC, London, 1972), p. 134.
2. cited in "Channeling Children, Sex Stereotypes on Prime Time TV," in *Women on Words and Images* (Princeton, 1975).
3. cited in Ewen, Stuart, *Captains of Consciousness* (McGraw-Hill 1976), p. 170.
4. Butler, Matilda and Paisley William, *Women and Mass Media* (Human Services Press, New York, 1980), p. 70.
5. Ibid.
6. Ewen, p. 153.
7. Packard, Vance, *The Hidden Persuaders* (Pocket Books, New York, 1980), p. 103.
8. Ibid, p. 102.
9. Ibid, p. 104.
10. Ibid, cited on page 237.
11. Courtney A. and Lockeretz S., "A woman's place: An analysis of the roles portrayed by women in magazine advertisements," *Journal of Marketing Research,* no. 8, pp. 92–95.
12. Estimate by media analyst Dr. Jean Kilbourne.
13. ABC interview with Kilbourne on "The Last Word." Other Kilbourne quotes from interview with author, November, 1982.
14. Cited in Ewen, p. 182.
15. Berger, p. 47.
16. Goffman, Erving, *Gender Advertisements* (Harper & Row, 1976), pp. 41–79.
17. Packard, p. 3.
18. Cited in Butler & Paisely, p. 77.
19. Estimate by Kilbourne.
20. Cited in Packard p. 277.
21. Ibid.
22. Butler & Paisley p. 100.
23. Kilbourne.
24. Ashcraft, Laurie speech before national American Marketing Association, February 1982, Mountain Shadows Arizona.
25. Berger p. 131.
26. Goffman, p. 37.
27. Interview on "The Last Word" November 23, 1982.
28. Packard, p. 246.

Authority figures in advertisements are usually men—even if it is just a masculine hand or voice.

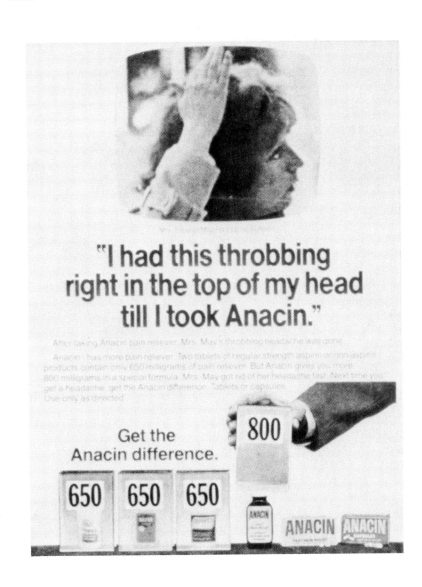

JAYNE AND JENNY STEWART'S FIRST DATE MADE THEM SO NERVOUS THEY SLEPT RIGHT THROUGH IT.

Most people experience some degree of apprehension the first time they have an appointment to see an Oral Surgeon. Not knowing quite what to expect, and wondering if it's going to hurt are important concerns.

There's no need to worry.
Fortunately, though, the Oral and Maxillofacial Surgeon not only is a specialist in dealing with problems of the mouth, teeth and jaws; he's also an expert in pain and anxiety control. Trained in the complete spectrum of procedures, from local anesthetics to sedation or general anesthesia. The choice depending on what is best for the patient.

In Jayne and Jenny's case, this meant administering

a general anesthetic since the thought of being awake during the removal of impacted wisdom teeth was upsetting. So they both woke up feeling relaxed and relieved.

Concern for your total health.
The span of an oral surgeon's specialty is a wide one. He's concerned, for example, with older patients unable to wear dentures. He treats accident victims with facial injuries. He cares for people with poorly shaped jaws. And treats people with wisdom tooth problems.

Just as meaningful, the oral and maxillofacial surgeon is actively involved in alerting the public

to hidden everyday hazards to our health. A prime example is the safety bar on the back of most school bus seats, a frequent cause of serious facial injury to children. Not only that, oral surgeons are advocates of the mandatory and proper use of sports safety equipment, goalie masks, mouthpieces and helmets. He also advocates the routine use of automobile seat belts. Because prevention is always the best policy.

Write to us.
For more information about this dental surgical specialty,

please send for our free brochure. Write:
The American Association of Oral and Maxillofacial Surgeons, P.O. Box 1024, Tinley Park, Illinois 60477.

And, remember, there's no reason to be anxious about a visit to an oral surgeon. After all, he not only specializes in taking away problems of the mouth, teeth, and jaws; he also specializes in taking away pain.

MERICAN ASSOCIATION OF ORAL AND MAXILLOFACIAL SURGEONS
NTAL SPECIALISTS WORKING TO INSURE YOUR TOTAL HEALTH

"Something's different with this Aqua-fresh."

"That's New Triple Protection Aqua-fresh."

1. **Fights Cavities.** New Aqua-fresh® has all the fluoride of the leading paste. In fact, no other toothpaste fights cavities better than New Aqua-fresh.

2. **Freshens Breath.** New Aqua-fresh has all the breath freshener of the leading gel.

New evidence 3. ➡ **Even Cleans Stained Film.** New Aqua-fresh has a formula clinically proven to remove stained film as it cleans teeth.

All concentrated in one toothpaste

New Triple Protection Aqua-fresh. The Complete Toothpaste.

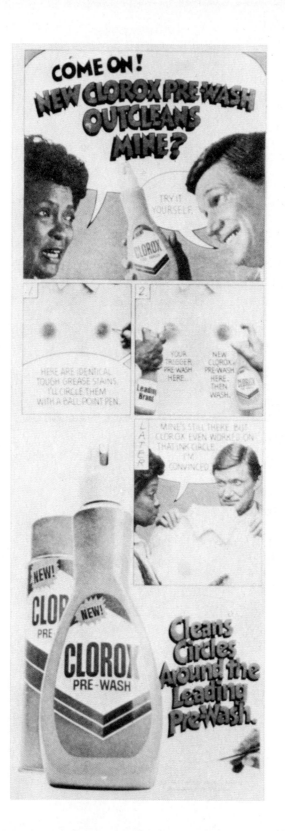

Women are most often shown as just housewives, or as some other family member, a
daughter, mother or granddaughter. Men
are shown in activities outside the home and
in a variety of roles.

"Yeah, I used your special fly. No!...it's bigger than that! Must be the
granddaddy of that one Harry got last year. I'd say it's about...well, let's just
say it's lucky we all like fish."
   A laugh. A smile. A fish story. Reach out and keep
faraway friends part of your life.

(A) Bell System

Diet aid ads often run right near those for luscious desserts, sending women mixed messages.

WHAT'S YOUR *Sara Lee* FANTASY?

"I had this fantasy that I was trapped inside a Black Forest and had to eat my way out." *Glenn Wolf*

Nobody doesn't like *Sara Lee*

Even professional women are still reduced to sex objects. Can anyone picture a professional man portrayed like this?

THE MAIDENFORM WOMAN.
YOU NEVER KNOW WHERE SHE'LL TURN UP.

The evidence is in and Pretty Me™ is the winner. Simply feminine, this front-close bra and matching bikini are lustrous super-satin with fan-shaped lace appliqués. Unquestionably natural in softcup (shown), underwire, or light fiberfill. Bras from $9. Bikini $6. In sensational colors. And that's the whole truth.

Pretty Me by Maidenform

Virginia Slims women flaunt their "liberation."

Virginia Slims recalls how the woman of 1910 brought a little warmth into the house.

VIRGINIA SLIMS *Lights*

You've come a long way, baby.

9 mg "tar" 0.8 mg nicotine av. per cigarette by FTC Method.

By relying on images, advertisements can be purposely misleading. "More" cigarettes are not always being, smoked; they simply fit in with the lively and attractive decor.

It's new. It's beige.

More
Lights
100s

More
Lights
100s

More
Lights
100s

Box 8mg

Ads today are increasingly using alluring female models—often with subtle sexual suggestions like "turn 'em on with frost & tip."

"Heard Secret Solid's so strong, a guy shouldn't pass it up."

"You picked a real winner, but Secret Solid's just for women. Sorry, fella."

If you think an antiperspirant for women can't be strong, wait until you try Secret® Solid. Secret Solid's made with the full strength a woman needs to help her stay fresh and dry all day. In fact, it's even strong enough for a guy. But Secret Solid glides on silky, smooth, dry—feminine. So it feels great under your arms. And with a pretty feminine fragrance or unscented too. Secret Solid. It's strong enough for a man, but made just for a woman.

HEADLIGHTS
turn 'em on with Frost & Tip®

Soft lights. Bright lights. Outasight lights. Turn on the headlights with Frost & Tip. Just pick your look, follow the exclusive "how to." Designer Cap and you've got the look. Your lights are on! With every hair richly colorstoned to turn on a shine. So turn on the headlights. And turn out beautiful. With Frost & Tip from *Clairol.*

Perfume sellers use the power of suggestion
by creating romatic fantasy worlds.

Only in the islands
do the most delicate flowers grow
a little wilder.

Island Gardenia by Jõvan.
Delicate. Exotic. Above all…Sensuous. Perfume or Cologne $6.

At cosmetic counters of fine stores everywhere. Jovan, Inc., 875 N. Michigan Avenue, Chicago, Illinois 60611 © 1982 Jovan, Inc.

SOPHIA®
BY COTY
Like the woman who inspired it,
always magnificent.
Never the same.

White Shoulders®
The best the world has to offer™

Evyan Perfumes, Inc.

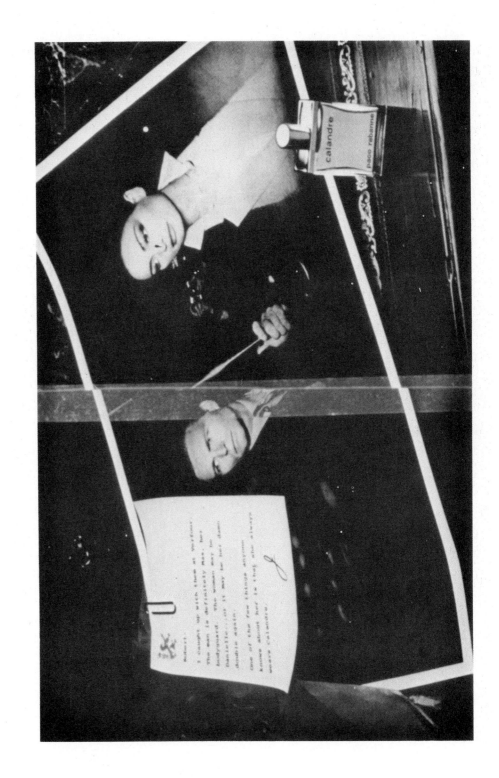

MS. magazine's "No Comment" column makes overtly sexist advertisers look foolish; but inside the magazine are the same damaging symbols found in other magazines and on TV.

NO COMMENT

Just what you need around the office.

The Viking Sauna. Designed by sauna experts. Manufactured with the highest quality sauna materials and controls. Available in a great variety of sizes. And pre-built to go up anywhere in a matter of minutes. We've got one that's just right for the corner of your executive suite. It operates on 120V standard power.

It's the perfect way to unwind after a rough day at the office. Its desert-dry heat works like a massage on the muscles. It stimulates circulation. Calms you down, tunes you up, relaxes like nothing else in the world.

Of course, you can always install one at home too. Your whole family will love it.

Call For Information
Whirlpool Baths – Spa's
Universal Gym Equipment

Viking Leisure Products
of Central Ohio

MS. MAGAZINE

advertisement appearing in *Ohio* magazine, submitted by Kathy Rhodes, Columbus, Ohio, and 10 other readers

NO COMMENT

TREAT 'EM GOOD AND THEY'LL TREAT YOU GOOD.

advertisement appearing in the Sunday Times Magazine, submitted by Beatrice S. Wehmeyer, Kezar Falls, Maine, and more than 150 other readers

California Avocados. Only 17 calories a sli[ce]

Would this body lie to you?

2

FASHION

"To choose clothes," writes Allison Lurie, "is to define and describe ourselves."[1] For centuries fashion has pressured women to define and describe themselves as weak and helpless ornaments, wearing clothes that hamper their activity and movements—and sometimes cripple them.

The Chinese used to bind their young girls' feet, deforming the bones to keep them "dainty." Moslems covered their women from head to toe in heavy white shrouds.

Victorian women wore so many layers of shifts, chemises and petticoats beneath their hoop skirts and long dresses that they could barely walk, let alone run. Beneath all that they wore corsets so tightly laced they often resulted in "chicken breast," a condition caused by the continual constriction of the ribs which led to insufficient respiration, fractured ribs, and injuries to the sternum and clavicle. "The lungs in the parts most compressed," says one account, "atrophied and collapsed."[2] It is little wonder that the Victorian succeeded in her attempt to look frail and "feminine," blushing and fainting frequently.

Looking back, those fashions seem absurdly outdated. But look around today. Until very recently, women commonly wore constricting skirts and girdles; many still totter around on spike heels and in tight skirts. "In Western societies the ubiquitous hobbling device for women has been skirts, usually accompanied by dysfunctional stilted shoes . . . 'female' apparel carries a universal symbolism of servitude—the badge of subservience," wrote Betty Lehan Harragan, in *Games Mother Never Taught You,* a study of how to succeed in the business world.[3]

Watch men and women walk along a crowded downtown avenue. Most of the women look constrained by the clothing they wear; while most men transcend theirs, they appear more comfortable, as if clothes were a natural part of their bodies.

Fashion can, and does, restrict women's ability to function—to run for a bus or take long walks. With high heels and straight skirts, said one woman, "I cannot run or walk fast."

While growing up fashion can hinder a girl's ability to compete in a boys world, to learn to compete and be assertive with boys in sports or climbing trees. "As a young girl, dresses were constricting, especially to a girl who did not like to just sit down all day. They did not give the freedom of pants," said a 27-year-old woman.

Or fashion can just make us uncomfortable: "In elementary school, it was painful to change from snowsuits or pants to our required dresses," said one woman. Another added: "I remember wearing skirts to school and being cold and uncomfortable when we had to sit on the floor."

Does fashion affect the way in which women are treated in the marketplace, by women and others? If we can apply what Betty Lehan Harragan and John Molloy, author of *The Women's Dress for Success Book,* say about dress and the workplace, then the answer is yes.

"There is no question in my mind that many women are held back in their job progress because of inattention to dress," wrote Harragan. "If your clothes don't convey the message that you are competent, able, ambitious, self-confident, reliable and authoritative, nothing you say or do will overcome the negative signals emanating from your apparel." (For women in the corporate world both she and Malloy recommend perfume and frilly dresses be left for after-hours; for work, classic looking suits and sensible low heel shoes are appropriate.)

Harragan's caveat about dress can be applied to women consumers: Just as women professionals need to earn respect from male bosses, so too do women consumers need the respect of auto repairmen, doctors, lawyers and salespeople.

That runs counter to what women have been taught since they were young. "Sex-typing in dress begins at birth with the assignment of pale-pink layettes, toys, bedding and furniture to girl babies and pale-blue ones to boy babies," said Lurie in her book, *The Language of Clothes.* "Pink in this context is associated with sentiment, blue with service. The implication is that the little girl's future concern will be the life of the affections; the boy's earning a living."[4]

Later on the young boy and girl often wear identical fabrics and cuts in their playwear. But the boy's clothes are usually made in darker colors and "printed with designs involving sports, transportation and cute wild animals. Girls' clothes are made in paler colors and decorated with flowers and cute domestic animals. The suggestion is that the boy will play vigorously and travel over long distances; the girls will stay home and nurture plants and small mammals," wrote Lurie.

The clothes a young girl wears may affect her later on as a consumer in two ways. First, those girls who cannot participate in sports or other "boy's" activities grow up less assertive with men than their 'tomboy' counterparts. (Though certainly other factors besides dress determine a young girl's activities.) "The presence of a girl 'all dolled up' is unreal," said Dr. Selma Greenberg of Hofstra University, who has studied how little girls behave and how adults respond to them depending on their dress. "She is unable to move. She is sweet. She is cute. Girls become too dependent on others' opinions of them." Today, of course, that is changing. Little girls commonly wear pants and comfortable clothing. But there is still a strong emphasis—particularly among peer-conscious teens—on wearing clothes, such as tight jeans and miniskirts, that handicap their activities.

Second, as fashion buyers, girls are taught to rank attractiveness over utility, comfort and quality. "Very young girls get a lot of attention if they participate in the expected behaviors," said Greenberg. "Girls get a lot more praise than boys . . . but for the wrong reasons. The praise is for appearing decorative . . . It has little girls worried when they are not praised because they are hooked on praise. Girls are praised on appearance. They are almost never praised on accomplishment. Boys are praised for activity; girls are praised for passivity. In clothing, they are praised for being decorative, not functional."

Women are most style conscious when they are young. Later in life they begin seeking practicality, comfort over design.

In Step, In Pain

Fewer women are sacrificing comfort and mobility for style than ever before in recent history. There is one huge exception to this trend: shoes. The pointed toe, high-heel shoes that women continue to buy—and the ones principally offered by manufacturers—not only hobble women but are dangerous (not unlike the Chinese practice of foot binding). Many women responding to our questionnaire complained about the limited choice and quality of women's shoes. "Tennis and casual shoes are okay," said one woman, "but dressier shoes to wear to work are *terrible*. They never fit well, the toes are too cramped, the heel area too wide, the arch in the wrong place. High heels for dancing and dress are total torture."

"Shoes are not very practical for working or for my health," said another.

"I just bought designer shoes—$100," said a 37-year old woman. "I wish you could see them now . . . "

Some of those responding refused to be taken in by what is considered fashionable. Others, however, admitted they dislike current styles but wear them anyway. "I hated wearing high heels," said one woman, "but I still do . . . [to] conform." Another woman added: "I was always into comfort—not pointy toes, high heels, etc. But sometimes I fell into 'style' and often regretted it."

Indeed, in 1973, when Dr. Claire Nader was doing research on shoe styles (platforms were than in vogue) she walked into the Better Shoes Department of Garfinckels' Department Store in Washington, D.C. and asked the salesman if he would help her find some comfortable shoes. His response was: "What's wrong with your feet? Do you have a problem?" Clearly he did not think that comfort was a consideration in most women's choice of shoes.

In between high heels, platform shoes were in style. The high heel, combined with a rigid, thick platform sole, interrupted the normal reflex pattern of walking, placing abnormal strain on the ankles, legs, and hips. The danger of falling was acute. The press reported that a Manhattan woman fell down a flight of stairs after she tripped on the high heel of her platform shoe, fractured a bone in her toes, and was on crutches for six weeks. Singer Kay Starr reportedly fell off a pair of backless clogs, broke two bones in her foot, and was in and out of a cast for three months. Platform shoes were also known to cause auto accidents by preventing the driver from distinguishing the accelerator from the brake.

Dr. Richard Benjamin of the Anacostia Foot Center in Maryland is mystified by women's willingness to continue wearing uncomfortable and dangerous shoes. "Women's shoes are built according to vanity and style. Men's are sensible. They work in their shoes, the shoes are built for work. Women's shoes don't correspond to the work they do." Benjamin, a podiatrist, says that 95 percent of his patients are women, and "they almost all have shoe related problems."

Here are some of the most common:

Fit: Many stores do not carry shoes that fit properly in length or width, said a saleswoman from the Modern Shoe Shop in Washington, D.C. "They only carry fashionable shoes in sizes 6-9 or 10. And they only carry medium (sometimes narrow) width. So women have to buy shoes that don't really fit well because they are not big (or small) enough and they aren't the right width." One woman who says her feet "are not typical" reports that years ago it was much easier to buy shoes for her unusual size.

Stuart Eisen, a manager of Boyce and Lewis shoe store in Maryland, says: "Women have this vanity thing about small feet. Not so much in our generation, but with women who are 55 or older. When they were young they didn't want a large foot (over size 7); now we'll see horrendous bunions on these women's feet. The toes had nowhere to go. The joint next to the big toe opens up and fills with calcium. Now they'll still try to squeeze their foot into a shoe that is too small. We won't sell a shoe if it doesn't fit properly. We try to re-educate these people."

Bunions, said Dr. Harold B. Glickman, president of the D.C. Podiatry society, are a malalignment of the first toe joint. "Calcium may then deposit in the space in the joint to aggravate the problems," he said. "Other problems related to women's shoes are corns, calluses, and lesions."

Pointed toes now in style can cause bunions, and so called "hammer toes." "The pointed-toe shoes caused women to turn to orthopedic shoes," said a saleswoman from the Orthopedic Shoe Service in Washington, D.C. "As a matter of fact, those pointed shoes were great for our business. There was a woman who was just in here this morning; those pointed toes had ruined her feet."

High heels have been in style on and off for years. As Stuart Eisen notes, they are popular because they make the leg sexually attractive: "The leg is longer and tighter. Some women [and men] think it looks more shapely; it puts pressure on the back of the calf to *make* it tight and shapely. Also, high heels elongate the leg by making the ankle seem like it merges with the leg."

But, here's what some experts say about the health hazards of high heels:

Eisen: "Low heels are much better for a person; they put less pressure on the lower back. You could kill yourself if you tried to run in high heels! Your foot just wasn't made to be standing on high heels . . . Anything over three inches is bad for the foot. . . . It puts a lot of pressure on your spine. Also, in heels, your legs are not relaxed. Your legs are tighter."

Benjamin: "High heels throw all of the weight on the ball of the foot. A woman then rotates the weight on the ball and off the big toe, causing further problems. The foot turns incorrectly and throws the knee out, the hip joint gets thrown off, and this might also result in back pain. Runners' knee problems, in fact, are often foot problems that become aggravated. Spike heels . . . and sandles provide no support for the arch. There is thus improper excessive motion of the foot, again causing corns and callouses, and even bunions."

Support. "The steel shank in a shoe is very important for support," said a salesman for Massey Shoes in Maryland. "The steel shank supports the [shoe and thus the] foot so your arches don't collapse. Almost all men's shoes have a steel shank. Women's shoes don't have them. . . . Some women's casual shoes will have a steel shank, but the fashionable ones with high heels don't."

Dr. Benjamin added: "In shoes with little support the little toe will bend back under the next toe. The toes are forced into contortions and the joints become malaligned."

"Women's stylish shoes are flimsy," said Dr. Glickman, "and offer no support or protection. They thus lead to sprained heels, sprained arches and sprained ankles, when women step off a curb for instance . . . . Women's shoes have no support for the medial arch; no [proper] shank; stylish shoes have none of these features."

Material. "Ladies shoes have a thinner sole and generally thinner leather all around. Men's are mainly leather. They absorb perspiration, they let the foot breathe," said Eisen.

"The shoe industry is the last vestige of male chauvinism left," said Dr. Glickman. "Now women can have a choice in their dress; slacks are okay; mini-skirts are out; the hem can be adjusted however a women likes . . . . Women are conditioned by the shoe industry to buy new shoes all the time that are just incorrect for the human foot."

True, shoes are about the last vestige of crippling, hobbling women's wear (though tight skirts and girdles worn by some could be added to that list). Unfortunately, though, women do still face discrimination in other aspects of their wardrobe.

Paying a Price for Style

"Letting the fashion industry influence your choice of clothes is a whopping mistake," says John Molloy in his *The Woman's Dress for Success Book.* "Any woman who thinks the fashion industry has her interest at heart is woefully wrong. The industry is interested in her pocketbook. And it will sell her, often at inflated prices, anything that will make money for the industry. It will sell her shoddy merchandise, and it will sell her tacky styling—anything to keep the cash register ringing."[5] Following are some details on the fashion industry's strategy.

The fashion industry—through magazines from *Seventeen* to *Glamour* to *Vogue*—exhorts young women to follow the latest fashion trend, to throw out their old wardrobe and buy a new one each year. To a large extent the strategy has worked. Women and girls spend 63 cents of each apparel dollar.[6]

Department stores are laid out to allure women shoppers. Anyone who walks in the store is immediately surrounded by products for women; the first floor is nearly always devoted primarily to cosmetics and women's accessories. "You sell more cosmetics than anything; the store would be crazy to put their best selling item behind the elevator," said a woman sales manager at a top East Coast department store. Cosmetics, she said, are the most profitable department, with women's accessories running a close second. "If you can't afford another piece of clothing, you buy cosmetics or a belt instead," she said.

In addition, women are encouraged to buy more than they can afford through lay-away plans. Those plans are not as common, or well-publicized in men's stores.

At her store only three small departments are devoted to boys and men; the rest to women and housewares, which are directed at women. She estimated that 75 percent of the store's advertising was aimed at women. A customer has to literally search for the men's wear. "A man comes in here looking for the men's department, a woman comes in looking," said a salesman at the store.

That may seem like an advantage to women: they have more variety, there is more to choose from. But, according to experts, women pay a high price for variety and rapidly changing fashions. In 1980 working women spent an average of $525 on clothes (one estimate puts the latest figures at $750); working men spend $250; and non-working women, with less available money, spent $155 a year.[7]

Part of that higher price is because women buy more clothes to keep up with fashion trends. But women also generally have to pay *more* than men for comparable quality. Consider a pair of Levi jeans. At one chain store (the Gap), men's jeans were priced at $18.95 unwashed and $25.50 prewashed. Women's jeans, which had a different cut and in some cases lighter weight fabric, ranged from $26 to $31. In addition, men could get a variety of lengths. "The men's are definitely a better buy," a salesman told us. Compare a medium-priced woman's blouse with a man's shirt—if they are the same price, the woman's blouse will probably be made of a lesser quality (polyester blend v. cotton) or lighter weight fabric with looser stitched seams. The same is often true in children's departments. As one 33-year-old mother said: "If I buy jeans for my daughter in the girls' department, they are $2–3 more than in the boys' department and often less sturdy."

The sharpest difference can be seen between women's and boy's clothes. For example, a woman's designer pullover shirt in one store was priced at $23–26, while in the boy's department it was $12. The woman's garment may have a slightly different cut but the amount and type of material used is the same.

The price gap between men's and women's clothes can increase as the quality goes up. The department store sales manager admitted: "If the workmanship for a man's garment compared to a like garment for women—if it is a comparable garment—the woman's will probably be a lot more money—$50 on the average."

"I resent the pricing mechanism," said one woman, "because my clothing is usually one-quarter the size of a man's outfit (I'm small and short). It uses less fabric, has fewer stitches, and should cost less."

Candid department store salespeople will tell you that the mark-up on women's and girl's clothing is higher than on men's and boys': "The mark-up is a lot higher in women's clothing," the manager of another, lower quality, department store admitted. "In the junior department the mark-up is 6-7 percent higher than boys'; in the women's department it is 4 percent higher than men's."

Other sales people insist that the manufacturers charge more for women's clothing. In many cases it is probably a combination of both. Women's clothes are "more expensive, without a doubt," said a representative from Oxford Industries, a clothing manufacturer.

Why do women's clothes cost more? One answer is that sellers know that women have been cultivated to spend more money on clothes. "Women will pay more than men," explained the woman department store sales manager. "Retailers know that boys, for example, can't spend $90 on a shirt. But a woman will buy that. It all depends on what the consumer will spend." A salesman in a men's department said: "A man is a harder sell. You have to convince him. . . . It's harder to get a man to part with his money." Another salesman added that contrary to women, "I don't think most men see something and say 'I must have that shirt.' "

Higher pricing also results from fashion changes. Men's fashions change gradually and in small ways: the width of the tie, length of the collar, the width of the lapels. Women's fashions change dramatically from year to year, and season to season. It may be the prairie look one year, miniskirts the next; olive green and gold in the fall, pastels by the spring. ("Wearing last year's shoes can ruin a businesswoman's day," one executive vigorously insisted.) "We will run with some items all season," said the menswear salesman, "whereas the women's floors often change every two weeks."

Women's departments do have more frequent sales—and markdowns are sharper—but overall, this high turnover is costly for women. Oxford industries' representative noted that the garment industry must undergo expensive retooling for large-scale fashion changes: "There is a high price to pay in flexibility for a higher degree of fashionability," he said. The expense of those changes are then passed on to consumers.

Trendiness is a risky business for manufacturers of women's clothing. "It's more volatile—you hit or miss," said Paul Priestlams, economist for the American Apparel Association. The men's industry, he said, tends to be more stable, a solid market not deeply affected by fashion and style changes.

Priestlams saw three reasons why, as part of the "retailers' marketing philosophy," women's clothes will continue to cost more:

1. Fashion change: High prices compensate for the losses accrued in unloading out-of-style goods and fashions that never caught on. "The ones you just can't give away," says Priestlams.

2. Variety: The cost of producing a wide range of women's clothes (lingerie in every color, dresses in hundreds of styles) is passed on to the consumer.

3. Women's market: With more women working, they have more money to spend, and according to the "retailers' marketing philosophy," they will continue to pay the inflated prices.

So why do fashions continue to change? First, when a new style becomes fashionable, the payoff is big. Retailers and manufacturers may take in enough profit to pay off bad years and then some. In addition, as the woman sales manager remarked: "Changes in fashion are very important to the department stores. The store that does the best is the one that can get to people who have the money to spend. Changes draw customers in; the new clothes on the mannequin draw them in."

This high turnover is also one reason behind the poorer quality often found in women's clothes. The second reason is the insistence by clothiers that women's only interest is looks, not durability. "Quality suffers," said Oxford's representative, "because you can't concentrate on quality when the line changes so often."

An unspoken assumption by clothing retailers and manufacturers is that since women's fashions change so often women do not want or need quality clothing. "Men are looking for quality goods they can wear for three or four years," said a department store salesman. And women aren't? "Women's fashions change from season to season," he said. Sometimes, the quality difference is apparent in the stitching of seams (men often have double stitched seams whereas women's are single-stitched) or the quality of the fabric. "I don't wear synthetics," said one woman, 33, "so sometimes it is easier to buy men's clothing synthetic free than women's."

Hosiery is a good example of how lower quality can cost women more. Style dictates that women wear nylons—pantyhose or stockings—that frequently run (and many women complain are uncomfortable.) The socks that men buy, however, last much longer. As a result men spend about one-third of what a woman spends on hosiery.

Women (and increasingly men) also are conned into paying extra money for designer-labelled wear of questionable quality. An employee for Ralph Lauren (who previously had worked for another name designer) told us that the quality of designer clothing does not measure up to the price you pay. In fact sometimes it is worse. (One of Lauren's belt lines was discontinued, in fact, because the factory, to save money, stopped reinforcing them with a top stitch. As a result the belt easily fell apart. Now the company has returned to using the reinforcing stitch.)

Consumers should also be aware that often what they buy has not been designed by the famous designer at all. Rather, the designer bought the line of garment from another factory and put his or her name on it. "There is a terribly high price to pay for a square-inch piece of cloth with some guy's signature on it." said the Lauren employee.

Some designer men's and women's jackets "are identical in fabric, style, button type, etc.," added a top costume designer and clothing expert in New York City. "Yet they differ in price by $100. Women's garments need a few extra steps to shape them to a woman's body, but not $100 worth of steps. A woman will spend more, that is why women's clothes cost more." She added that the advantage of designer wear is that generally the garments are not trendy, they will not wear out as fast, and they won't shrink, stretch, fade or bleed when washed and dried.

The most stark example of quality difference between women's and men's wear are shoes. The price of women's shoes varies tremendously. One salesman estimated the range at anywhere from $9 to $200. Men's shoes do not vary as much, generally ranging from $30 to $70. The quality of women's shoes—with a few exceptions—ranges from not-so-bad to lousy. "Men's shoes are *much* better," said Stuart Eisen of Boyce and Lewis. "They are all leather or mostly leather. Women's are made of man-made material. Women's prices may be lower, but men's quality more than makes up for the cost. Men's are more durable, last longer and support better. Men's shoes include many features that women's do not. Men's shoes are almost like prescription shoes; they include a metatarsul bump in the sole of the shoe, formed for the sole of the foot. Also, the sole has ridges and bumps inside to form to the contour of the foot. They are better made and better for the feet." And, as mentioned earlier, men's shoes generally have a metal shank for support, women's don't.

As any woman who has bought summer shoes knows, they do not last more than a few months of arduous wear. "It's those strappy, high-heeled things that almost always break," complained one shoe repairman. "Women buy more shoes—often at the expense of quality. They'll bring in a lot of cheap shoes, plastic ones, wooden ones that crack . . . Men just don't buy these."

Shoe repairmen have seen more than their share of poor quality women's shoes. "Women's spikes are coming back in," said one. "Those little heels get caught on the sidewalk. They pay $160 for a pair of the best shoes, and you know they're going to bring them in to be repaired . . . You know women's shoes."

Said another: "Women's shoes fall apart more. The heel structure is made really thin, flimsy. Women's shoes are sold strictly for money deals. Men know more about shoes. They have a knowledge about buying what's good. Women'll buy anything. You never see a man wearing wooden shoes. Women will put anything on their feet. How could the government let them put these things on the market? Some are so flimsy I can't repair them."

* * *

The position of women consumers is improving, particularly in fashion. "The concept of buying fewer but better garments has emerged," said a report by the Celanese Fibers Marketing Company,[8] and many manufacturers and retailers are responding. "Greater numbers of women are showing that they will spend their dollars on quality goods that are functional despite the rising costs of our inflated economy . . . 45 percent of all women are buying fewer apparel items but of better quality and expect them to last."

But price and quality discrimination remains. Women still have to pay, on average, more money than men to get the same quality in their clothing. "Women's clothes," said Oxford's rep, "will never be like men's—quality or price wise."

PROFILE OF POPULATION AND EXPENDITURES ON APPAREL

Market Group	Age Group	1979 U.S. Population		1979 Apparel Expenditure At Retail	
		Millions	% Dist.	Billions	% Dist.
Men's Market	(19+)	73.2	33%	$19.3	26%
Boys' Market	(4–18)	27.2	13%	6.7	9
Total		100.9	46%	$26.0	35%
Women's Market	(15+)	88.4	40%	41.4	56%
Girls' Market	(4–14)	18.4	8%	4.4	6%
Total		106.8	48%	$45.8	62%
Children's & Infants' Market	(0–3)	12.5	6%	2.2	3%
TOTAL MARKET		220.2	100%	$74.0	100%

U.S. Trade Policy
Hearings before Sub. Com. on Trade
Com. on Ways & Means—House   June 26 & July 21, 1980

TAKING CHARGE

Manufacturers look for styles that are economical to produce; they look for a cut that can be mass-produced easily. Such garments often cut down on detailing, economize on fabric and omit steps in construction.

You should become more aware of the "loose threads" in the fashion industry and learn how to avoid them. Here are some things to look out for:

Fabric

√ Amount of fabric: High quality garments are made with more fabric to allow for ease of movement. Often manufacturers skimp on the amount of fabric in order to get more garments out of an allotted amount of cloth. Garments that are not cut generously enough will split at the seams when you are active.

Also, well-made clothing will match at the seams.

√ Shape of fabric: Better made garments have a more sophisticated cut made of many parts. Generally, the more pieces in a garment, the better it is constructed. Also look for clothes are cut "on the grain" of the fabric and joined on the grain.

√ Types of fabric: There are many different grades of fabric. They range from 50 cents a yard to $50. Synthetics are usually less expensive than natural fibers. Rayon and nylon are the highest quality synthetics. The less expensive synthetic fibers, however, have some advantages: They are easy to wash and wear. Although they will not last as long as natural fibers, they require little maintenance. Higher quality clothing is made of natural fiber. Cotton, silk and wool last longer than synthetics and are more durable. Natural fibers "breathe" and do not trap perspiration and odor.

√ Thread: Plastic threads should be avoided. Polyester, cotton and silk threads are far more durable.

√ Lining: Better quality garments are lined. Check to see that the lining is material comparable to the garment's fabric. Comparable materials will move together and stretch together. Incompatible fabrics will buckle and gap and may not respond similarly to washing and drying.

√ Seams: Well-made seams have a large seam allowance so you can alter the seams and let them out. Poorly made seams have a small seam allowance on the inside of the garment with loose edges. Such unfinished seams will fray.

√ Hems: Quality men's clothes will not have finished hems on the pants leg. This option is just beginning to appear in women's clothes. The garment length is more easily adjusted to your height when the end of the fabric is left unfinished.

√ Buttons: Buttons should be sewn on securely. Good clothes come with extra buttons and an extra sample of the same color thread. Buttons in outerwear and rainwear are secured with a clear plastic button on the inside of the garment to make the button more sturdy.

√ Button holes: Look for finished button holes, not just slits.

√ Fastenings: Buttons and fastenings should be large enough to accommodate the garment. Small hooks and eyes won't work well on a skirt.

Shoes

If you want quality, healthful shoes, here are some things to look for:

√ Proper fit: "The shoe has to be large enough," says Eisen. "It has to be the corrrect size with plenty of room for the toes. The ball of the foot should be where it belongs, at the widest part of the shoes."

√ Cushioned insole, for comfort and protection.

√ Steel shank for support. A steel shank should run from the heel to the toes. "It gives the shoes support when you walk. The shank holds the shoe up and holds the foot up. Women's shoes, because they are lighter weight, usually have a fiber shank which is not as strong," said Eisen.

√ Buy leather. "Leather breathes and stretches," says Dr. Benjamin. "Vinyl and other synthetic materials retain heat. If you spend a lot of time on heated surfaces, the retained heat will cause the foot to sweat. Rashes and athlete's foot will result." Leather soles, he added, are also better than synthetic soles. "I buy good leather," said one woman who indicated she was happy with the quality of her shoes. "I take care of them, repair them, clean them, and they last two–three years."

√ Low heels. From the point of view of your feet, *no* heel is best. If you feel you must wear heels, two inches should be the maximum.

Dr. Benjamin adds this advice: "Buy shoes in the afternoon or evening when blood has been rushing to your feet all day and they are swollen. Then the accurate size can be fit. Buy sensible shoes, with no more than a two inch heel. Have them wide enough for the toes, and have good support in the medial arch. The shoe should be firm, not tight. The arch [of your foot] should have support."

FOOTNOTES

1. Lurie, Allison, *The Language of Clothes* (Random House, NY, 1981) p. 5
2. Lauer, Robert H., Jeannette C., *Fashion Power,* (Prentice Hall, N.J. 1981) p. 213
3. Harragan, Betty Lehan, *Games Mother Never Taught You: Corporate Gamesmanship for Women,* (New York, 1977) p. 275.
4. Lurie, p. 214
5. Molloy, John T., *The Women's Dress for Success Book* (1977)
6. based on figures from American Apparel Manufacturers' Association.
7. Celanese Corporation figures, cited in Barbara Toman, "Department Stores Start Adding Seminars and Services to Attract Working Women," Wall Street Journal, July 19, 1982, p. 17.
8. "Women Take a Look at Apparel Retailing," Celanese Fibers Marketing Company, January, 1982.

3

CONSUMER SERVICES

*"A few years ago . . . my family was traveling across the country in our station-wagon," says a 20-year-old college student. "My father had gone to the bathroom and so he was gone when the gas attendant came out to service our car and it appeared that my mother was out-of-state, traveling alone with several children. When the attendant checked the car he told my mother that a serious engine repair would have to be done immediately. When my father came back to the car, the gas attendant retracted his statement."

*"I had a 1970 Maverick," reports a 29-year-old Massachusetts woman, "and I brought it into the gas station for inspection because in Massachusetts you have to have your car inspected twice a year. The man in the gas station went over the car and said that I needed an incredible amount of work done on the car before he would pass it. There was something to do with the transmission and something to do with the exhaust system. All I thought was that I had a loose headlight and that he could replace the faulty wiring in it. But he slapped a red sticker on the car and said that I could only drive for five days with the red sticker. He said, 'you have to come in here to have the repairs done. Anybody else will rip you off.' The repairs were going to cost $500.

"Having not had a car much on my own—basically all I could do was put oil and water in it—I called up my father. He told me to bring the car home. He fixed the headlight and [apparently] . . . what that mechanic had told me was ridiculous . . . He brought it in for the second inspection and they asked my father, 'gee, why do you have a red sticker?' And they passed the car."

*"I was charged for brake pads which were not really installed," reports a 44-year-old female accountant.

*"Several times I have been told expensive work needed to be done," said a 28-year-old woman, "only to find out from another source that only a very minor repair was needed."

*"When I was taking the car for a muffler estimate," said one woman, "the mechanic told me all the pipes needed replacing. When I questioned the necessity, because to me the majority of the pipes looked fine, he claimed they were

bad. Upon getting a second opinion, I found out I was correct and that only the muffler itself needed any replacement."

Both men and women fall victim to unscrupulous servicemen—home improvement contractors, electricians, plumbers, and auto repairmen. About 40 cents of every dollar spent on auto repairs, for example, is spent on fraudulent or incompetent repairs, according to the National Highway Traffic Safety Administration. (As one woman caustically remarked when asked if she had ever been cheated or misled by an auto repair shop: "Who hasn't?") In the early 1970s, the Senate Subcommittee on Antitrust and Monopoly uncovered evidence, substantiated by hundreds of letters from consumers, that many auto mechanics will cheat you, if you let them. Home maintenance also draws a large number of consumer complaints to the Better Business Bureau.

Women can be particularly vulnerable to these practices. For instance, after dark a mechanic might tell a woman that her battery, fan belt or spark plugs, or all three, are about to go, and that she will never make it home. It is an effective tactic on an unsuspecting female.

Women are at a disadvantage in the consumer service arena for several reasons. First, on average women do not have the training of their male counterparts in mechanical equipment or home repair. Remember those weekends when your father took your brother under his wing and began teaching him the fine art of changing spark plugs and fixing fan belts while your mother set you to household chores like vacuuming or mopping the floors?

Though that imbalance is slowly changing, many of us don't know an alternator from a muffler; a circuit switch from a gas meter. That can put anyone at a severe disadvantage. If you do not know what a carburetor does, how are you going to know if that repairman is telling the truth when he asserts that the carburetor is what's causing the problems with your car? (Of course, no one but a mechanic can know for sure, but with some background, you will have a better idea if the repairman is telling the truth.) Without proper training, you begin losing control over the situation; all you can do is trust a total stranger to be honest about your home or your car.

Since we never watched the service game being played while we were growing up, many of us never learned the rules. When is a written estimate needed? Is the estimate binding? What is a warranty and what should it cover? What recourse is there for fraud? Some women may not even know that there are rules, so they don't ask about them before they start.

Second, even when women are well-versed in things mechanical, servicemen tend to assume that they aren't; and, often just as incorrectly, they assume that men are. Sometimes this perception can lead to fraud—a repair shop assumes it can take advantage of an unknowledgeable customer. Other times, that perception results in insufficient help or explanations. "I feel I don't get full explanations because it is assumed that I would not comprehend," said a 28-year-old married woman. "I find that if I research first and go in knowing what I am talking about it works wonders. On the other hand, my husband knows nothing about cars, did no research, and they direct conversations to him, use shop talk, and he doesn't know what they are talking about!"

"When I take my camera into the store I am treated like I am incompetent and inept," said a 23-year-old woman, "when in fact, I probably know just as much about the camera as the salesman."

Women's lack of mechanical expertise, combined with the stereotypes of women perpetuated in the media, make some repairmen simply assume that women as a group are stupid. They might give you a disbelieving look when you try to explain what is wrong, or they might flirt and tell you not to 'worry your pretty little head', or they might just ignore you. Either way the message is clear: You are not being taken seriously.

"Men [in repair shops] generally tend to assume that because I am a woman I am 1) dumb generally; 2) not knowledgeable about machines; and 3) gullible to come-ons and soft soap," said one woman.

"I feel I have [been treated differently than men] because men have the attitude that a woman knows nothing about mechanical equipment, so she is treated with an air of impatience," said another.

"They don't listen to you," complained a 53-year-old married woman. "Some mechanics speak to me as if I was mentally retarded," said a 28-year-old, "even *before* I have revealed my ignorance about cars."

A 36-year-old school teacher added: "Repairmen often assume that women won't know what they are talking about. Many of them also feel free to flirt with female customers or call us 'dear.' "

One woman recounted this experience: "A stereo salesman treated me like what I complained of was improbable—if not impossible. So I sent my boyfriend in with the same problem, and an adjustment was made on the component."

The auto and home repair industries are still dominated by men. Since they have so few female colleagues, it remains easy to assume that women are not capable of handling even the most fundamental mechanical problems. Lynne Witteveen, a home repair specialist from Santa Cruz, California, recounted her experience in attempting to break into that male-dominated profession: "I applied to be a union carpenter, and I was laughed out of the union hall, they whistled at me, and made jokes. I didn't know what to do. Finally I said, 'to hell with you guys,' and I started my own business," called MS. FIXUP.

Witteveen teaches home repair courses, popular particularly with women, at several junior colleges. The females in her classes, she says, "say they are fed up with being treated like idiots."

But, as she admits, part of the problem is that women often flaunt their ignorance and helplessness, prompting repairmen to respond predictably. "If you go into that helpless, whiney routine, they are going to treat you like that," said Witteveen. If you learn about your home (or car), she added, and can at least tell a plumber "the hot water line is broken," rather than, "that funny little pipe . . ." you are likely to achieve better results.

"This is the thing that men have put over on us for years—that there is a mystique about fixing a pipe," she said. "It takes a fair amount of coordination, but there is no mystique."

The third reason women can be more vulnerable in the consumer services arena is that they are not always as assertive as their male counterparts. As we discussed in the fashion chapter, passivity is emphasized in young girls as they grow up, while activity is emphasized in boys. We were rewarded for being docile and sweet; boys had to fight for attention—with achievements and competition. "Boys, as it were, have to push their way to manhood, girls merely have to unfold," wrote Erving Goffman.[1]

Unfolding is not particularly good training for playing the consumer game. It takes boldness and assertion, a fighting spirit, and some calculated moves. When push comes to shove, an untrained woman can be easily outwitted.

Sometimes it *is* easier to fall into the role of compliant female than to assert one's rights. It is easier to play dumb than to put in the time and effort needed to learn about the parts of your car or your home. It is easier to flirt rather than demand efficient and effective service. But it is not likely to bring good results. In fact, that kind of behavior sends off the message that you are ripe-picking for an unscrupulous repairman.

Lack of assertiveness, combined with lack of knowledge, can result in an intimidating situation for anyone. For women in the consumer world, it can be debilitating. A study on women's tastes in cars, commissioned by Conde Nast publications, concluded that women "appear to be far more intimidated by the prospect of dealing with car salesmen than men."[2]

Many normally independent women—women with jobs who live alone and pay their own bills—bring along a male companion when they shop for an auto or stereo, or bring in merchandise for repair. "I'll always take a guy with me," said the women who took her 1970 Maverick in for an inspection and was told she required extensive repairs. "He will usually just stand there and not say anything. But just having a guy with me—a male presence—really helps. It stinks, I guess, and I felt like a chicken. But money is money."

Other times, if a woman fails to receive a satisfactory response on a defective product, she sends in a man to take over the fight. "There have been a few times when I have failed and had to send [my husband] in as back-up," said the 36-year-old school teacher. "But those instances are becoming less frequent. A woman must be much tougher than a man to get respect."

To what extent nationwide women are treated differently than men as consumers is not known: unfortunately there are no comprehensive statistical studies. It is a difficult situation to study, though many women believe they are more mistreated than men. But one trend seems to emerge from the women we contacted: Those women who consider themselves assertive, even pushy, also report that they receive better treatment from complaint departments (and often repair shops) than their husbands or boyfriends. So do the women who say they have taken courses and/or read books about their cars, homes, stereos and so forth.

Here are some responses from women who know how to play the consumer game:

*"I insist on equity and justice in the situation," said a 57-year-old retired school teacher. "And I follow up a situation quickly, with proof. I usually write a letter of complaint, outlining the facts, etc."

*"I'm more controlled, yet firm, about my expectations," said a 27-year-old single.

*"I am more insistent and demanding than anyone else," said a 29-year-old married woman.

*"My husband and sons feel that I am much more positive and insistent that my rights be respected," said a 50-year-old mother of three.

*"I do [receive more responsive treatment than my husband] as I demand accuracy and justice," said a 50-year-old mother of two.

*"I think that my initial visits to *any* repair place (I have experience with auto and construction/home repair) has meant simplistic and vague (sometimes disbelieving) reactions to my explanations of the damage. This attitude generally changes, though, when I begin asking questions, using jargon. For those situations, where treatment has remained vague, I found replacement repair

50

persons/shops. Note: Whenever possible, I become familiar with situations *before* I have to deal with problems, i.e. car maintenance courses, carpentry courses."

*"In self defense, with all kinds of repairs, I have learned to ask the estimated cost in advance, get any guarantee in writing, press them to itemize, and ask enough questions to indicate a deep interest in not being overcharged," said a 58-year-old woman. "Also, speaking up assertively is very important. Nothing can be taken for granted—i.e. that they'll just do their job, as they usually would for a male customer."

TAKING CHARGE

There are some general rules for playing the consumer services game that women should keep in mind. Some more of the specifics—on car and home repair—will follow.

√ *Be assertive, but not aggressive.* Unfortunately, service shops tend to look upon men who raise their voices as authoritative, but women who raise their voices as bordering on hysterical. But don't cower. Look the attendant in the eye and keep in mind: you are paying this person for a service, and you deserve both competency and efficiency.

√ *Communicate clearly.* Men thrive on 'logic'; so when you are explaining the problem you might want to number each item ("One, the car stalls at intersections; two, there is a clicking sound on the front left hand side . . .") Describe the symptoms of your defective merchandise carefully: sounds, smells, how long the problem has existed. Before you go into a repair shop or call a repairman into your home, think through the problem and symptoms, and write them down.

√ *Ask for the repairman's initial estimation of the problem.* Later, after a diagnosis, but before work begins, get a final diagnosis. If he or she is reluctant to explain everything to you, it may be a sign that you should go elsewhere. If you think the repairman is reluctant to explain the problem to you because of your sex, why not try saying something like, "Are you afraid I won't understand this because I am a woman? Actually, I am perfectly capable . . ." It might be disarming enought to elicit a response.

√ *Learn about your home and car.* Take courses, read books, or have a friend teach you. This, of course, does not mean that you are preparing to do the actual repairs on your home or car, but you will be able to better protect yourself from fraud; and you will earn a repairman's respect with your ability to engage in an intelligent conversation about the problem. Using the jargon of the trade will let the repairman know you are not an easy mark.

√ *Don't try to guess in order to sound intelligent.* If you don't know what the problem is, just carefully describe the symptoms.

√ *Shop around.* Get two or three estimates on major repairs. It could save you a lot of money.

√ *Be a crafty negotiator.* If, after reviewing the estimate (including the parts or material required, the labor costs, and the time required to complete the job), you think the price is too high, tell the person it sounds a little steep and that you are going to shop around some more. A smart contractor or repair shop may bring the estimate down considerably rather than lose business. If you have shopped around, you should have a ceiling figure in mind: go for considerably less than that price in order to reach the desirable figure.

√ *Don't let incidents of incompetence or fraud slide.* If you are a victim of unfair or deceptive practices, you should lodge a complaint with your city or state consumer protection office. You may want to recover damages in Small Claims Court (See Auto Repair Checklist for details).

Home Repair Checklist

Choosing a contractor

√ Check to see if the contractor is licensed if your state requires it, and ask for his or her record. A licensed contractor is no guarantee of great service, but you will have the satisfaction of knowing the person is not a fly-by-night and has something (the license) to lose. For women at home alone, it is some measure of protection against harm (though certainly not fool-proof). An unlicensed repairmen or company could be less scrupulous.

√ If your state has no licensing law, ask the Better Business Bureau about the contractor. Drop him from your list if the Bureau has many complaints about him.

√ If possible, ask a friend who was pleased with some recent work for the name of the contractor.

√ Ask the contractor you are considering hiring for the names of five or six people in the area for whom he has done work; then call those people and ask about the quality of the work, how accurate the initial written estimate was, and whether the contractor responded promptly to any requests for corrections.

√ Don't hire someone that tries to high pressure you into signing a contract.

√ Develop contacts with licensed plumbers and electricians on whom you can count in emergency situations.

√ Make sure the contractor you hire is the one that will do the work; some companies subcontract much of their work.

√ Make sure the company provides liability and compensation insurance to protect you in the event of an accident.

√ If a warranty is offered, read it carefully: Is it "full" (giving the consumer unconditional rights) or "limited" (putting conditions on the rights of consumers)? Does it spell out the terms and conditions in language you understand? Who is responsible for the warranty: the dealer, contractor or manufacturer? What is the duration of the warranty?

KEEPING TABS

√ Get written estimates on costs—make sure it includes all labor and materials, and any promises that the contractor made orally. Be wary if the contractor insists on open-ended increases. But you should also be aware that written estimates are just that, estimates. Expect some fluctuation in the final price, generally about 15 percent, but make them prove their case.

√ Obtain a breakdown of when payments are to be made. Be wary if a contractor asks for a substantial part of the bill before the work is near completion. Find out how much money you lose if you cancel the job.

√ Several days into a major job, ask the permit office to send out inspectors (usually free of charge). Provided the work meets your approval and that of the inspectors, let it continue. If not, have it stopped until the changes are made. After completion of the project, request another inspection. Only then should you initiate or complete payment. Never sign a completion agreement until you are satisfied with the work.

√ If you are alone in the house at the time a contractor is working, you may want to alert a neighbor or friend. Keep an eye on the workers; know where they are and what they are doing at all times.

Auto Repair Checklist

Choosing a shop

√ Take care in choosing a repair shop. It can save you money, time and nerves in the end. One way to go is to find a certified mechanic. The National Institute for Automotive Service Excellence (NIASE) tests and certifies mechanics. Certification is not automatic and an estimated 30 percent of the tests taken are failed. There are about 156,000 mechanics nationwide that are currently certified. But certification by itself is not always a good guarantee.

The Washington (D.C.) Consumers' *Checkbook* (put out by the Washington Center for the Study of Services) rated Washington-area shops and found little correlation between certification and customer satisfaction.[3] "One explanation for this surprising result," said *Checkbook's* authors, "is that NIASE certifies only the competence of individual mechanics. Competence of one, or a few, mechanics in one or more service specialties [engine repair, automatic transmission repair, etc.] does not guarantee competence of a shop's other mechanics, much less their diligence and honesty."

Shops are certified by the American Automobile Association (AAA), which is supposed to inspect for the appropriate equipment and customer conveniences, and examine staffing and quality control procedures. AAA-approved shops offer a 90-day or 4,000-mile parts and labor warranty to AAA members. But again, that certification is not a good guarantee of quality work. "The AAA-approved shops we evaluated," said *Checkbook,* "look better, but only slightly better, than other shops on our quality measure."

Customers should take other factors into account: the fixed prices and labor rates of the shop (by the way, low prices are not any guarantee either); the attitude of the repairmen; and most importantly whether your friends or family members have used the shop before and been satisfied with the work. There may also be rating services, like Checkbook in Washington, for your area.

√ Be wary of specialty shops that advertise services such as "free towing" or bargain brake jobs. Good shops, which depend on regular customers, don't have to advertise deals.

√ Keep in mind that only dealers are authorized by their auto companies to perform warranty repairs, but don't ask them to do nonwarranty work until you shop around. It is a good idea to check the independent garages in your area. Unlike dealerships or gas stations, they have nothing to sell except repairs.

KEEPING TABS

√ When you bring in your car for repairs, take along a written list of the problems, and keep a copy for yourself.

√ When you describe the problem be as specific as possible, As mentioned earlier, you should describe the symptoms—sounds, smells, feel of car—and when they actually happen (i.e. in cold weather, when the car is stopped, etc.) If you find it difficult to describe, get someone in the shop to go on a test drive.

√ Always get a written estimate before work begins that includes parts and labor, and an estimate of when the work will be completed. Never sign a blank repair order. Cross out the blank lines after the work you request is filled in.

√ Be precise when you order a tune-up. It is a vague term that sometimes means the serviceman will perform a lot of "repairs" you don't need and neglect other items. A tune-up should include a compression check of all cylinders; a check of all engine electrical connections, a check (and often replacement) of ignition points, condenser and plugs, and finally, resetting of all ignition and carburetor adjustments.

√ Be wary of the mechanic who finds ailments in your car that you did not ask to be fixed. Keep a schedule of routine maintenance so that you can check his suggestions against work recently done on your car.

√ If your suspicions are aroused, don't authorize additional repairs until you have had another diagnosis. You may find it is worth it.

√ If you pay for repairs that are not done properly, try to get the shop to do the job without additional charge. Speak directly to the service manager (not the service writer who wrote up your original repair order). Ask the manager to test drive the car with you so that you can point out the problems.

√ The Federal Trade Commission suggests using a credit card on auto repairs as a protection against faulty or unnecessary work. If you pay by check, by the time you find out about the problem it may be too late to stop payment. Cash is certainly gone. "According to federal law," says the FTC, "if you have a problem with goods or services purchased with your credit card, you have the same legal rights in dealing with the credit card issuer as you have with the auto mechanic. In other words, because you have the right to withhold payment from the auto mechanic for sloppy or incorrect repairs, you *also* have the right to refuse to pay the credit card company. Of course, you may withhold no more than the amount of the repair in dispute."

√ If you cannot get the problem resolved, says the National Highway Traffic Safety Administration (NHTSA) in its *Car Book*,[4] "take the car to a mechanic you trust for an independent examination. Get a written statement defining the problem and telling how it can be fixed. Give your repair shop a copy."

√ If there is a complaints handling panel in your city, present your problem there. The panel generally can give assistance. Or contact the Better Business Bureau which will, in some regions, mediate complaints. If the BBB is passive, hold them to higher standards of concern for comumers. At the very least the Bureau will enter your complaint into its files on the particular shop.

√ NHTSA also suggests you call or write your local 'Action Line' newspaper columnists, or radio or TV broadcaster. Send a copy of the letter to the repair facility.

√ If none of that elicits an adequate response from the repair shop, you can bring suit against the facility in Small Claims Court. The fee for filing such an action is small and you generally represent yourself without a lawyer, saving legal fees. Check with your state to find out what the dollar limit on claiming damages in Small Claims Court is. Your local consumer affairs office or state attorney general's office or the clerk of the court can tell you how to make such a claim.

FOOTNOTES

1. Goffman, Erving, *Gender Advertising* (Harper and Row, NY, 1976) p. 38
2. Conde Nast, "The Women's Market (New York, 1981), p. VIII
3. Center for Study of Consumer Services, *Washington Consumers' Checkbook: Auto Repair* (Washington, D.C.), pp. 16–17.
4. National Highway Traffic Safety Administration, U.S. Department of Transportation, *The Car Book*, Jan., 1981, pp. 44–45.

THE PROBLEM:
The auto mechanic who tries to "Take you for a ride."

THE SOLUTION:
Remember your family.

4

HEALTH

A prominent woman physician once remarked that a doctor-patient relationship is like a marriage—each side has unrealistic expectations and assumptions about the other. The relationship between a woman patient and a male doctor has particular strains. Many women complain that male physicians do not treat their ailments seriously, frequently suggest emotional causes for physical pains, and over-drug and over-operate. Doctors retort that too many women come to them with "trivial" discomforts and pressure them for unnecessary prescriptions. Some women patients complain that male doctors are condescending. And many male doctors reply that women come to them looking for a demi-god, a masculine authority figure who can cure their every physical and emotional pain. As the communication gap grows, the chances that womens' health needs are being met narrow.

The obstacles that block women from receiving competent and understanding care from male doctors are deeply rooted in both society and the medical field. The practices of any profession, including medicine, are a reflection of the society that created it. The societal stereotypes and biases against women—that they are less intelligent, feeble, and more prone to emotional disorders—have carried over into the medical profession since its inception.

Ancient Greek physicians developed the theory that the emotional disorder "hysteria" was brought on by the female reproductive system—the word "hysteria" in Greek translates literally as "belonging to the womb." Throughout history male doctors performed hysterectomies and clitorectomies on women to "cure" mental and emotional disorders.

Just over 100 years ago, a well-known physician, Dr. Issac Ray, argued that *all* women were likely to fall victim to hysteria, insanity, and criminal behavior: "With women it is but a step from extreme nervous susceptibility to downright hysteria, and from that to overt insanity. In the sexual evolution, in pregnancy, in the parturient period, in lactation, strange thoughts, extraordinary feelings, unseasonable appetites, criminal impulses, may haunt a mind at other times innocent and pure."[1]

Now, with women playing a more forceful role throughout society, no one would publicly express those kinds of thoughts even if they had them. But the lingering remnants of these attitudes are still visible—in the doctor who talks down to women patients, who withholds information, and who dispenses unnecessary mood-altering drugs. "They think we're short and slight and have high-pitched voices so we must be children," said Dr. Estelle Ramey, an endocrinologist at Georgetown University. Female patients perpetuate that attitude by assuming a helpless role.

Women are the largest consumers of health care in the country:[2] they have babies, their reproductive systems are more unpredictable, and they generally are the ones who take children to the doctor. They receive 60 percent of all drug prescriptions in the country.[3] Women also face physically and emotionally traumatic operations such as mastectomies and hysterectomies. Yet, the deliverers of healthcare in the U.S. are almost exclusively male.

Over the last decade, the relationship between male doctors and female patients has begun to change. Women have spoken up and their doctors have become more sensitive to their needs, more aware of their capabilities. The influx of women into the career world is chipping away at long-held biases. "The main change has been in what women themselves are doing," said Dr. Ramey. "When women came in wanting to be treated like children—and many women demanded that—he [the doctor] responded in kind. Now more and more women are going to doctors with a different attitude: They want to know what, why, how and when."

More and more women are also seeking out female practitioners. Nearly every day Dr. Ramey receives calls from women asking her to recommend a good doctor. Not too long ago, when she suggested a female doctor to a female patient, the universal response was: "I'd feel more comfortable with a man." Now she receives the opposite reaction. "Women gynecologists are booked solid," said Ramey, "and the men are getting annoyed."

A 29-year-old single woman adds: "Until I found my new doctor, I had to endure cold forceps, cold stirrups, etc., at the hands of male gynecologists. Not so at my clinic, as it is staffed mostly by women. But I have to wait several hours after each scheduled appointment time to see a doctor as they are so busy with women who are fed up with male gynecologists."

Male gynecologists can avoid such warnings at their own risk; the ob-gyn field is suffering financially because of the drop in the birth rate. It is becoming a buyer's market.

CAVALIER DOCTORS

"If a physician cannot come up with a diagnosis, it is always 'emotional.' After running in circles for almost 15 years, one doctor finally discovered that my thyroid was malfunctioning. Until that time all my complaints were 'emotional.' "

—68-year-old woman

Many women responding to our questionnaire felt their doctors treat them like children and refuse to respond to their questions adequately. This was a complaint directed primarily, though not solely, at male doctors. "I have encountered two very unempathetic male ob-gyn's," remarked one women, "one of whom went beyond that to maliciousness."

"I prefer a concerned doctor and those seem to be women doctors," said a 25-year-old administrative secretary. A 53-year-old married woman described woman physicians as "more understanding" and men as "more condescending." Previous studies have demonstrated that women physicians tend to spend more time with each patient and to show more interest in the patient's social background and problems.[5]

A 33-year-old woman described her experience with a male physician when she decided to switch from the Pill, because of the risks associated with it, to another form of birth control. "I went to my doctor inquiring about the diaphragm and tubal ligation. He *refused* to discuss either with me. He advised me he only recommended the Pill for women and didn't deal with other forms of birth control . . . He vehemently opposed tubal ligation. His comment to me— and I was so angry that I still remember this—was: 'What if you meet a nice boy who wants to have babies—then you'd regret it.' I've always been clear about not wanting children and I haven't changed my mind in that time. But he was clearly unwilling to accept the fact that I knew my own mind and could make that choice for myself. His thinking obviously indicated that what a man in my life wished would have to take precedence . . . Later I found a woman [doctor]—she's wonderful, open to anything I wanted. I got a diaphragm. She was willing to do the tubal ligation, which I decided against only because I didn't want to subject my body to a surgical procedure."

"It's Only Psychological"

Similarly, doctors often treat women's pains less seriously than men's pains, attributing the woman's ailment to emotional distress or pyschological disorders. Women *are* much more likely to show up in a doctor's office with a less serious ailment than a man, who has likely been brought up to view going to a doctor as a sign of weakness. "Often men will overlook minor pain while women will go to the doctor for a cure," said Dr. Lawrence Schneiderman of the University of California, San Diego. For women, the result is like the boy who cried wolf. Often, emotional problems are discussed or override the physical ailment.

The problem is compounded because male doctors cannot experience a woman's pains. Schneiderman and his colleague, Dr. Karen Armitage studied the medical files of 52 men and 52 women who had sought treatment from male doctors for five minor ailments such as headaches and lower back pains. They found that "men received more extensive workups than women in all five of the complaints." Male physicians, the two concluded, "tend to take illnesses more seriously in men than in women."

WOMEN ON DOCTORS

(remarks from women who responded to our questionnaire)

Doctors *"downplay my physical pain. There's not great concern to end the pain; almost the belief that excruciating pain is normal."*

—24-year-old charity fund raiser

"Once with a specific physical complaint, the physician asked me if I thought it might be psychological instead of physical. I was offended by the question and yet perhaps it had some validity. I wonder if it would have been asked of a man."

—38-year-old health clinic manager

"For four years I was going to the doctor for a pain in my chest. They began to tell me that it was in my mind until I asked them what was on my x-rays. They found out I had gall stones."

—25-year-old mother of two

"Female ob-gyn's are more sympathetic [than males]—and they don't call you 'dear.'"

—45-year-old educational gerontologist and mother of three

"Several male gynecologists have been insensitive and patronizing"

—35-year-old educator

"I must say, female doctors I have met seem less secure and more often seek consultation. Also their detachment is very obvious. They work hard at avoiding emotional involvement."

—50-year-old mother of two

"Male gynecologists sometimes adopt a very condescending or fatherly attitude."

—50-year-old mother of three

"Male doctors have been much more straight forward and clinical in approach. I also know my attitude has been different. I am much less likely to have a lengthy discussion with a male gynecologist especially if the problem is indistinct and difficult to describe."

—28-year-old, single

Underestimating a patient's complaints can have—and has had—dire consequences. One 53-year-old woman was told her problem was just psychological; later another doctor diagnosed it as a serious physical problem. "If a physician cannot come up with a diagnosis," said one woman, 68, "it is always 'emotional.' After running in circles for almost 15 years, one doctor finally discovered that my thyroid was malfunctioning. Until that time all my complaints were 'emotional.' "

A 22-year-old from Massachusetts described how she learned the hard way about "doctors who attach labels to symptoms they are not capable of diagnosing." She was having pain in her lower abdomen and visited her doctor. "I complained about severe pain and was told it was psychological," she said. It turned out to be "a blood clot in my uterus that caused me so much pain I could not straighten out my body. A male ob-gyn insisted it was psychological even though I could pinpoint exactly where the pain was located . . . Serious complications resulted from that neglect."

A 29-year-old woman reported that when she was 21 she had a case of bronchial pneumonia. The doctor she saw first told her: "It's probably in your mind. You probably take after your mother. She's the nervous type too." Another woman's "psychological" lower abdominal pain turned out to be a cyst.

In looking for psychological reasons behind ailments, doctors can go to extremes. One 24-year-old woman reported that her gynecologist administered a piercingly personal questionnaire before her first visit. Among the questions asked:

*How many sexual partners have you had?
*Male or female partners?
*How many partners at *one* time?
*What is your favorite sexual position?

Drugs

Diagnosing symptoms as "emotional" or "psychological" leads logically to prescribing mood-altering drugs. Doctors write more than 200 million prescriptions each year for tranquilizers, sedatives, painkillers and stimulants. Women account for most of those prescriptions.

Cynthia Maginniss started taking Valium when she was 16-years-old, just after her mother died.[6] The next several years of her life were a blur. Her gynecologist prescribed Valium when she was depressed and bored as a young housewife. Later he gave her Valium and Darvon for cramps, then Valium during a pregnancy. After the birth of that child, her second, she was depressed and anxious and developed colitis. Her family doctor gave her a relaxant and another painkiller. "My doctors never asked me what else I was taking and didn't tell me what I was being given," said Maginniss.

After hallucinations, bad dreams, walking into walls and suicide attempts, Maginniss finally sought help from a drug counseling organization, Women-Together, Inc. of Glassboro, N.J. Her doctors had never warned her about the dangers of the drugs they prescribed, nor did they worry about her addiction. Cynthia Maginniss had become a helpless child. There are millions of women like her in the U.S. (More information would be available to women about the drugs they take if manufacturers were required to insert basic information about the drug and side effects into each package. The Carter Administration

WOMEN ON DOCTORS

"There is a big difference in approach between male and female doctors, especially in attitudes. Male doctors see female patients as subjects, making it hard for you to relax. Female doctors are more compassionate and understand women's concerns."

—27-year-old, single

"Male doctors tend to talk down to me with a condescending tone."

—25-year-old TV reporter

"I have visited three different gynecologists. The men were understanding and sympathetic; the woman was a butcher."

—23-year-old student

"I definitely detected a difference in approach, especially by gynecologists. When I went to a male gynecologist about three years ago I was nervous and unsure. The doctor explained none of the procedures with me. Then I went to another male gyn. He kept trying to push the Pill on me (when I decided to become 'sexually active'). Last year I went to a female gyn. at my school's clinic. She explained all the procedures and discussed preventive medicine with me."

—20-year-old college student

"Female gynecologists generally are more willing to answer questions and develop alternatives to many health problems women have."

—40-year-old Washington D.C. woman

"If I had to do it over, I'd certainly have female obstetricians. I found the males domineering, brusque, non-informative, not really relating to me as a person or really 'on my side.' However, I must also note there were among these three or four truly respectful and caring [male] doctors . . ."

—58-year-old mother of three

"I feel that my doctor does not volunteer enough information about side effects. Other people, male and female, have said the same. I always consult the PDR when prescribed a new drug."

—divorced woman

began such a pilot program. The Reagan Administration, however, has ended it.)

Doctors claim that women ask for mood-altering drugs. Some do, of course. But a doctor could say no, and certainly should carefully explain risks and possible side effects. Whatever the reason, it is clear that women receive many more of these drugs than men. One study in Ontario, Canada found that doctors prescribe psychotropic (mood-altering) drugs almost twice as often to women as to men.[7] More than twice as many women than men received prescriptions for anti-depressant drugs.

A 68-year-old woman reports that her doctor attempted to push tranquilizers on her to make her "feel good." She wrote: "As a matter of fact one even gave me a free sample and when I asked if this was a tranquilizer, he became very angry and demanded that I just take it, which I did not. In another case, I got a prescription. Again, when I asked what it was, he said I should just take it. It would make me feel good. So I asked the pharmacist, who confirmed my suspicion. Whereupon I tore the prescription to shreds—*that* made me feel good."

Women responding to our questionnaire mentioned over and over that their doctors had not warned them about the side effects of drugs, some of which were potentially dangerous. "It was only after looking up Indocin [which my doctor had given me] in the PDR [Physician's Desk Reference] that I found out it can cause stomach and intestinal bleeding and other nasty side effects," said one woman. A 68-year-old woman reported that she had *never* been warned about the side effects of drugs. Another woman added: "Doctors I have had in the past have informed me [about side effects] but only *after* I asked questions."

A 29-year-old woman reports that her doctors never told her about the drugs they prescribed "which is why I purchased a home guide to prescription drugs long ago. Family and friends now check with me when given a prescription as *their* doctors don't give details either." "It's difficult to get enough information from physicians," complained another.

A 50-year-old woman from Washington, D.C. reports that she is usually informed of side effects. But, one doctor did not inform her, and "although the drug was not dangerous it had unfavorable side effects of which I was not told. I stopped taking the drug and changed doctors. I was furious!"

Why are male physicians reluctant to share such vital information with their women patients? Part of the problem is that doctors do not routinely offer such advice to men *or* women. But, experts say, doctors tend to be less defensive when men ask questions about the drugs. "I think doctors don't tell women about the side effects because they think we are so whifty we would develop these side effects out of our own minds, something like that," said Cynthia Maginniss. "They have a very sexist attitude about women. I think they would tell me, 'because a man has to go to an important job every day, but women just stay home. And so what if they get a little dizzy?' "

One male physician gave his own answer to this question when he testified on the issue of informed consent to oral contraceptive use before a Congressional committee and asserted that many women are too flighty to understand the most elemental biological facts. "A misguided effort to 'inform' such women leads only to anxiety on their part and loss of confidence in the physician ... They want him [the doctor] to tell them what to do, not to confuse them by asking them to make decisions beyond their comprehension."[8]

Over-operating

At one time the following joke was popular in medical school:
Question: What are the symptoms for a hysterectomy?
Answer: A Blue Shield card and $200.

Doctors have offered up hysterectomies—surgical removal of the uterus—to women as the solution to problems ranging from birth control to backaches. Too often the only purpose this major operation has served is to line the doctors' pockets. Hysterectomies rank high on the list of several million unnecessary operations performed each year.

As I was sitting in Dr. Estelle Ramey's office, she received a call from a woman, a stranger, who had just been told by her doctor that she had fibroids, small tumors, on her uterus and would have to undergo a hysterectomy. The woman wanted a second opinion. Ramey gave her the name of a woman physician she knew and trusted, and who was conservative about recommending operations. "It used to be that when they found you had fibroids, they just yanked your uterus," said Ramey after she got off the phone. Fibroids are common among women and are usually benign tumors. But doctors often felt that it was easier to remove the entire uterus than to treat the fibroids.

According to figures presented by the Health Research Group in 1975 congressional testimony,[9] the number of women having hysterectomies increased by 25 percent between 1965 and 1973. Moreover, studies conducted over the 25-year period from 1948 to 1973 have consistently found that between 32 and 39 percent of the hysterectomies conducted were unnecessary. This included sample populations from New York to California. By age 70, according to government data based on 1973, fully 45.3 percent of all U.S. women will have hysterectomies. Significantly, women who use Health Maintenance Organizations reported only about half that many hysterectomies.

This very high incidence of hysterectomies is symptomatic of a broader problem of over-operating in the society. According to the Health Research Group research, surgery rates for all operations rose 22 percent in the period from 1965 to 1973. Disc operations, for example, rose 74 percent. As was the case for hysterectomies, "the odds of having these operations in a pre-paid HMO (where the fee-for-service incentive is minimized and peer review is prominent) are considerably lower," said Dr. Sid Wolfe, director of the Health Research Group.

Hysterectomies have been used for a variety of less than adequate reasons. The operation has been used on women seeking a form of birth control. Other times the operation has been performed to relieve menstrual discomfort. "No more monthly curse, no napkins, no Tampax, no accidents, no embarrassment, no poring over a calendar to see when a trip is feasible," said Dr. Joseph H. Pratt Jr. of the Mayo Clinic in a concise summary of that school of thought.[10] Dr. Ralph C. Wright, a gynecologist who supports routine hysterectomies, argues that the operation is needed to prevent uterine cancer. "When the patient has completed her family," he says, "total hysterectomy should also be performed as a prophylactic procedure. Under these circumstances, the uterus becomes a useless, bleeding, symptom-producing, potentially cancer-bearing organ and therefore should be removed . . . To sterilize a woman and allow her to keep a useless and potentially lethal organ is incompatible with modern gynecological concepts. Hysterectomy is the only logical approach to surgical sterilization of women."[11]

Certainly a removed uterus cannot become cancerous. But Wright omits that the death rate for hysterectomies, estimated by Washington D.C.'s Health Research Group in the mid-1970s, is higher than the death rate for uterine/cervical cancer.[12] According to those figures, and statistics compiled by the American Cancer Society on uterine/cervical cancer, 1,000 out of every 1 million women annually undergoing hysterectomies die, whereas 100 out of every 1 million uterine or cervical cancer cases are fatal. Additionally, many of those cancer deaths could be prevented with regular Pap smears and gynecological exams.

A hysterectomy, in many cases certainly, is necessary, but it is a major operation that should not be treated lightly. Women who are told they should undergo this operation should always get a second opinion, preferably from a doctor who is conservative about operations, before they undergo the danger, trauma and expense involved.

WHAT DOCTORS LEARN ABOUT YOU

"The idea of suffering is an essential part of her life . . . The traits that compose the core of the female personality are feminine narcissism, masochism and passivity . . ."

—gynecology textbook.

In Medical School

Though the textbooks in medical schools have vastly improved over the last decade, most of the practicing physicians in the field today—particularly gynecologists and obstetricians—were weaned on some shocking portrayals of women. A glimpse at some of these can help women understand the attitudes of those doctors that they complain are "patronizing" or assume that their physical pains are psychological. Here's some of the rules medical students were taught about you:

You are neurotic. Dr. J.P. Greenhill, in the popular 1971 text, *Office Gynecology,* asserted that women's pains are mostly in their head. "Many women wittingly or unwittingly exaggerate the severity of their complaints to gratify neurotic desires."[13] Indeed, according to Dr. Mary Howell, medical school lecturers generally refer to hypothetical patients as "he"—except when they talk about ailments originating in the mind, for which they use "she."[14]

Doctors, Greenhill advises, should look to personality factors for complaints ranging from menstrual disorders to pelvic pain. Among the questions to be asked: "Does the patient accept herself as a woman?"

In the 1971 text, *Obstetrics and Gynecology*,[15] the female patient is portrayed as "anxious" and "fearful," particularly during pregnancy when she may "fear that the rewards [of pregnancy] will be damaged or denied because of past sins." This type of neurotic fear may result in injury during childbirth, so the book recommends labor-inducing drugs for "most" patients, despite the possible dangers of such drugs. And though studies indicate that over three-quarters of all pregnant women experience morning sickness, one text describes this nausea "as classified with neurosis. . . It may indicate resentment, ambivalence and inadequacy in women ill-prepared for motherhood . . ." Addressing that book, Drs. Jean and John Lennane of Prince Henry Hospital in Australia later noted that women on oral contraceptives containing estrogen experience similar nausea: Are they "resentful, ambivalent, and inadequate because they are *not* pregnant?" the doctors asked.[16]

The inability of men to experience the pains of women's reproductive systems may explain in part why so many medical school texts written by men and classes taught by men until recently perpetuated the myth that it is all in the female head. One study explained away dysmenorrhea—painful menstruation—as wholly or partly psychological: "It is generally acknowledged that this condition is much more frequent in the 'high-strung', nervous, or neurotic female than in her more stable sister."[17]

Another text observed that "[f]aulty outlook . . . leading to an exaggeration of minor discomfort . . . may even be an excuse to avoid doing something that is disliked."[18] That "faulty outlook" behind dysmenorrhea occurs in about half of all women and there is no scientific evidence to back up assertions such as these.[19]

Those myths are perpetuated by lecturers. Dr. Margaret Campbell surveyed female medical students in the early 1970s and got responses like these:

> *"In the classroom there are a number of teachers that will tell jokes against women—make them synonymous with neurotic, etc. More of this was evident in the urology and gynecology blocks—'the mentality of women is dominated by their reproductive function'—than others."
> *"Women patients [are] frequently viewed as 'hysterics' with accusing looks at female students . . ."
> *"In lecture there are demeaning references to 'old ladies' and 'hysterical mothers'. . . ."
> *"Re: 'hysterical women' as a self-explanatory category—a constant problem for medical management—we need to learn how to handle."
> *"Frequent comments [are] made concerning the female 'hypochondriacs' we will confront."

You are a child that views doctors as gods. Gynecology texts have portrayed women as unable to comprehend even the basics of medicine, implying that they want to blindly put their trust and faith in their doctors without asking questions. In the 1968 text, *The World of the Gynecologist,* Dr. C. Russell Scott states: "If like all human beings, he [the gynecologist] is made in the image of the Almighty, and if he is kind, then this kindness and concern for his patients may provide her with a glimpse of God's image."[21] (Parental authority is deeply rooted in the medical profession. The AMA's code of ethics, adopted in 1847, urged doctors to "unite tenderness with firmness and condescension with authority

. . . to inspire the minds of their patients with gratitude, respect and confidence.")

By overstepping the traditional female role (e.g. childrearing, household duties, or losing the man in your life) *you can endanger your health.* Dr. Greenhill asserts in his text that a woman's inability to menstruate "may occur in women who consciously or unconsciously cannot accept womanhood. This condition is commonly noted in 'tomboys.' " Older women are also susceptible to such ailments, the texts advise. *Obstetrics and Gynecology* observes, "Post-menopausal women who have been separated from the significant men in their lives . . . may have vaginal bleeding."[22] (In reality, that may be a sign of uterine cancer.)

The physician is advised to begin gauging a patient for personality disorders when she first walks into the office. Says *Obstetrics and Gynecology:* "The physician notices whether the patient is reacting to the interview in a feminine way or whether she is domineering, demanding, masculine, aggressive." The normal woman, says the text, "sacrifices her own personality to build up that of her husband."

In *Gynecology: Essentials of Clinical Practice* by Thomas H. Green, Jr., MD, the gynecologist-to-be is told how to counsel newlyweds. "If the sexual inadequacy on the part of the wife stems from a fundamental immaturity and inability or failure to assume the normal adult female role in the marital relationship, [the gynecologist] may be able to help by gradually imparting to her the nature of what her role should be." That role is to "make herself available" for the fulfillment of the greater "instinctive sexual drive of the male" and to "preserve the family unit as a happy, secure place for both man and wife and for the rearing of their children . . . Herein lies her power and purpose . . . Only by understanding and assuming this role can a woman throw off her childhood inhibitions and taboos and attain the feminine maturity essential to a happy, successful marital adjustment."[23]

You enjoy pain. "The idea of suffering is an essential part of her life," the same text says of the female patient. "The traits that compose the core of the female personality are feminine narcissism, masochism and passivity . . . Too much feminine narcissism without masochism produces a self-centered woman." Apparently, women depend on abuse and pain for sexual satisfaction.

The book recommends that gynecologists conducting surgical incision of the hymen on women who experience acute pain during intercourse avoid anesthesia to demonstrate "to the patient that she is quite capable of withstanding the discomfort . . . pain . . . is usually a valuable part of therapy."

Classroom antics reinforce sexist images of women. Campbell's survey found that sexist jokes were pervasive. "Remarks and pictures—slides of pin-ups or seductive nudes or Playboy bunnies—are often used at the beginning or end of class lectures to break tension or 'gain rapport.' Comments about female sexual practices, habits and preferences are given as embroidery overlaid on factual material related to the clinical practice of medicine. It is assumed that any man has the right to regard any woman—colleague or patient—as an object of sexual interest."

Here is a sampling of responses to the survey:

*"Woman's place is in the home."

*"Wouldn't you know a woman would say that?"

*"In the 1st 2 yrs. of medical school, when large lectures were the rule, it was very common for lecturers to begin sessions with little jokes, invariably

with women as the butts, in an attempt to gain rapport. This, of course, encouraged the men in my class to adopt a similar attitude toward women, and whenever any attempt was made by women in the class to point out this humiliation, they were further belittled."

*"The head of the Ob-Gyn department tells obscene degrading jokes while performing surgery and considers it his right to tease black nurses about bizarre sexual habits in front of 10 other people during surgery."

"While it is true that medical trainees are taught—implicitly—that all patients are somewhat demanding, irrational, and of course less valuable as persons than the wise doctors who make life-and-death decisions, it is clear that patients who are also women are doubly demeaned," Campbell wrote.[24] "Patient status plus female status makes one a very poor creature indeed, and one is likely to provoke some annoyance or irritation from the physician."

In Medical Journals

It is not surprising that doctors turn with regularity to mood altering drugs for their female patients. Each day in medical journals doctors are bombarded with advertisements from drug companies, many of which directly or indirectly urge such treatment.

Past ads have introduced such characters as the *female* college student, distraught by "today's changing morality and the possible consequences of her new freedom . . . apprehensive about unstable national and world conditions," afflicted by "a sense of lost identity in a strange environment." For her Hoffman-LaRoche Laboratories recommends Librium "to help free her of excessive anxiety."[25] There has been the housewife "caged" by mops and brooms: "You can't set her free," Wyeth Laboratories tells doctors, "But you can help her feel less anxious"—with Serax, a tranquilizer.[26]

More recently a woman has been pictured as up to her ears in pills—carrying on a lucrative advertising tradition of identifying women with pills. "Theirs"— the advertiser's—of course is the better one.[27] In another ad, a woman is smiling on a merry-go-round, just like a child.[28]

The content of such ads is particularly alarming because doctors rely heavily on drug advertising for information. Often they are the primary means to keep up on new medicines.

As the Health Research Group notes in its 1982 book, *Stopping Valium,*[29] most doctors "receive little formal training in the pharmacology of psychoactive drugs (such as Valium), and most of what they learn about them comes from sources originating within the drug industry. Advertising in medical journals and direct mail advertisements, and conversations with drug company salespeople or detailmen are the principal sources of information about tranquilizers for many doctors."

The group adds that "during the late 1960s and early 1970s Valium and its cousins were heavily advertised for use in coping with the normal activities of life . . . Most advertisements which promoted Valium and its cousins for 'tension and anxiety' depicted women; other advertisements, which promoted Valium as an adjunct in treating muscle spasm, depicted male athletes."

In 1980 the federal Food and Drug Administration called a halt to advertising such drugs as a remedy for the tensions of everyday life by requiring drug companies to include this statement in product labelling setting forth the indication for the use of the drug: "[Name of anxiolytic] is indicated for the management of anxiety disorders or for the short term relief of the symptoms of anxiety. Anxiety or tension associated with the stress of everyday life usually does not require treatment with anxiolytic."

Today, says the Health Research Group, "simple anxiety and muscle spasm are no longer the only reasons given by drug companies for prescribing a tranquilizer such as Valium. Rather, physicians are implicitly encouraged to view almost every human ill as an occasion for such a prescription."

Sexual Abuse

In very rare instances, a doctor's distorted image of his female patient can translate into sexual abuse. One woman visiting her family doctor to find out why she had a ridge of puffy, red bumps running down the nape of her neck was told she had a tipped uterus and asked to lie back for a pelvic examination. Feeling uneasy about the way the doctor was touching her, the woman asked for her husband to come in. The doctor just told her to relax and "think about being on a beach with waves and water." Finally, she shouted "stop," got dressed, and ran out. Later she was one of several women to testify against the doctor and his license to practice medicine was revoked.[30]

In another case a 21-year-old woman went to her doctor complaining of abdominal pains.[31] Instead of asking for a urine sample—which she expected since she had a history of bladder infections—the doctor asked her if she was on the Pill. He told her to undress and left the room. She noticed his coat was unbuttoned when he returned. "I got on the table," she testified in a subsequent court case, "and he began examining me. Then he told me to take a deep breath and suddenly I felt something very wrong. At first I thought I was imagining it—I tried to dismiss it from my mind . . . But it wasn't my imagination. I tried to move away, to move farther back on the table, but he kept telling me, 'move back down.' Finally I jumped off and there he was, giving me visual evidence that something *was* wrong."[32]

Women Doctors

Complicating a female patient's relationship with her doctor is that women practitioners have not been fully accepted into medicine as equals with men. In 1871 the president of the American Medical Association, Dr. Alfred Stille, complained that certain "women seek to rival men in manly sports and occupations and the 'strong-minded' ape them assiduously in all things, even in dress. In doing so, they may command a sort of admiration toward a higher type than their own." He later said his organization would give "the people" women physicians "if they wanted them" hoping these "women would never embarrass us by a personal application for seats in this Association."[33] Added the editor of the *Journal of the American Medical Association* in 1900: The "whole question of woman's place in medicine hinges on the fact that when a critical case demands independent action and fearless judgment, man's success depends on his virile courage, which the normal woman does not have nor is expected to have."[34]

A leading American gynecologist, Dr. Augustus Gardner, took a more paternalistic view in 1872, claiming that, "more especially is medicine disgusting to women, accustomed to softnesses and the downy side of life . . . Rightings and tumults, and blood and mire, bad smells and bad words, and foul men and more intolerable women she but rarely encounters, and then, as a part of the privileges of womanhood, is permitted and till now, compelled, to avoid them by a not, to her, disgraceful flight."[35]

Women medical students still face the legacy of those attitudes from some of their peers and colleagues—whether it is a derogatory remark about the desirability of woman doctors, or a slight from an instructor. When students break up into groups of four—generally three men and one woman—"women very frequently report that the attending physician speaks only to the men," said Dr. Ramey. "If she makes a comment he ignores it or brushes it off. That happens quite frequently . . . It's changing, especially because a lot of these guys [instructors] have their own daughters in medical school now. Most doctors have learned to be more sensitive, but there's always a few."

Dr. Howell's surveys in the early 1970s revealed that male medical students feel deeply threatened by their female peers. One student observed: "The terms 'castrating' and 'hysterical' are used surprisingly often on us. We often hear 'I would never marry a woman doctor.' " In one case a histology instructor demonstrating the digestive system, asked for two women assistants. He added hydrochloric acid to some food to produce its by-product. He asked the women to clean up the "shit" and said "that's the place of women in medicine." The men thought it hilarious.

Once out of medical school, women have a difficult time beginning a practice; male doctors often will not let them into their group practices. "One doctor insisted his wife would be up in arms if they let in a woman," said Dr. Ramey. "Women doctors are really not regarded as first-class members of the club."

The number of both female doctors and medical students has sharply increased in the last decade, with more women in general practice, ob-gyn, psychiatry and other fields. But few are surgeons—the top of the medical social strata.

Perhaps one of the most overt displays of discrimination against female practitioners—and patients—is the stubborn opposition by a small portion of the medical profession to the use of certified nurse-midwives. Midwifery is not a new profession. Indeed, female midwives delivered babies until the late 17th century, when men began assuming the function. Men gradually drove women from midwifery through the use of version—turning a malpositioned baby in the uterus to enable its delivery—and forceps. Version had been used for centuries—Cleopatra taught it in the first century A.D.—but it had fallen into disuse by midwives in the Middle Ages who were afraid of being accused of witchcraft if the baby was born dead or deformed.

That fear was real. German witch-hunters were particularly vengeful toward midwives: "The greatest injuries to the Faith as regards the heresy of witches are done by midwives; and this is made clearer than daylight itself by the confession of some who were afterwards burned," said one inquisitor.[36] Later in Massachusetts, the first woman executed for witchcraft was Margaret Jones, a physician and midwife.[37]

Men found that delivering babies could be a lucrative practice. They began taking over the field and barred women from medical schools. Childbirth became an operation, with doctors routinely using instruments and drugs to speed up labor. As Gena Corea reports, in her book, *The Hidden Malpractice* one unorthodox doctor in the 19th century complained about male obstetricians: "Instead of assisting the efforts of nature they go to work like a galley slave tugging at the oar."[38]

Nurse midwives have begun to reappear in increasing numbers and women seeking emotional support and less expensive healthcare are beginning to turn to them. On average, from conception through delivery, an obstetrician spends a total of three and a half hours with a patient and charges about $900. Nurse-midwives spend an average of about 26 hours with a patient during the same period at an average cost of between $500 and $800.[39]

Professional nurse midwives are registered nurses, graduates of midwifery training programs and are certified by the American College of Nurse Midwifery.

Though not expressly outlawed by any state, in many areas midwives are discouraged from practicing by hospitals that refuse to give them access to hospital beds for their patients. "It cannot surprise you that many women either for financial or emotional reasons prefer the services of a nurse midwife," said Patricia Bailey, Federal Trade Commission member. "Why can't those women, wherever they live, get admitted to a hospital for delivery or for emergency services?"[40]

TAKING CHARGE

For years women quietly assumed the role of a child in their relationships with doctors; some actively played it out, never asking questions, blindly placing their faith in male physicians, not wanting to know more than what the bills told them.

That has begun to change. Women are demanding treatment as intelligent adults. Some are switching to female physicians; others are simply equalizing their relationship with male doctors. Part of that can come by changing the way you think:

√ *Look upon your doctor as an employee, not a god.* For too long the medical profession has been placed on a pedestal, beyond reproach. Like all sciences, medicine is fallible. So are the human beings who practice it. (The excerpts from textbooks previously mentioned are proof enough of that.) Medicine is like any consumer service: You pay the bills, you have a right to expect quality.

√ *Ask Questions.* If something makes you feel uneasy—you don't see the necessity of a certain operation, you are worried about the side effects of a drug— ask for an explanation. Doctors who have nothing to hide should be willing to explain; if not, it may be a sign that this doctor is not for you.

Inquire about a diagnosis or prescribed drugs even if you trust your physician; it can help you become more informed about your health and medical practices.

√ *Don't let your physician confuse you with big words.* Get an explanation in terms you can understand and explain to your own family members.

√ *Describe your symptoms carefully and in detail.* As Ruth Cooperstock notes in her study of women and psychotropic (mood-altering) drug use, "contributing to the higher consumption of psychotropic drugs by women is that women frequently define their symptoms poorly, and the physicians' frustrated responses to these vague symptoms cause them to view these symptoms as 'trivia.' "[41]

√ *Get a second opinion* on operations, whether or not you question your doctor's diagnosis. It is an accepted practice and your doctor should not mind. If he or she does, it may be a sign that you *should* ask another physician. Also, it is worth remembering that in Health Maintenance Organizations, where the fee incentive for additional surgery has been removed, the overall surgery rates are far lower than comparable systems. As Dr. Wolfe notes, "All comparative studies consistently show that people 'served' by fee-for-service physicians have twice as many operations overall."

√ *Report improprieties.* If you feel your doctor has acted improperly toward you, demand an explanation. If you are not satisfied with the reason, don't let the incident slide. Report it to your state's medical licensing board. You may well not be the only person complaining about the doctor. If the board has enough evidence, they can move against him or her. If not, they will at least be alerted to a potential problem.

√ *Shop Around.* Like any consumer service, you should make an informed choice about doctors. If you are not satisfied with your doctor, set up an appointment for consultation (not an examination) with another. Dr. Margaret Bridwell of the University of Maryland Health Center adds this: "On your first consultation, make sure you are clothed and sitting upright. Often doctors will have you undress and be lying on your back, feet in stirrups, before they will talk to you. That automatically puts you at a disadvantage."

√ *Start a referral network at your local club.* It is difficult to find the names of good doctors, particularly if you are new in town. (A woman doctor reports that women who contact the American Medical Association's local chapter simply get a list of five names, chosen completely at random.) You can help yourself and other women by getting a network going at your club or organization in which you keep a list of doctors around town who are sympathetic to women's needs.

A list of women's health clinics and organizations appears in the appendix of this book.

Asking one's friends for advice is a much better means of deciding on a doctor, agrees Dr. Mary Howell, "inquiring especially about the doctor's willingness to teach and to answer questions, about the availability of the doctor and the nurse who works for him or her." She adds:[41]

"Before visiting a doctor, one should ask over the telephone about short-notice availability. It is less than helpful to visit a physician regularly for checkups only to find that it is impossible to be seen by the doctor when [you or your] child is ill.

"One should, of course, ask about fees. In addition, one should ask about the usual waiting time for an appointment, whether siblings are welcome in the office and what hospitals the doctor uses for in-patient care."

√ *If you don't like a doctor's service, let him or her know.* Howell suggests you can write a letter to the doctor (or clinic or hospital) "indicating the reasons for your dissatisfaction and asking for a meeting to discuss problems." Another method, she says, "is not to pay bills for care that seems to be careless or attitudinally inappropriate. This is perfectly reasonable if you do not wish to use that source of medical care again. For many, however, there are few or even no alternatives but to work with the only doctor or clinic in your community. While not paying bills on a matter of principle is a powerful weapon, it is also likely to be so alienating to the professionals that it will make future dealings very difficult if not impossible."

√ *Take more responsibility for your own health,* and cut down on your need for formal healthcare. Smoking is the number one health problem facing women in the 1980s. "Within three years," said the 1980 report of the President's Advisory Committee on Women, "deaths from lung cancer in women will surpass those from breast cancer." Sound nutrition and exercise is vitally important to good health: are you and your children meeting those requirements? Are the meals served at your child's school healthful and well-balanced?

√ *Become an informed consumer.* "To fulfill a collaborative role in all aspects of her healthcare, education is mandatory," said Catherine Fogel, a nurse from North Carolina.

"Greater knowledge of health can help parents pass along good health habits to their children," said the President's Advisory Committee on Women in 1980. "Only then will we break the vicious cycle whereby uninformed children become uninformed adults who then raise uninformed children."

A list of important reading material on health can be found in the appendix.

FOOTNOTES

1. Ray, I., Mental Hygiene, (Hafner Pub. Co., NY, 1968; facsimile of 1863 edition) p. 54.
2. Ramey, Dr. Estelle R., "How Well is American Medicine Meeting Human Needs?" Cedar Lane Forum on Medicine and Society, Oct. 1, 1981 (Bethesda, MD).
3. "Women's Dependency on Prescription Drugs," Hearings before Select Committee on Narcotics Abuse and Control, U.S. House of Representatives, Sept. 13, 1979.
4. Cited in Ramey address.
5. Ibid.
6. House testimony, pp. 4–19.
7. Cooperstock, Ruth, "A Review of Women's Psychotropic Drug Use," Can. J. Psychiatry, Vol. 24 (1979).
8. "Oral Contraceptives," Hearings before the Subcommittee on Monopoly of the Committee on Small Businesss, U.S. Senate, 1970.
9. Wolfe, Sidney, testimony before the House Subcommittee on Oversight and Investigations on Unnecessary Surgery, July 15, 1975.
10. Cited in Learned, Deborah, "The Epidemic of Unnecessary Hysterectomy," *Seizing our Bodies* (Claudia Dreifus, ed., Vintage, 1977) p. 199.
11. Ibid.
12. Ibid, p. 200.

13. Greenhill, J.P., *Office Gynecology* (Yearbook Medical Pub. Inc., Chicago, 1971).
14. Dr. Mary Howell, the first woman associate dean at the Harvard Medical School, conducted surveys of medical students in the early 1970s on their attitudes toward female colleagues and patients. Her findings can be found in the article "What Medical Schools Teach About Women," included in the appendix of this book, and *Why Would a Girl Go Into Medicine* by Margaret Campbell (Howell's pseudonym.).
15. Willson, J.R., MD; Beecham, C.T., MD; Carrington, E.R., MB, *Obstetrics and Gynecology,* 4th edition, (St. Louis, 1971) chapters four and eight.
16. Lennane, Jean K. and John R., "Alleged Psychogenic Disorders in Women—A Possible Manifestation of Sexual Prejudice," *New England Journal of Medicine,* Feb. 8, 1973.
17. Menaker, J.S.; Powers, K.D.; "Management of Primary Dysmenorrhea" *Obstetr.-Gynec.,* 20: 66–71, 1962).
18. Jeffcoate, T.N.A., *The Principles of Gynecology,* Third Ed., (London, 1967) pp. 684–686.
19. Lennane, Jean and John.
20. see note 14, *Why Would a Girl Go Into Medicine?*
21. Ibid.
22. Ibid.
23. Green, Thomas H., *Gynecology: Essentials of Clinical Practice* (Boston) p. 436.
24. Campbell, "Why Would a Girl Go Into Medicine?"
25. Ad appeared in the *Journal of the American College of Health Assoc.,* June, 1969, vol. 17, #5.
26. Ad appeared in *Medical Aspects of Human Sexuality,* Dec., 1969.
27. Ad appeared in *Medical World News,* June, 11, 1979.
28. Ad appeared in *The American Journal of Psychiatry,* Aug., 1979.
29. Bargmann, Eve; Wolfe, Sidney; Levin, Joan; and the Public Citizen Health Research Group, "Stopping Valium," Washington, D.C., 1982.
30. Kelly, John, "Sexually Abusive Doctors," *Ladies Home Journal,* June, 1979, pp. 55–6. Kelly's research is based on court testimony and court documents.
31. Ibid.
32. Ibid.
33. Fishbein, M., *A History of the American Medical Assoc.,* (Phil., 1947) pp. 82–85.
34. Ibid., p. 218.
35. Barker-Benfield, G.J., *The Horrors of the Half-Known Life: Male Attitudes Toward Women and Sexuality in Nineteenth Century America* (New York, 1976) p. 87.
36. Kramer, Heinrich and Sprenger, Jacob, *Malleus Male Ficarum: The Hammer of Witches* (London, 1968) p. 128.
37. Corea, Gena, *The Hidden Malpractice: How American Medicine Treats Women as Patients and Professionals* (New York, 1981) p. 222.
38. Ibid, p. 225.
39. Bailey, Patricia, Testimony before the Subcommittee on Commerce Tourism and Transportation of the Committee on Energy and Commerce, U.S. House of Representatives, April 1, 1982.
40. Ibid.
41. Cooperstock, p. 29.
42. Howell, Mary, *Healing at Home: A Guide to Health Care for Children* (Beacon Press, Boston, 1978) pp. 241–265.

5

FINANCES

CREDIT

> "A widely-held view in the mortgage lending community is that single women must present a stronger paper position than single men. Their credit and status must be more secure than those of men of the same status, and their credit histories must be more closely scrutinized. ... The myth generating this stringency holds that the female is inherently unstable and incapable of conducting her own affairs."
> —U.S. Civil Rights Commission, 1974

Ten years ago financial institutions commonly denied women credit solely because they were women. It was not an accurate or fair way of judging a customer's creditworthiness, of course, but it was an easy way, based on the same stereotypes and myths about women that are rooted elsewhere in the economy.

The thinking of the financial institutions went along these lines: A woman is generally flakey and unreliable. If she works, she is probably going through a phase that she will outgrow once she decides to settle down and bear children, at which time she will stop repaying her loans. If she is single, she cannot be trusted to manage her own financial affairs. If she is divorced, she is in an unstable economic state. In any case, she is a bad credit risk.

Before the passage of the Equal Credit Opportunity Act in 1975, women, and their families, faced a dismal situation. If a married woman worked outside the home, loan officers would discount all or part of her income in considering the family's credit application. That practice hurt many families, particularly minorities, since more and more married women were taking full or part-time jobs. In one case in the early 1970's, a Puerto Rican couple—both 29 years old, both school teachers with no children—had a joint income of $20,000 a year. They applied for a $16,000 mortgage on a $20,000 home and were told their income was insufficient; the wife's income had been discounted because she was at a child-bearing age, even though she had the same employment credentials as her husband. They later received a mortgage from a savings and loan, where only half the wife's income was considered, giving them an adjusted income of $15,500.[1]

Popular at credit institutions in those days was the so-called "baby-letter," a physician's statement attesting to one of the partner's sterility, their use of approved birth control methods, of their willingness to go through with an abortion. If a woman of child-bearing age could not produce the document the cost of future children would be taken into account when considering a credit application, and credit was often denied on that basis.

As a survey conducted by the U.S. Commission on Civil Rights found, "baby-letters" were not a uniform institutional policy and therefore depended "entirely on the attitudes of individual loan officers."[2] Branch managers in two lending institutions told the commission that they required baby-letters before they would consider all the income of a young wife. However, the central office of these same institutions differed over the need for such a letter.[3]

Women with jobs considered "nonprofessional"—such as a store clerk, secretary or bank teller—would be severely penalized. Less of her income was considered in applying for credit than, say, a business executive, nurse or teacher. The underlying assumption was that professional jobs, and the women who hold them, are more stable than women with "nonprofessional" jobs. This bias was greater against nonprofessional women than men.

Here's what the Civil Rights Commission found in Hartford, Connecticut in 1970:[4]

*"One lending institution official said that his rule of thumb in crediting wife's income was that, if the woman is in her child-bearing years, she must hold a professional position, and even then, not more than 50 percent of her income would be credited. He would not under any circumstances, however, count any income of a woman in her child-bearing years who held a blue-collar job."

*"A branch manager of another lending institution stated that he allows 50 percent credit toward the income of a working wife under 35 and 100 percent for a working wife over 35, regardless of the type of job she holds, provided she has been employed for at least one year."

*"Another branch manager of the same institution, however, stated that he would never allow 100% of the income of a female blue-collar worker. Jobs in that category, he said, are unstable."[5]

Before the passage of the Equal Credit Opportunity Act, single women—whether unmarried, divorced or widowed—had the most difficult time obtaining credit. Banks preferred married couples to individuals of either sex. Though all married persons were considered more stable "because, among other things, he (she) has responsibilities holding him (her) to his (her) obligations," unmarried women had a much tougher time obtaining credit than unmarried men.

"A widely held view in the mortgage lending community," the Commission said in 1974,[6] "is that single women must present a stronger paper position than single men. Their credit and status must be more secure than those men of the same status, and their credit histories must be more closely scrutinized. ... The myth generating this stringency holds that the female is inherently unstable and incapable of conducting her own affairs." As a result, creditors were reluctant to grant a mortgage loan to women, and often required a male co-signer.

Lenders used a variety of excuses to back up that practice. In one case, a loan official insisted that normally "a man would do the repairs himself whereas a woman has to hire someone."[7] For the unmarried woman, they cited the possibility of marriage and pregnancy—ignoring the fact that a marriage could well improve a woman's financial position. "One branch manager went so far as to assert that an unmarried woman could obtain a loan *only* if she had a professional career," said the Commission.[8]

Separated and divorced women faced a different bind. The finances of separated women are generally in limbo, and creditors shy away from ambiguous situations. For divorced women, creditors often refused to consider alimony and child support payments as income, even if there was a long history of reliable payments. Often it seemed that just being divorced was cause enough to deny a loan. One 51-year-old divorcee with no children wanted to buy a small $20,000 home in 1971. She had an excellent credit record, two department store accounts, had worked at an insurance company for 15 years, and had a $8,600 salary. She applied at four different savings and loan institutions for a $15,000 mortgage; she was willing to make a downpayment of $5,000. She was turned down at one, with no explanation given. At two others, she was told she did not "fit their formula." She finally obtained a 25-year, 7.5 percent mortgage from a fourth.[9]

Congress Takes Action

Credit has become an important part of the American way of life. More than half of all families in this country, of all ages, income levels, and occupations use consumer credit. By 1970, consumer credit was used in about 40 percent of all personal consumption expenditures, and excluding service credit, close to half of all retail purchases.[10] Since then the use of credit has expanded dramatically.

In 1975, Congress passed the Equal Credit Opportunity Act (ECOA) to end the severe economic handicap faced by women unfairly denied credit. As is often the case with such legislation, it was not just concern for the women facing discrimination that built support for the bill, but also a realization by the financial industry that it was hurting itself by refusing to lend to women. Statistical studies from as far back as the 1940's show that women were often better credit risks than men.[11] Women's banks, founded as a response to women's obstacles in obtaining credit, had begun tapping a huge new credit market. It was another sign to established creditors that they were missing a potentially lucrative business.

In essence, the ECOA outlawed discrimination in any aspect of credit transaction because of sex, marital status, race, religion, national origin, or age (if you are an adult). But the law did not end all lending discrimination against women. "Obviously, there is not 100 percent compliance, or there would be no need for enforcement by the regulatory agencies," said Jean Noonan, the Federal Trade Commission's program advisor for the ECOA. The Federal Trade Commission, one of twelve agencies charged with enforcing the Act, receives several thousand complaints about credit discrimination each year. Private groups, such as the Women's Law Project in Philadelphia, also report large numbers of complaints from women. Sometimes that discrimination is a result of a loan officer's long-held biases; other times it is a result of misinformation on the part of the woman customer. Here are some common examples of discriminatory practices and misunderstandings today:

*In 1977 lenders issued a one-time notice to joint-account holders, telling them they had the right to set up a separate credit rating, in compliance with the ECOA. Only 10 percent responded, according to Noonan. Most married women with joint accounts failed to do that, either because they never saw the notice (their husbands intercepted it), their husbands objected, or they simply did not understand its importance. Now divorced or widowed women are discovering they have no credit rating.

One woman, the manager of a store in her mid-30's, was separated from her husband and had tried to obtain credit on her own. She had maintained her maiden name, but creditors insisted they had no credit record on her. As it turned out, all the joint accounts and loans taken by the couple were reported only in his name.

*In another case a woman purchased a car together with her husband. They applied for the loan on it using both names. Later, she discovered that there was not any documentation of that car loan on her record. "I informed her," said Sharon Askew of the Women's Law Project, "that according to the ECOA she did have a right to have the credit reported in her own name, and when the title was independent of the loan, she could have the title changed by the Department of Motor Vehicles. The title, of course, is what shows who has ownership of the vehicle. The loan agency keeps the title until the loan is paid off; they actually own the car until the loan is paid off."

*Many women are still told they require their husband as a co-signer in cases where it is prohibited. (For details on when this is prohibited see "Taking Charge" at the end of this chapter.) "We hear complaints from women who have been told that they must get their husband's signature when applying for individual credit," said Noonan of the FTC.

*Often women, particularly elderly women, are denied credit for discriminatory reasons, but they have no way of telling if the denial is legitimate, said Noonan. "Although discrimination is occuring blatantly, it is not always clear to the woman in the situation whether or not she has been given accurate reasons for denial. We aren't hearing cases of women being told that they don't qualify for credit because they are women. Yet, this does not mean that sex discrimination does not occur."

*Rarely, women are still asked about their birth control practices or plans for having children when applying for a loan. "That practice still goes on," said Rosemary Rosso, of the Federal Trade Commission's Cleveland office. "But women do not know that these questions are unlawful."

*Divorced women still have a tough time getting credit if they do not have a job. In Dallas, a separated woman who received an income of $50,000 a year from her millionaire husband, was turned down for credit cards everywhere because she was unemployed. Now she has found an effective solution to the problem: she threatens to sue when her applications are turned down.[12]

*Some loan officers are patronizing or just plain sexist toward women clients. When a woman seeks a loan with her husband, for instance, she may find that she is ignored, left out of the transaction. One 38-year old married woman observed the attitude of the loan officer toward her: "I was less important and less of a participant than my husband." Another woman recalled her employment in a bank several years ago where men would commonly make comments like, 'she's got nice legs, we'll give her a loan.' Though that behavior is more rare today, it does still occur. One woman told *Business Week* in 1980 about her experience when she attempted to obtain a $5,000 bank loan to expand her Houston talent agency. "She prepared an optimistic, 73-page financial prospectus for the forthcoming year" said *Business Week*, "but was turned down by three banks on the ground that she had no collateral." On her fourth try, the woman reported, the loan officer admired her prospectus and said: 'What you need, honey, is a sugar daddy. Go out and find yourself a nice boyfriend, and we'll take care of that.' "[13]

TAKING CHARGE

Unlike in other sectors of the economy, in credit women have a useful and effective defense. The main problem is that most women do not know their rights under the ECOA. Your ability to point out your legal rights to a reluctant creditor might make the difference in a credit decision. The law has worked for others, such as the Connecticut woman who wrote to the company which had denied her credit, telling them of her rights under the law and that a carbon copy of her letter was going to the state's Commission on the Status of Women. She received her credit card.[14]

Equal Credit Opportunity Act

First it is important to note what the ECOA does and does not do. It does prohibit discrimination in any aspect of a credit transaction because of your sex, marital status, race, religion, national origin, or age (if you are old enough to contract). This means that a creditor may *not* use any of these facts as the reason to:
    *discourage you from applying for a loan;
    *refuse you a loan if you qualify;
    *lend you money on terms different from those granted another person with similar income, expenses, credit history and collateral.
The ECOA does apply to all creditors who regularly extend credit, including banks, small loan and finance companies, retail and department stores, credit card companies and credit unions. However, the ECOA does not guarantee anyone an automatic right to credit. It simply requires a creditor to apply the same standards of creditworthiness equally to all applicants. In other words, it seeks to guarantee equal credit *opportunities*.

As Emily Womach, president of The Women's National Bank in Washington, D.C., notes, many credit institutions do not communicate well with their women customers. Often, a woman may think that she had been denied credit because of her sex or marital status when, actually, she simply has not met the institution's standard of creditworthiness (i.e. your ability and willingness to repay the money advanced to you). A creditor must be assured of this before granting credit, and the ECOA does not change this standard.

Even women's banks, which were a response to women's credit access problems, have strict standards of creditworthiness which any of their credit customers must meet. The difference is that they may be more willing to explain their standards and help their customers determine how to meet that standard than traditional lending institutions.

To determine creditworthiness, creditors examine your income, including salary, saving and investments and any other sources of income. They look for signs of stability, such as type and length of employment, length of residence and whether you own a home. They may also look at your credit history to see how much you owe, how often you have borrowed in the past and how well you have managed to repay those debts.

Furthermore, creditors may set their own standards of creditworthiness, as long as they are not based on prohibitive criteria. Some institutions have higher standards than others, just as some institutions provide certain types of credit but not others. One institution may grant credit while another institution will refuse credit on the same set of facts.

Commonly Asked Questions

Here are some commonly asked questions about the ECOA with advice on what you should do, based on information from the FTC and Jean Noonan:

Q. I never saw the notice issued in 1977 telling me I could set up a separate credit rating. I am married and have only joint accounts with my husband. Can I still set up a separate credit record?

A. Yes. And the time to do this is while you are married. It is much harder for a divorced or widowed woman to claim a credit history.

Q. How do I do this?

A. The first thing to do is notify in writing all your creditors who report credit history, give the account number and the name under which the account is listed and say that you want the credit history under that account reported in *both* names. Women should be very careful to identify themselves as Mary Smith, not Mrs. John Smith. If you identify yourself as Mrs. John Smith, you will have no credit history because credit bureaus drop off the title and are left with "John Smith and John Smith." Mrs. John Smith is a social title, not a legal name. And it does not identify you. It identifies the person who at this moment is John Smith's wife.

Q. Aren't separate credit ratings given automatically?

A. If you have opened an account since July 1 or June 1, 1977: yes. That is supposed to be done automatically if you are listed as an authorized user or you are contractually liable (you signed the contract). That is, for example, if the man was requesting a Sears card, if he designated his wife as an 'authorized user,' Sears should report it in both names. Or if it was an account in which

80

you were both contractually liable (you both signed) it should be reported in both names.

Frequently both names do not appear on the application. Both names *must* appear on the application either as joint responsible parties or as one designated party and one 'authorized user.' If a husband requests a credit card and two come in the mail and he gives one to his wife, she signs the back and uses it (this is called a 'courtesy card' or an 'authorized user account') she has a right to that credit history, even though it is a courtesy card. But she has to make sure the creditor knows she is using it; just signing the retail slips is not enough.

Q. How do I know my credit history is being properly reported?

A. Go to the credit bureau in your area that reports credit history and request a copy of your credit bureau report. (They are required by law to disclose the contents. They are not required to make a carbon copy.) You should then make sure your credit history is accurate and complete. This is also your opportunity to make sure the history is reported in your name.

Q. What do I do if my credit history report is inaccurate?

A. Write to the creditors who do not appear in your file. Also, tell the credit bureau that the information in your husband's file belongs to you as well and they should transfer it. They will agree to transfer it if a) your husband designated you as an authorized user of the account, or b) you are contractually liable for the account.

Q. What about if I am divorced?

A. When you apply for credit as a divorcee or widow, you can insist and require that creditors consider the record you shared with your ex-husband.

Q. Will my ex-husband's bad credit rating affect my applications for credit?

A. Women get to claim good credit that was his, and so they have to claim the bad—unless you can prove why the bad history on the account should not reflect your creditworthiness. For example, if you are separated, live apart, and no longer use the credit card, and your husband has run up unpaid bills on his signatures, you could make a good case for disclaiming his credit history.

Q. Does the ECOA cover business as well as consumer credit?

A. Yes. However there is one major exception: a creditor may request information on your marital status. There are also other provisions that treat businesses differently, but which are not impediments to seeking credit.

Q. How do I know I have been discriminated against?

A. The ECOA lays out very specifically what a creditor may and may not ask, may or may not consider when processing your application, and may or may not require about co-signers. It is important that you familiarize yourself with this information.

You will find that important information, provided by the FTC, on the Equal Credit Opportunity Act, at the end of this section. (More appears in the appendix of this book.)

A SAMPLING OF WOMEN'S CREDIT COMPLAINTS RECEIVED BY THE FEDERAL TRADE COMMISSION*

A woman who resided in Utah for four years recounted her experiences with The Model Finance Company when applying for credit. In a letter to the Utah FTC she wrote:

"Talking with [the manager] . . . he asked me questions pertaining to my state of origin and my reasons for coming to Utah. At no time did he ask me my length of residence in Utah, my name, or pertinent credit information. After finding that I was originally from North Carolina, he stated that he had enough trouble with people from Utah, that he couldn't go trusting people from out of state. I have lived in Utah for four years. . . . I do not believe his actions are in accordance with the Equal Credit Opportunity Act."

***

A woman in Denver received a charge card in her married name from Montgomery Ward. Her husband was the co-applicant. Her credit limit was $150 and all bills and advertisements were addressed to her. She paid every bill.

When she and her husband separated she wrote to Ward's billing office in Shawnee, Kansas and asked them to continue the card in her name only. "I destroyed my ex-husband's card," she wrote in a letter to the FTC. "I never received a reply from Wards, but I continued to receive letters saying my credit limit had been raised to a final total of $900." After her divorce was settled, wards changed her bill to her maiden name, at her request. But she never received a credit card in her new name.

Several months later, she was informed by phone that her name had been dropped off the account and it had been transferred to her ex-husband in New Jersey. "I was told that if I wanted credit, I would have to fill out a new application. If they had a reason for their actions, they refused to tell me," she recalls. "My credit rating, although limited, is excellent. My ex-husband is another story. The Fourth National Bank in Wichita hired a detective . . . to locate him in Key West, Florida so they could repossess the car. American Express has contacted Wards several times trying to find his current address so they can collect from him. I have been employed by the same firm for 5 years and lived in the same town for 7 years. He has drawn unemployment off and on during the past year and lived in at least four states in the past year. . . . It appears their only criteria for granting credit is sex."

***

A Florida woman and her male partner applied for a loan to finance a mortgage. Within two weeks she received a call from the loan officer saying the loan had been denied. "We both subsequently called the CBI Credit Bureau and asked for reports to be pulled on both of us. My partner received his report

*Obtained through the Freedom of Information Act.

three days later. I have yet to receive mine," she wrote in a letter to the FTC's Atlanta office.

They made an appointment with the loan officer to find out exactly what the problem was. She knew her credit was good. "He informed us [the problem] was credit. He looked at the report my partner had and showed him the problems. I asked the loan officer, since the decision was based on credit, did they get a favorable report for me? He said, 'frankly, in order to save time, we didn't have your credit report in the loan committee meeting.' I asked him why my credit was not weighed as equally as my partner's. He informed me that they were interested in saving time and my report was not back from the Bureau," she wrote in her complaint letter.

She was never told why her good credit was not weighed as equally as her partner's credit difficulties.

***

One young woman in Boston provided a classic example to the Massachusetts FTC office detailing the comparative treatment she and a fellow male employee received from the G. Fox Company.

"I have proof that I am being discriminated against," she wrote in a letter to the FTC after being rejected for the G. Fox Co. charge card. "I am a single, white, middle-class female. I am 21-years-old and have been employed by City Trustbank in Bridgeport, CT. for one year and two weeks. Before I applied for this charge I had no credit at all, and still do not. I work along side another teller. He is a single, Puerto Rican, middle-class male. He is 20 years old and has been employed by City Trust for approximately 2–4 weeks less than I. I have proof that he has never had any credit whatsoever. He told me that he received his charge account from both G. Fox and D. M. Reads about one month after his application was received. His sole purpose in acquiring charge cards was to build his credit, and likewise with me. But I was rejected and his were accepted."

***

A woman from Los Angeles, California wrote to the Los Angeles FTC Office with this complaint about the credit policies of General Motors:

"When [my husband and I] purchased our car in 1978, we asked to have both of our names listed on the loan agreement. The sales representative refused, saying that there was only room for one name, and that name was supposed to be the husband's. Being ignorant of the laws governing credit and failing to read further in the contract which contained room for a co-buyer, we did not pursue the matter. As the term of the contract drew to a close, I realized that I have been making payments for a car for almost 3 years without improving my personal credit history. My husband wrote to General Motors Acceptance Corporation (GMAC) asking them to report our account in my name also. They refused."

***

A woman in Los Angeles was denied credit at Deaden's Department Store. In a letter to the FTC she describes the "humiliating" manner in which the store managers and loan officers treated her:

"I called the store's credit department before applying and asked the representative how much credit do they allow persons receiving state aid. She told me it depends on what I wanted . . . I told her I wanted a washer and drier set that cost $718. . . . She said I needed ⅓ down. Just to be sure I [brought in] $400 . . . which is more than 50%. I talked to the salesman, he asked me if I had ⅓ of the balance. I told him, 'yes.' He said, 'Fine. That's all you need and someone in the credit department [will] process [your] application.'

"I had to wait 45 minutes in the credit department, while two other customers were waited on but who came in after me, and both got what they wanted. (One of them who received state aid.) When a representative finally waited on me she only granted me $100, without verifying my income. I receive money each month and live with relatives . . . so I don't pay rent. I would have gladly put the $400 down. This is unfair. I feel I could afford the monthly payments.

"The loan officer never punched my name in the computer or even asked for verification of my income. She said she would have to talk to her supervisor . . . [H]er supervisor just looked out his window at me and wrote on my application '$100.' I never knew that you could look at a person and determine if their credit is good when you have 10 computers and 100 telephones to check on people. Any fool could look at my application and see I was eligible plus I had over 50% of the balance. But just my luck, all the fools were off today!"

***

Sandra, a businesswoman in Omaha, Nebraska, applied for a $2,000 business loan in 1982 to start a "Mary Kay" cosmetic business. She offered as collateral a motorcycle valued at $3,500. After being told that the Household Finance Corporation did not offer loans to start or support businesses, she applied to the same office for a $750 personal loan. (She again offered the $3,500 motorcycle as collateral). On both applications she listed herself as the sole applicant and did not mention a spouse as a co-signer.

The loan officer told her that if she wanted the loan she should file a joint application with her husband because he "would not loan money to a woman to sell cosmetics." She was denied credit after overhearing the branch manager tell her loan officer not to deal with her and to tell her that her file had been lost. When Sandra charged that the denial of her application was based on her sex and marital status, she was verbally abused by the manager who proceeded to call the police.

***

A Virginia woman who had been divorced for four years was tired of "being constantly reminded" of the overdue payments she had with Montgomery Ward on a charge account in her husband's name. "Finding that my ex-husband wouldn't take the responsibility of the payments, even though the court held him responsible, I just could not take the pressure along with other responsibilities, so I assumed the task," she explained in a letter to the department store.

She was earning $85 a week as an Early-Childhood teacher. Yet, she managed to keep making payments after changing the account into her own name. "Many times the sacrifices were very great, but at last I succeeded in paying off the account in June, 1981," she said.

The next Christmas, bicycles went on sale. "My son wanted one so badly," she recalled. She couldn't pay cash, so she arranged to pay for a bicycle in four equal installments. "I took the sales ticket to the credit department for approval. Would you believe the discrimination I received was so embarrassing? The reason they gave for refusing my credit was 'being at the Mr.'s [her husband's] request.' . . . I had been divorced for more than two years, and paid off the account myself!," she wrote. Had it been up to her husband to pay the debts, she informed the store, they would have had to use a collection agency.

"I was in tears, and went straight to J.C. Penney and got a bicycle. . . . Such discrimination is a disgrace. May God have mercy on those who back such rules as these," she wrote.

***

A woman writing to the Cleveland Regional office of the FTC had this to say about the Household Finance Corporation's denial of her loan application for household furniture:

"I cannot believe that at age 39, after handling all of the personal finances throughout my 13-year marriage and not only making sure bills have been paid on time but early, that I should suffer the injustice of being denied credit because I am separated or divorced. My salary as a secretary . . . is $900 a month and I receive $232 per month from my husband for support of our daughter. I cannot believe that $1,132 per month is not a 'safe' enough salary to make a $70 per month loan payment.

"Where is a woman in my position to start when trying to establish credit in her own name? When calling the credit bureau in Lorain, I found that I only have two credit listings in my own name, Penneys and Sears. I also have a Visa card, a loan with West Beneficial Finance Corporation in Elyria, and an account with N.P.C. from Pennsylvania. My husband's listings are numerous, having received all the 'good credit' that I have worked this past 13 years to establish. Is this justice?"

***

Federal Enforcement Agencies

National Banks
Comptroller of the Currency
Consumer Affairs Division
Washington, D.C. 20219

State Member Banks
Federal Reserve Bank serving the district in which the State member bank is located.

Nonmember Insured Banks
Federal Deposit Insurance Corporation Regional Director for the region in which the nonmember insured bank is located.

Savings Institutions Insured by the FSLIC and Members of the FHLB System (except for Savings Banks insured by FDIC)
The Federal Home Loan Bank Board Supervisory Agent in the district in which the institution is located.

Federal Credit Unions
Regional office of the National Credit Union Administration serving the area in which the Federal credit union is located.

Creditors Subject to Civil Aeronautics Board
Director, Bureau of Enforcement
Civil Aeronautics Board
1825 Connecticut Avenue, N.W.
Washington, D.C. 20428

Creditors Subject to Interstate Commerce Commission
Office of Proceedings
Interstate Commerce Commission
Washington, D.C. 20523

Creditors Subject to Packers and Stockyards Act
Nearest Packers and Stockyards Administration area supervisor.

Small Business Investment Companies
U.S. Small Business Administration
1441 L Street, N.W.
Washington, D.C. 20416

Brokers and Dealers
Securities and Exchange Commission
Washington, D.C. 20549

Federal Land Banks, Federal Land Bank Associations, Federal Intermediate Credit Banks and Production Credit Associations
Farm Credit Administration
490 L'Enfant Plaza, S.W.
Washington, D.C. 20578

Retail, Department Stores, Consumer Finance Companies, All other Creditors, and All Nonbank Credit Card Issuers
FTC Regional Office for region in which the creditor operates or
Federal Trade Commission
Equal Credit Opportunity
Washington, D.C. 20580

Complaints may also be referred to the Civil Rights Division of the Department of Justice, Washington, D.C. 20530.

The Equal Credit Opportunity Act and . . .

WOMEN

u and your husband apply for a loan. The application
enied because of "insufficient income." You think this
ans that your salary was not counted. What do you
)

u are single and want to buy a home. The bank turns
 down for a mortgage loan, even though you feel sure
t you meet its standards. What do you do?

ur charge account is closed when you get married.
u are told to reapply in your husband's name. What do
 do?

u may have a complaint under the Equal Credit Op-
tunity Act, a Federal law which prohibits discrimina-
 against an applicant for credit on the basis of sex,
ital status, race, color, religion, national origin, age
 other factors. This pamphlet describes the provisions
he Act (and the regulation issued by the Federal Re-
'e to carry it out) that apply to sex and marital status
 that affect you as a woman who wants credit.*

 Equal Credit Opportunity Act does not give anyone
automatic right to credit. It does require that a creditor
ly the same standard of "creditworthiness" equally to
pplicants.

What Is Creditworthiness?

ditors choose various criteria to rate you as a credit
. They may ask about your finances: how much you
1, what kinds of savings and investments you have,
t your other sources of income are. They may look
igns of reliability: your occupation, how long you've
n employed, how long you've lived at the same
ress, whether you own or rent your home. They may
 examine your credit record: how much you owe,
 often you've borrowed, and how you've managed
 debts.

 creditor wants to be assured of two things: your
ty to repay debt and your willingness to do so. The
al Credit Opportunity Act does not change this
dard of creditworthiness.

---

h men and women are protected by the ban against discrimination
ause of sex or marital status.

What Is Equal Credit Opportunity?

The law says that a creditor may not discriminate against
you — treat you less favorably than another applicant for
credit — because of your sex or marital status.

**Just because you are a woman, or single, or
married, a creditor may not turn you down for a
loan.**

The rules that follow are designed to stop specific abuses
that have limited women's ability to get credit.

Applying for Credit — Questions About Your Sex or Marital Status

A creditor may not discourage you from applying for
credit just because you are a woman, or single, or
married. When you fill out a credit application, you
should know that there are only certain questions a
creditor may ask about your sex or marital status.

- You **may not** be asked your sex on a credit application — with one exception. If you apply for a loan
to buy or build a home, a creditor is **required** to ask
your sex to provide the Federal Government with
information to monitor compliance with the Act.
You do not have to answer the question.

- You **do not** have to choose a courtesy title (Miss,
Ms., Mrs.) on a credit form.

- A creditor **may not** request your marital status on
an application for an individual, unsecured account
(a bank credit card or an overdraft checking account, for example), unless you live in a community
property State or rely on property located in a community property State to support your application.*

- A creditor **may** request your marital status in all
other cases. But, you can only be asked whether
you are married, unmarried, or separated (unmarried includes single, divorced, or widowed).

---

*Community property States are: Arizona, California, Idaho, Louisiana,
Nevada, New Mexico, Texas, and Washington.

Rating You As A Credit Risk

To make sure that your application is treated fairly, there are certain other things that a creditor may not do in deciding whether you are creditworthy.

Specifically, a creditor **may not:**

- refuse to consider your income because you are a married woman, even if your income is from part-time employment.

- ask about your birth control practices or your plans to have children. A creditor may not assume that you will have children or that your income will be interrupted to do so.

- refuse to consider reliable alimony, child support, or separate maintenance payments. However, you don't have to disclose such income unless you want to in order to improve your chances of getting credit.

- consider whether you have a telephone listing in your own name, because this would discriminate against married women.

- consider your sex as a factor in deciding whether you are a good credit risk.

- use your marital status to discriminate against you.

However, there are some closely related questions that are permitted. In order to estimate your expenses, a creditor may ask how many children you have, their ages, and the cost of caring for them, as well as about your obligations to pay alimony, child support, or maintenance. A creditor may ask how regularly you receive your alimony payments, or whether they are made under court order, in order to determine whether these payments are a dependable source of income. You may be asked whether there is a telephone in your home.

And finally, a creditor may consider your marital status because, under the laws of your State, there may be differences in the property rights of married and unmarried people. Such differences may affect the creditor's ability to collect if you default.

Extending Credit — Your Own Account

The law says that a woman has a right to her own credit she is creditworthy. If you are getting married, remembe that you can keep your own credit accounts and cred record.

Specifically, a creditor **may not:**

- refuse to grant you an individual account just be cause of your sex or marital status.

- refuse to open or maintain an account in your firs name and maiden name, or your first name an your husband's surname, or a combined surname.

- ask for information about your husband or ex husband, unless:

  — you're relying on his income

  — he'll use the account or be liable for it

  — you're relying on income from alimony to sup port your application

  — you live in a community property State or rely o property located in a community property Sta to support your application.

- require a co-signer or the signature of your spous just because you are a woman or married (wit certain exceptions when property rights are in volved).

If your **marital status changes,** a creditor **may not** re quire you to reapply for credit, change the terms of you account, or close your account, unless there is some ind cation that you are no longer willing or able to repay you debt. A creditor **may** ask you to reapply if your ex husband's income was counted to support your credit.

Establishing a Credit History

Married women often have had trouble establishing cred records because all debts were listed in their husband names. A new rule will help women build up their ow credit records.

The rule applies to information that creditors furnish to credit bureaus or other creditors about any account used by both husband and wife or on which both are liable. Such information must be reported in the names of each spouse.

The law also provides new guidelines for considering credit histories. It says that if credit history is used in rating your application, a creditor **must:**

- consider the available credit history on any account you hold or use jointly with your husband.

- consider any information that you can offer to show that a **favorable** credit history on any account in your husband's name reflects your own credit history accurately.

Some women have been denied credit simply because an ex-spouse was a poor credit risk. The law also says that a creditor **must:**

- consider any information that you can offer to show that an **unfavorable** credit history on any account you shared with your spouse does not reflect your own credit history accurately.

Another Federal law, the Fair Credit Reporting Act, gives you the right to get a summary of your credit history from a credit reporting agency and to correct any inaccurate information in it.

Notice and Penalties

A creditor may not stall you on an application. You must be notified within 30 days of any action taken on your application. If credit is denied, the notice must be in writing and it must either give specific reasons for the denial or tell you that you can request such an explanation. You have the same right if a credit account is closed.

If you are denied credit, first find out why. Try to solve the problem with the creditor, and show you know about your right to equal credit opportunity. If the problem can't be solved and you think that you've been discriminated against, you can sue for actual damages plus a penalty if the violation was intentional. The court will also award you reasonable attorney's fees if there's been a violation.

The Most Important Rules

- You can't be refused credit just because you're a woman.

- You can't be refused credit just because you're single, married, separated, divorced, or widowed.

- You can't be refused credit because a creditor decides you're of child-bearing age and, as a consequence, won't count your income.

- You can't be refused credit because a creditor won't count income you receive regularly from alimony or child support.

- You can have credit in your own name if you're creditworthy.

- When you apply for your own credit and rely on your own income, information about your spouse or his co-signature can be required only under certain circumstances.

- You can keep your own accounts and your own credit history if your marital status changes.

- You can build up your own credit record because new accounts must be carried in the names of husband and wife if both use the account or are liable on it.

- If you are denied credit, you can find out why.

To Find Out More

If you think you have been the victim of discrimination in connection with credit, you may want to contact the appropriate Federal enforcement agency for advice and help. These agencies and the types of creditors regulated by each are listed on the back of this pamphlet.

(Board of Governors of the Federal Reserve System, Washington, D.C. 20551)
(May 1977)

The Equal Credit Opportunity Act

...and AGE

Federal Enforcement Agencies

National Banks
Comptroller of the Currency
Consumer Affairs Division
Washington, D.C. 20219

State Member Banks
Federal Reserve Bank serving the district in which the State member bank is located.

Nonmember Insured Banks
Federal Deposit Insurance Corporation Regional Director for the region in which the nonmember insured bank is located.

Savings Institutions Insured by the FSLIC and Members of the FHLB System (except for Savings Banks insured by FDIC)
The Federal Home Loan Bank Board Supervisory Agent in the district in which the institution is located.

Federal Credit Unions
Regional office of the National Credit Union Administration serving the area in which the Federal credit union is located.

Creditors Subject to Civil Aeronautics Board
Director, Bureau of Enforcement
Civil Aeronautics Board
1825 Connecticut Avenue, N.W.
Washington, D.C. 20428

Creditors Subject to Interstate Commerce Commission
Office of Proceedings
Interstate Commerce Commission
Washington, D.C. 20523

Creditors Subject to Packers and Stockyards Act
Nearest Packers and Stockyards Administration area supervisor.

Small Business Investment Companies
U.S. Small Business Administration
1441 L Street, N.W.
Washington, D.C. 20416

Brokers and Dealers
Securities and Exchange Commission
Washington, D.C. 20549

Federal Land Banks, Federal Land Bank Associations, Federal Intermediate Credit Banks and Production Credit Associations
Farm Credit Administration
490 L'Enfant Plaza, S.W.
Washington, D.C. 20578

Retail, Department Stores, Consumer Finance Companies, All other Creditors, and All Nonbank Credit Card Issuers
FTC Regional Office for region in which the creditor operates or
Federal Trade Commission
Equal Credit Opportunity
Washington, D.C. 20580

Complaints may also be referred to the Civil Rights Division of the Department of Justice, Washington, D.C. 20530.

If you are denied credit, first find out why. Remember that you might try to renegotiate credit terms — such as the length of the loan or the size of your downpayment — if some aspect of creditworthiness connected with your age puts you at a disadvantage. Try to solve the problem with the creditor, and show you know about your right to equal credit opportunity.

If the problem can't be solved and you believe that you have been discriminated against, you may sue for actual damages plus a penalty fee if the violation was intentional. The court will also award you reasonable attorney's fees if there's been a violation.

To Find Out More

If you think you have been the victim of discrimination in connection with credit, you may want to ask the appropriate Federal enforcement agency for advice and help. These agencies and the types of creditors regulated by each are listed on the back of this pamphlet.

If you need help in locating sources of credit in your community, you may want to contact a local consumer education group or association of retired persons.

Board of Governors of the Federal Reserve System
Washington, D.C. 20551
(May 1977)

The Equal Credit Opportunity Act

. . . and Age

You retire this year at age 63, planning to fulfill a lifetime dream of sailing on the seas. But, despite a good credit history and a comfortable income, you find that the money you can borrow would barely buy a rowboat. What do you do?

On your 65th birthday you receive a notice to reapply for your credit card at a local department store. Your financial situation is unchanged from last year. What do you do?

You may have a complaint under the Equal Credit Opportunity Act. This Act prohibits discrimination against an applicant for credit on the basis of age, sex, marital status, race, color, religion, national origin, and other factors.

This pamphlet describes the provisions of the Act (and the regulation issued by the Federal Reserve to carry it out) that prevent your age from being used against you when you need credit.

Rating You As A Credit Risk — The General Rules

Creditors use various criteria in determining the types of loans they will make and the creditworthiness of the people to whom they will lend. They want to be assured that you are both able and willing to repay debt. They will therefore ask questions about your income, your expenses, your debts, and your reliability. Do you have savings and investments? Do you own your own home? How long have you lived at your current address? What is your credit history?

The Equal Credit Opportunity Act does not prohibit a creditor from using such criteria. It does not give anyone an automatic right to credit or require that loans be made to people who are not good credit risks.

Under the law, a creditor may also ask how old you are. However, the use of this information **is** restricted. The law says that **your age may not be the basis for an arbitrary decision to deny or decrease credit if you otherwise qualify.** You may not be turned down for credit just because you are over a certain age.

A creditor also may not:

- refuse to consider your retirement income in rating your credit application.

- require you to reapply, change the terms of your account, or close your account just because you reach a certain age or retire.

- deny you credit or close an account because credit life insurance or other credit-related insurance is not available to persons your age.

Some creditors rely on a system of credit-scoring to rate you as a credit risk. Based on the creditor's experience, a certain number of points is given to each characteristic which has proved to be an accurate predictor of creditworthiness. The Equal Credit Opportunity Act permits a creditor who uses such a system to score your age. But:

- if you are 62 or older you must be given at least as many points for age as any person under 62.

Special Considerations

Age has economic consequences. If you are young and just entering the labor force, your earnings are likely to grow over the years. On the other hand, your expenses

are probably rising too, and you may not have built up much of a credit record to rely on. As you near retirement age, you are likely to face a loss in income over the next few years. On the other hand, your expenses are probably decreasing too, and you may have a solid credit history to support your application.

All of this information could have an important effect on your creditworthiness, but not all of it will show up on a credit form.

The law therefore permits a creditor to consider information related to age that has a clear bearing on a person's ability and willingness to repay debt. Consider the following example:

- Jones applies for a mortgage loan for 30 years with a 5% downpayment. Jones is 63 years old and his income will be reduced when he retires in two years. The loan is denied.

Jones might meet the bank's standards if the downpayment were larger, if the loan had a shorter term with higher monthly payments, or if savings and investments — or other assets easily converted to cash — could be offered as security for the loan.

If you think there may be a connection between your age and the factors used to determine creditworthiness, you should go to your credit interview armed with alternatives and ready to supply whatever information will help your chances for credit.

If Credit Is Denied

A creditor may not stall you on an application. The law requires that you be notified within 30 days of any action taken on your application. If credit is denied, this notice must be in writing, and it must either give specific reasons for the denial or tell you of your right to request such an explanation. You have the same rights if a credit account is closed.

There's a new Federal law, the Equal Credit Opportunity Act, that bars discrimination in all areas of credit. As a professional or small businessman you may be subject to this law. You should determine promptly whether you are a creditor under the Act and, if so, what you must do and not do to be in compliance with it.

Are You a Creditor?

You are a creditor if you regularly and in the ordinary course of business grant to your customers the right to defer payment for goods or services they purchase from you. Merely honoring a credit card issued by someone else does not make you a creditor for purposes of the Equal Credit Opportunity Act.

Do You Grant Only "Incidental Credit"?

Incidental credit is credit that:

(1) is primarily for personal, family, or household purposes;

(2) is not granted under the terms of a credit card account;

(3) is not subject to any finance charges or interest; and

(4) is not granted under an agreement allowing the debtor to repay in more than four instalments.

> All creditors are subject to the Equal Credit Opportunity Act. If you grant only incidental credit, you are subject only to the rules described in this pamphlet. If you grant other kinds of credit, you should refer to Regulation B, a copy of which may be obtained from the Federal Trade Commission, Legal and Public Records, Room 130, Washington, D.C. 20580.

Rules About Incidental Credit

General rule. The purpose of the Equal Credit Opportunity Act is to ensure that credit is made available fairly and impartially. The law prohibits discrimination against any applicant for credit because of race, color, religion, national origin, sex, marital status, or age, or because the customer receives income from any public assistance program, or because the customer has exercised rights under consumer credit laws. These are the "prohibited bases" under the law.

Creditors may continue to evaluate credit applicants on the basis of their willingness and ability to repay. However, the law does impose certain restrictions on the questions you may ask and the way you consider information. You should review your application forms and your procedures for taking and evaluating credit applications, to make sure you are complying with the following specific rules and that in general, you apply your standards of creditworthiness evenly.*

Rules on obtaining information. When a customer applies for credit, you may **not:**

— ask the applicant's sex, race, color, religion, or national origin.

— ask about birth control practices or plans to have children.

You may collect this information when it is needed for a specific purpose not related to credit—for example, when it is part of a medical history.

Rules on considering information. In deciding to grant credit, you may **not:**

— consider any of the prohibited bases. There are certain exceptions: for example, you may consider age and receipt of public assistance to the extent these factors may affect continuity of income, or other aspects of creditworthiness.

*The law does **not** impose on incidental creditors (as it does on other creditors) any recordkeeping or notice requirements.

— use assumptions or statistics about childbearing or family size.

— discount or exclude income of the customer or the customer's spouse because of sex or marital status or any other prohibited basis.

— discount or exclude income from part-time employment, retirement benefits, or alimony, child support, or separate maintenance payments. However, you may consider the probable continuity of any income.

— take into account whether a telephone is listed in the customer's name. However, you may consider whether there is a phone in the customer's home.

If you consider a customer's credit history, you must include accounts which the customer holds or uses jointly with a spouse. You should also consider any information a customer can offer to show that a reported credit history is unfair, inaccurate, or incomplete.

Other rules on extending credit. You also may **not:**

— discourage a customer from making a request or application for credit because of a prohibited basis.

— refuse to grant a creditworthy married person an individual account.

— refuse to keep an account in a maiden name or a combined surname if the customer requests it.

— close or change the terms of a standing credit arrangement merely because your customer's marital status has changed or because the customer reaches a particular age or retires.

Penalties

Penalties. The law allows persons who have been discriminated against in connection with credit to sue for actual damages and punitive damages. Liability for punitive damages is limited to $10,000 in an individual action, and to $500,000 or 1% of the creditor's net worth, whichever is less, in class actions.

FOOTNOTES

1. "Credit Discrimination," Hearings before the Subcommittee on Consumer Affairs of the Committee on Banking and Currency, U.S. House of Representatives, Part 1, June 20-21, 1974, p. 258.
2. Ibid, p. 256.
3. Ibid.
4. Ibid, pp. 260–261.
5. Ibid.
6. Ibid. p. 267.
7. Ibid.
8. Ibid, p. 269.
9. Ibid, pp. 273–274.
10. Keesling, Karen, "Credit Availability to Women," Library of Congress Congressional Research Service, Washington, D.C., 1977, p. 1.
11. "Where Credit is Due, an Update," *WEAL Washington Report*, v. 7, #3, June, 1978, p. 5.
12. "Women Still have a Hard Time Getting Credit," *Business Week*, Dec. 1, 1980, p. 135.
13. Ibid.
14. Ibid.

INSURANCE

> ". . . women pay considerably more for health insurance than men. One Iowa study found that women pay as much as 50 percent more—*excluding* maternity coverage—than men for identical policies in health insurance."

While sex discrimination has been outlawed in the credit industry, it continues unabated in the insurance industry. A bill now in Congress would ban the use of race, color, religion, sex or national origin as a basis for discrimination in insurance and annuities. But most of the insurance industry has rallied in strong opposition to the legislation, predicting dire consequences for both the industry and for women. Supporters of the bill, like Republican Senator Robert Packwood of Oregon say those arguments are meritless—they listened to the same predictions from the credit industry during hearings on the ECOA, predictions that turned out wrong.

The insurance industry uses a person's sex in deciding rates, coverage and the types of insurance offered. But sex is an inappropriate measure. "Classification by sex is not only unfair and burdensome to women, but also it is a largely irrelevant, artificial classification," said Gayle Melich of the National Women's Political Caucus. "Criteria other than sex—such as smoking, medical history, driving record, occupation or recreational activities—are better indicators of the insurer's potential risk."[1]

Indeed, one firm, the Commercial Union Insurance Company, completely revamped its auto policies, basing rates on such factors as driving experience, driving record and car safety—not age, sex or marital status—and has found the system suitable to both customers and the company.

The insurance industry agrees that other characteristics more accurate and fair than the gender of a customer can be used. But many of those indicators are subject to change, while sex, generally, is not. A woman's weight may go up, her health may decline, they argue, but she will always be a female and subject to the "norms" of female life.

Why, then, doesn't the insurance industry use characteristics such as religion—Mormons live longer; or race—whites live longer? "Indeed," said Robert T. Freeman, Jr., president of Consumers United Insurance Company, "it hasn't been all that many years since insurance companies *did* base their rates on race. White Americans were charged one amount for life and health insurance. Negro Americans were charged a much higher amount."[2] Today that practice is not tolerated. Why, then, is it permissible to base rates and access to insurance on sex?

Sex discrimination can penalize men as well. In auto insurance, for instance, young men are forced to pay a higher rate than women because as a group they have higher accident rates. However, that practice penalizes men who are safe drivers. A more fair system would base rates on a person's driving record.

Disability Insurance

Most sex-based insurance practices work to the disadvantage of women. Disability insurance is a prime example. Until recently, disability coverage often was not even available to women. Now, when it is available, it generally excludes payments for disability from pregnancy, childbirth or miscarriage. Part-time workers, 72 percent of whom are women,[3] have only limited access to disability insurance; homemakers who required housekeeping and/or child-care when they become disabled, are generally prevented from obtaining coverage at all.

"Even where disability insurance is in fact available to women," said Melich, "women pay more than men for identical coverage." In addition, waiting periods, the period before benefits are payable, are generally longer for women. The "benefit period," the time during which benefits are paid to the insured, and the "basic period," the time the worker is considered totally disabled, are shorter for women. "For instance," said Melich, "a male in a low-hazard occupation can obtain a policy with a benefit period of ten years. The policy of a woman in the same hazard classification is usually limited to a two-year benefit period."[4]

Elizabeth S. Morrison, manager of financial services for Herget and Company, Inc. described her experience in writing disability policies for women:[5]

> I write many disability policies for women and more and more frequently my client is a woman who is the product of a recent divorce. Often she has been married 20 or more years to a professional and, if she worked early in her married life, she has not worked recently.
>
> Now she must re-enter the job force, usually with non-existent or out-of-date skills. She will often start out taking a job with a small business or nonprofit organization that does not offer disability coverage. It is very hard to get her adequate disability coverage, not because she isn't qualified or because she isn't in good physical health, but because during the stress of the separation and/or divorce, she saw her physician for assistance and

almost certainly was given Valium. In addition, her doctor probably recommended she seek counseling and she got psychiatric help during the period of separation.

Thus, said Morrison, even though counseling is beneficial to her health, "that fact that she had this counseling is very openly used against her by the insurance industry. She is seen as 'unstable' and frequently is declined disability coverage. The head underwriter for one of the major Mutuals for whom I used to write disability told me that the company felt that if one saw a psychiatrist under 12 times, that was all right. If one went 12–20 times, that was questionable; and if a client went over 20 times, it indicated a severe problem and therefore the company saw the applicant as a high risk. Many women clients with whom I have worked saw a psychiatrist approximately once a week over the year of their legal separation prior to their divorce. This, in insurance circles, makes them a 'high risk.'"

Morrison added that though an insurance company would certainly treat a man in that position the same way, "it is very unlikely that in our society, the man's doctor would prescribe Valium, and also it is not the usual pattern for a man to get psychiatric support during a separation."

As Morrison notes, although this type of discrimination is not specifically sexual, it is societal and thereby creates a clear "secondary" discrimination against women.

Health Insurance

Similarly, women seeking health insurance are at a disadvantage. Pregnancy, for instance, is rarely covered adequately. Although the 1978 Pregnancy Disability Act required coverage of pregnancy by employee group policies, in individual and private group policies maternity coverage is still routinely excluded. In addition, maternity benefits are frequently subject to waiting periods of up to 10 months.

Insurance companies claim that pregnancy is a voluntary condition. However other "voluntary" disabilities resulting from vasectomies and prostatectomies are usually covered for men.

Finally, women pay considerably more for health insurance than men. One Iowa study found that women pay as much as 50 percent more—excluding maternity coverage—than men for identical policies in health insurance.[6] As Morrison explained: "In most cases, individual disability policies do not include maternity, yet maternity is included in the company's justification for higher rates. This is obviously the height of discrimination or 'double jeopardy.'"[7]

Life Insurance

In determining life insurance policies, firms use mortality rates—that is, probable life spans—of individuals based on their sex. In some ways this practice hurts men: Since they have, on average, a shorter life span than women they must pay higher premiums for the same amount of life insurance, or receive less coverage for the same premium. But, ironically, the burden of that discrimination usually falls on *women,* since most men designate women as their beneficiaries at the time of death. A widow, for instance, would have to live on the smaller benefits if her late husband could not afford the higher premium.

(Even the use of mortality rates is somewhat biased and inaccurate. Though premium rates for women are usually calculated on the basis of male mortality rates plus, the average life expectancy of a woman is actually six to nine years greater than for a man.)

The problem with using sex-based mortality rates, said Gayle Melich, is that "by classifying an individual as part of a large and diverse group, such as all women, the perceived needs of that individual are bound to be distorted. Statistics show that, while women do tend to outlive men, the difference is relatively small. In one study, less than 14 percent of the women did *not* match the death ages of the men."[8] The similarities are certainly more significant than the differences. In 1978 the U.S. Supreme Court ruled that the treatment of individuals as merely components of large groups like race, religion or sex should be prohibited because "there is no assurance that any individual woman or man . . . will actually fit the generalization."[9]

A more equitable means of distributing health, disability, auto, and life insurance should be based on "all-American experience tables" said Robert Freeman. "That would take into account such factors as life and health styles, occupation and other personal choices that directly affect mortality and morbidity."[10]

If you are interested in supporting the elimination of sex discrimination in the insurance industry convey your recommendation to your senator urging a yes vote on S. 2204, the Fair Insurance Practices Act; or ask your representative to support H. 100, the corresponding bill in the House.

FOOTNOTES

1. Melich, Gayle, executive director National Women's Political Caucus. Testimony on sex discrimination in insurance before Senate Commerce, Science and Transportation Committee, July 15, 1982.
2. Freeman, Robert T. Jr., president of Consumer United Insurance Company. Testimony before Senate Commerce Committee, July 15, 1982.
3. Melich, p. 2.
4. Ibid.
5. Morrison, Elizabeth S., manager of financial services, Herget & Company, Inc. Testimony before Senate Commerce Committee, July 15, 1982.
6. Senate Committee on Commerce, Science and Transportation, "General Background: Discrimination in Insurance," p. 4.
7. Morrison, p. 2.
8. Melich.
9. *Los Angeles Department of Water & Power v. Manhart,* U.S. Supreme Court, 1978.
10. Freeman, p. 5.

PENSIONS

As in other sectors of the economy, company or union pension plans have built-in biases against women. Far fewer women than men benefit from private pensions. (1980 figures showed that 27 percent of men over 65 received benefits from their pension plans, while only 10 percent of women over 65 did.) The bias in pension law is one reason why most of the single people over 65 who live below the poverty line are women.[1]

Since Congress passed the Employee Retirement Income Security Act (ERISA), the federal pension law, in 1974 the situation has improved. But women still face some deeply rooted obstacles. Pension plans are not designed to meet the needs and interests of women in our economy:

Employment: Half of the women employed in the private sector work in the retail and service industries, which have the lowest pension coverage.[2] Women are also more likely to be employed in small firms, which have fewer benefits, and which may not be insured (so if the pension fund runs into financial trouble, you may not be entitled to any benefits). In addition, the millions of American women who are solely homemakers are not entitled to benefits in their own right, unlike in many European countries.[3]

Salaries: On average, working women still earn much less than men: Lower salaries mean lower benefits.

Part-Time Work: After having children many women want to work part-time. Under ERISA, to be included as a participant in a pension plan, an employee must work 1,000 hours a year before they can get that year credited to their benefits (about six months of full-time work.)

Length of Employment: Even if you are covered by a plan, you will not receive benefits when you retire unless you meet certain legal requirements. One is a specified length of employment. The simplest and most popular option is to require 10 years of service. Both men and women lose benefits under this system since Americans change jobs so often. But women move even more quickly. Men change jobs an average of every 4.5 years, while women change an average of every 2.6 years.[4]

Everyone should know how private pensions work and what they are entitled to. Too many women have found themselves retired with no pension benefits, or divorced or widowed with no share of their spouse's benefits because of plan requirements they knew nothing about. Here are some tips on the pension game (for details you should *read* your or your husband's pension booklet, do not rely on what others tell you):

Tenure: Your pension will have a required length of service before benefits can be accrued. Find out what it is. In addition, the pension does not have to count all your years of service: those years of service before age 22 need not be counted.

Death: If the employee dies before reaching retirement in some cases benefits will be forfeited. If death is before early retirement age, all benefits will probably be forfeited.

Security of the fund: If the pension plan encounters serious financial trouble or does not have the money in the fund to pay all earned benefits, the Pension Benefit Guaranty Corp., insures many plans.[5] However, not all plans are insured. A major exception to the rule is the pension plan in a small professional office, which often is not insured. Find out if your plan is insured.

Breaks in employment: Pension benefits can be lost because of an interruption in employment—either voluntary (i.e. maternity leave) or involuntary (i.e. layoff). ERISA has set complex rules for defining breaks in service and the circumstances under which benefits may be lost. But the general rule is that an absence shorter than one year may not be recognized as a break in service. Find out the specific rules of your plan.

Survivor benefits: There are no precise statistics on the number of widows receiving pension benefits (the figure was put at less than five percent before ERISA was passed, requiring some plans to include them). But it is clear that many widows still receive nothing from their spouse's pension plan. If you are married, be sure you know what survivor benefits are provided by your husband's plan.

Divorcee benefits: ERISA does not give a divorced spouse a right to any of the pension earned during marriage, but your state's laws might. Check with a lawyer.

Individual Retirement Accounts

Recent legislation, including the Economic Recovery Tax Act of 1981, has made changes in the regulations for individual retirement accounts (IRAs), some of which may be helpful to women.

Now you may establish and contribute to an IRA even if you are covered by another plan. It may be a good way to protect yourself, particularly if you won't reap the full benefits of your pension.

The maximum contribution to an IRA by an individual worker was raised to $2,000 a year, all of which is tax-deductible. Furthermore, the 15 percent of earnings limitation was dropped. Not only will this change help women build larger retirement accounts, but it will help those who work part-time.

Spousal IRA's were authorized in 1977. With such an account, an individual can allocate part of his/her IRA contribution to a spouse without her own earnings. Tax deductions are authorized for additional contributions up to $250 above the maximum individual contribution. However, in 1981, the requirement that half the contribution be allocated to the spouse was dropped. Thus, a worker may take full advantage of the tax deduction by allocating only $250 to the spouse's account while contributing $2,000 to his own account.[6]

Divorced women with no earnings will be able to contribute unearned income to an IRA in some circumstances. Specifically, divorced women who had spousal IRA's prior to divorce in some cases may be able to make tax deductible contributions of alimony, or a combination of alimony and earnings, up to $1,125 a year.[7] This may not be too helpful to many women since most women receiving alimony may not have excess money to put into an IRA.

FOOTNOTES

1. Women's Equity Action League, *Pension Reform: Retirement Security for Women, A 1980 Fact Sheet,* Washington, 1980.
2. Benson, Helene A., *Women and Private Pensions,* U.S. Dept. of Labor, Washington D.C., 1980, p. 3.
3. Leonard, Frances, "Older Women and Pensions: Catch 22" *Golden Gate University Law Review,* v. 10, p. 1193.
4. Fierst, Edith U., "Why Congress Zapped Pensions for Women," *Graduate Woman,* Nov/Dec 1981, p. 17.
5. Reid, Heddy F. and Ferguson, Karen W., *A Guide to Understanding Your Pension Plan,* Pension Rights Center, Washington D.C.
6. Fierst, Edith U., "Women's Retirement Income and the Three-Legged Stool," *Journal of Legislation,* v. 8, Summer 1981, p. 273.
7. Ibid, p. 274.

For further information on pension plans and your rights under ERISA:
U. S. Department of Labor, LMSA
Office of Communications and Public Services
Pension and Welfare Benefit Programs
200 Constitution Ave., N. W.
Washington, D. C., 20216

Women and Private Pension Plans
What You Should Know About Pension and Welfare Law

Pension Benefit Guaranty Corporation
2020 K Street, N. W.
Washington, D. C. 20006

Your Guaranteed Pension (explains termination insurance for single employer
plans)

Pension Rights Center
1346 Connecticut Ave., N. W.
Washington, D. C. 20036

public interest organization which provides several publications for small
fee

A Guide to Understanding Your Pension Plan
Pension Facts
Women and Pensions (quarterly newsletter)

Women's Equity Action League
805 15th Street, N. W.
Washington, D. C. 20005

Women Growing Older: Facts (packet of eight fact sheets on economic issues
available for small fee)

Superintendent of Documents
U. S. Government Printing Office
Washington, D. C. 20402

The Pension Game: The American Pension System from the Viewpoint of
the Average Woman by Sarah Kaltenborn
IRA's Plan for Your Retirement

Federal Trade Commission
Bureau of Consumer Protection
Washington, D. C. 20580

Frank Talk About IRA's, A Buyer's Guide

For specific questions about your pension plan or a determination of whether
your plan meets government standards:

Internal Revenue Service
Employee Plans Division
1111 Constitution Ave., N.W.
Washington, D. C. 20224

OR

U.S. Department of Labor
Labor-Management Services Administration
Area Offices

ATLANTA, GA 30367
1365 Peachtree St., N.E.
Tel: 404-881-4090

BOSTON, MA 02108
110 Tremont St.
Tel: 617-223-6736

BUFFALO, NY 14202
111 W. Huron St.
Tel: 716-846-4861

CHICAGO, IL 60604
175 West Jackson Boulevard
Tel: 312-353-7264

CLEVELAND, OH 44199
1240 E. Ninth St.
Tel: 216-522-3855

DALLAS, TX 75202
Griffin and Young Streets
Tel: 214-767-6831

DENVER, CO 80294
1961 Stout St.
Tel: 303-837-5061

DETROIT, MI 48226
231 W. Lafayette St.
Tel: 313-226-6200

EAST ORANGE, NJ 07018
576 Central Avenue
Tel: 201-645-3712

HATO REY, PR 00918
Carlos Chardon St.
Tel: 809-753-4441

HONOLULU, HI 96850
300 Ala Moana
Tel: 808-546-8984

KANSAS CITY, MO 64106
911 Walnut St.
Tel: 816-374-5261

LOS ANGELES, CA 90012
300 N. Los Angeles St.
Tel: 213-688-4975

MIAMI, FL 33169
111 N.W. 183rd St.
Tel: 305-350-4611

MINNEAPOLIS, MN 55403
100 North Sixth St.
Tel: 612-725-2292

NASHVILLE, TN 37203
1808 West End Bldg.
Tel: 615-251-5906

NEW ORLEANS, LA 70130
600 South St.
Tel: 504-589-6173

NEW YORK, NY 10278
26 Federal Plaza
Tel: 212-264-4830

PHILADELPHIA, PA 19106
601 Market St.
Tel: 215-597-4961

PITTSBURGH, PA 15222
1000 Liberty Ave.
Tel: 412-644-2925

ST. LOUIS, MO 63101
210 Tucker Blvd.
Tel: 314-425-4691

SAN FRANCISCO, CA 94105
211 Main Street
Tel: 415-556-2030

SEATTLE, WA 98174
909 First Avenue
Tel: 206-442-5216

WASHINGTON, DC 20006
1730 K Street, N.W.
Tel: 202-254-6510

6

LEGAL

Muriel*, a 46-year-old housewife from northern California, wanted out. In the years since she had moved out West with her husband John her marriage had been rocky. Now it was unbearable. John, an aerospace scientist, was distant and moody. He was taking out his personal frustrations and anxiety on Muriel and their 16-year-old son, who was already a discipline problem. Heavy drinking turned John violent. At one point, John beat their teenage son and then kicked him out of the house, threatening to kill him if he returned. The son later turned up halfway across the country. "He was going through a terrible time," Muriel said of her husband, "and we got the brunt of it. He would say things like it was my fault that he wasn't more successful and that I had betrayed him by having children. Well, we had three kids and he had a lot to do with it."

During that period, even when drinking heavily, John continued to work, sometimes putting in close to 20-hour days. "His family was a front," said Muriel, "something he was told he was supposed to have. That was back in the '50's when to be a young successful executive at one of these companies you needed a wife and children. So the thing to do was pretend you had a family."

After finally gaining the courage to seek a divorce, Muriel looked up an attorney in the area, the husband of a woman with whom she worked. "I did not have a family attorney," she said. "We didn't even have so much as a will. I was scared to death." The attorney agreed to take her case but wanted $500 up front as a retainer fee. He estimated the entire case would cost about $8,000. He was right.

Although John made a comfortable living and Muriel had taken a part-time job at a local university, she had no access to that much money. John kept tight reins on the family's funds. "It had gotten to the point where he would put down $60 to $100 a week, and those were the house funds for everything—for

*The story of Muriel and John is true, however, their names have been changed to protect their privacy.

five of us," she said. John paid the water and utility bills and made the monthly payments on their suburban home. Gradually he stopped paying even those bills. "That was one of the things that prompted me to go out and take legal action," Muriel said. "They were going to turn off the electricity."

Muriel was in a bind that faces women across the country when they seek legal help. She could not qualify for free legal help from the federally funded Legal Services Corporation because her husband's income was too high. Even private law firms and clinics that use a sliding fee scale, adjusting their bills to a client's income, generally base their fees on family income, not what is available to the woman. Technically she was in the middle to upper middle income bracket; in reality she was in poverty.

Muriel was fortunate. She borrowed money from her well-off brother to pay for the divorce. But many wives without full-time jobs have nowhere to turn. "The biggest single problem for women in any legal service is that number one, their incomes are determined for any kind of representation—whether it is a sliding fee basis or a legal services basis or whatever—by family income," said Marcia Rochofsky of the Edhuld and Rochofsky law firm in Milwaukee, Wisconsin. "And most women, in my experience, do not have equal access to the family fund."

Rhoda Rivera, a family law attorney in Ohio, agrees. "The largest problem that women face when trying to get legal assistance is money," she said. Often lack of funds can prevent women from obtaining important legal help. A 44-year-old woman involved in a divorce case said she "couldn't afford a lawyer's fee to fight for custody of her children." Another woman added: "I work but don't make enough to afford a lawyer—yet I don't qualify for [federal] legal aid."

Even women who do have access to the family's money often have to consult their husbands about large expenditures. Such a relationship, of course, could be particularly sticky if the expenditure is a lawyer for a divorce case, for example. Whether by restricting her access to bank accounts or insisting that she get permission before spending large sums, husbands can, and do, keep their non-working wives financially handicapped.

"It is not really a class issue," said Rochofsky. "In fact, I would say that working class women tend to have more access to some money than the upper classes." Working women do have an income of their own. But even many of them find access to family money difficult. "Many of those women have to turn that paycheck over," said Rochofsky, who has represented clients for seven years. "Some of them even have to raise their family on that paycheck because their husband drinks [away his own paycheck] or spends it for himself. But at least they have some funds available."

In some cases, a husband will convince his wife that because of the expense they should both use the same attorney in a divorce case. As a result, said Rivera, the woman "then is not represented." She also has no recourse against an unfair settlement. Often in child custody cases, said Laurie Wood, executive director of the National Center on Women and Family Law (NCWFL), the man can afford to hire an attorney but a woman cannot.

In recent years, women whose family income falls below the poverty line have turned to the local offices of the Legal Services Corporation (LSC) for help. But now that assistance is in jeopardy. The Reagan Administration has sought to eliminate the agency. Though Congress has rebuffed those requests, it has severely cut the agency's budget. Staff will drop by nearly one-third by the end of 1982.

Establishment of the LSC in 1974, supplanting earlier legal services efforts by the Office of Economic Opportunity, fleshed out the nation's constitutional principle of "equal justice under the law." Both Democrats and Republicans supported its establishment. The American Bar Association (ABA) has supported the LSC and opposed its budget cuts.

Former ABA President David Brink has told a Senate subcommittee: "[W]hen we deliver legal services to the poor, we do not give welfare or charity. We do no more than return to them what is already the heritage of all citizens of this unique democracy—their rights: rights to remedies, rights to justice, rights to counsel."[1] As writer David Riley reported in 1976, "there are 380,000 lawyers in the U.S. or one for every 600 people. But only 5,000 serve the 35 million poor—one for every 7,000."[2]

Two-thirds of the nation's poor are women; three-quarters of those on public assistance are women. Women constitute 72 percent of the elderly poor. So budget cuts in the legal aid program primarily hurt women; over two-thirds of LSC clients are women.[3]

And while funding for LSC offices has sharply declined, their case loads are sharply up. As a result, in many areas LSC attorneys are only giving prompt attention to high-priority family law cases, such as clear danger from physical violence. The waiting list for other cases is months, sometimes years, long. So even if a woman qualifies for prompt, free legal help, she may not be able to obtain it.

THIRD CLASS JUSTICE

"I've seen too many women switching to me from a male attorney [because he was] very patronizing. Some have been abusive verbally if the woman had an opinion of her own . . . "

—attorney Marcia Rochofsky

Money is the first impediment facing women seeking legal help; the second is obtaining fair and effective representation. The legal field, like other professions, is dominated by men. And finding one who understands the particular problems of women can be difficult.

Those problems can be enormous. A woman who has been married 20 years and faces a situation like Muriel's probably has never, or rarely, worked full-time. She has a high-school diploma, or perhaps finished her college education before she married. She has two or three children who may need substantial financial support for a college education, or medical and dental bills. Without a husband's salary, she is ill-equipped to support herself and her children.

Consider Muriel. When she married she was a teacher. She finished her college education in 1950. Until taking her part-time job at the university she had never worked outside the home during her 21 years of marriage. Since she had moved from the Midwest she did not have a California teaching certificate. There was no argument over custody of the children—her husband did not want them. So she faced the cost of raising three children, and the unexpected expense of extensive psychiatric care for her eldest son.

Most judges, of course, are also men with little understanding of women's needs, nor experience in the day-to-day raising of children. One incident, though seemingly minor in importance, starkly illustrates that ignorance. A woman facing what she considered an unfair divorce settlement recounted how she angrily asked the presiding judge: "What in the world do you think it costs to clothe a four-year-old child? How much, for example, do you think a pair of child's shoes cost?"

The judge replied: "Well, I guess you could get a good pair of kid's shoes for $4."

Quality children's shoes today range in price from about $16 to $35.

Women in divorce proceedings are at another disadvantage. Most have never encountered an attorney or a courtroom until that time of deep distress. The legal system is shrouded in mystery. As often as not a woman does not know the attorney she chooses. She almost certainly does not know the judge.

The language is strange and new. So are the concepts. "Lawyers," said Rochofsky, "are one of the elite classes in this country. We write the laws, we interpret the laws. No one but us can understand most of them. It is a preservation of that sense of secrecy. And while men are out in the world making a living or being professionals or whatever, and paying attention more, women tend to be less attuned—even working women—to business and the legal aspects of our society."

Lori R. went to an attorney for the first time when she was 40-years-old. She was married to a well-paid, high level U.S. government official and lived in a $400,000 house. Her daughters were grown but a 14-year-old son still lived at home.

At the time, Lori was suffering from severe emotional trauma. She knew her husband was seeing another woman. At home he brutalized Lori. "Everyone thought he was the greatest guy around," said Lori. "But they didn't know he used to bang his head against the wall and then bang my head against the wall." Distraught and unable to sleep she began abusing tranquilizers and alcohol. She had a nervous breakdown, made attempts at suicide and was hospitalized for a period.

Amidst all that she had to handle the logistics of divorce, something about which she knew nothing. She put her trust in a local attorney and signed the settlement agreement without fully understanding what it meant to her future. "I was crying and on tranquilizers," she said. "I just said 'anything is fine, just get it over with.' I didn't know I had signed a final agreement." But she had, and with it, she had lost the house, alimony and child support, and all retirement benefits except $27 a month. "Now I can just barely make it on my salary. I have no way to retire, no way to buy property," she said.

After she had recovered from her emotional distress two years later, she went back to try to obtain a better settlement. Her attorney insisted he had lost all her papers. He refused to return her calls. So she went to another attorney. After having lunch with her first lawyer, he told Lori he would take on her case—provided she pay a $5,000 up-front retainer fee. That was out of the question for Lori; she couldn't afford it. She was forced to drop the matter.

Family law is where most women come in contact with the legal system. "Perhaps no other branch of law is as crucial to women's welfare if not survival," wrote attorney Joanne Schulman of the NCWFL.[4] "It encompasses fleeing a battering husband; attempting to feed a family on an inadequate child support order that the father refuses to pay and the court refuses to enforce; finding housing because the woman lost the family home in divorce; facing landlords who refuse to rent to her because she is receiving public assistance, has children, or is fleeing a battering husband and the landlord does not want 'trouble.'"

Family law is a complex, difficult field. Yet attorneys consider it the least prestigious aspect of law. It does not have the glamour and high salary of, say, corporate law and it requires involvement in emotionally-charged personal conflicts. "It is the dirtiest," said Rachofsky, "people getting emotional instead of arguing rationally." Therefore only a few, committed lawyers specialize in family law. Many attorneys do divorces and child custody cases as a sideline, for extra money. So women clients often find themselves with a lawyer who does not have the necessary expertise—or compassion.

"A lot of attorneys do divorce work as 'bread and butter,'" said Rachofsky. "They see divorce work as easy money. . . . Therefore, most people who do divorces, in my opinion, are not experts and are therefore not qualified to handle the complexities of the divorce laws. In many states you need an expertise in tax laws. We need to understand the psychology of families and children and parenting roles. We have to deal with the medical profession in terms of child abuse and abuse of wives. We have to understand all the property laws. . . . It's a lot. It involves real estate, wills, inheritance, social security, probate law, welfare. [Family law] is very complex, and most people don't deal with it fairly."

Some women feel they face discrimination from male lawyers. A 37-year-old woman who had a legal dispute with her landlord remarked: "Women lawyers are more understanding. Men lawyers don't let you have any say-so. They know everything. They don't give a damn."

Certainly some male lawyers may discriminate against women. But the problem runs deeper. The training lawyers receive, combined with most women's lack of experience with legal matters and, often, their state of distress when they first come in contact with the legal system, creates an inherently unbalanced situation.

"A . . . well-known occupational hazard of lawyers is their tendency to become contentious and to develop such associated traits as being arrogant, deceitful, and punitive," wrote David Riley. "Chicago law dean Soi Mentschikoff tells wives of first year law students, 'your husbands are going to change: their personalities are going to change in law school. They'll get more aggressive, more hostile, more precise, more impatient.' Law school develops an imperious impatience toward people with cobwebs in their minds. The constant atmosphere of contest and debates puts a premium on one-upmanship and a zero value on modesty. Law school is the one place of learning where an appropriate 'I don't know' is almost never heard in a classroom, out of fear of professional ridicule and the need to display the appearance of competence and confidence."[5]

That attitude, of course, can cause problems for male as well as female clients. "The attorney we had did not represent our interests well, he just wanted to get it over with," said one woman. "This attitude was present when both my husband and I were present. Both of us were not as assertive as we should have been. We also should have reported him to the bar." But women can face a double bind.

Rachofsky first went into family law because she felt women received unfair treatment from male lawyers. Her experience since then has reconfirmed her beliefs. "I've seen too many women switching to me from a male attorney [because he was] very patronizing. Some have been abusive verbally if the woman had an opinion of her own that tended to differ from the lawyer's."

Those attorneys, she said, "are more condescending. I think they are more prone to give orders without explanations. Not that the actual advice might be different, but there's a lack of explanation, there's a lack of information given. I would presume that it is under the assumption that 'the poor little woman' wouldn't understand anyway." On the other hand, she said, "a businessman client or even a working male client is going to get more background information, more [of a] factual basis. He might even be offered a choice. Or maybe not but at least the lawyer is more responsive to his [questions]."

A 58-year-old mother of three who has had legal assistance for a divorce, a will, administration of an estate and tax advice, reports that male lawyers in other than family law "have shown generally patronizing and chauvinistic attitudes, with a few exceptions. . . . However, I did feel they had client loyalty. With [family] lawyers my experience was not only extreme chauvinism and intimidating attitudes but also lack of client loyalty . . . I was told not to take notes on what he was advising me. (I did anyway.) I was described as 'distraught' when I objected to coercion. I was told what a fine fellow my husband (the adversary in the case) was. I was told I 'did not deserve' a lump-sum amount. Also [he told me] to sign a disputed joint tax return or he 'would cease representing me.' And about my daughter, age 15, I was told 'to see that she kept her legs together' . . . I was not properly informed, not consulted regarding choices, frequently intimidated, grossly lied to and grossly overcharged."

With a paternalistic approach the lawyer succeeds in stripping the woman of control over her situation. She is not handed a choice, but a decision. Without substantive input into the case, she comes out the loser, emotionally and financially. In some divorce cases, "attorneys will tell women 'Well, this is the settlement, I think you ought to take it,' or 'This is the best I can do for you, and if you don't sign it go somewhere else,'" said Rochofsky. "As opposed to saying 'This is what the other side is offering, I think it is a good idea, I think it is a fair settlement, let me know if you like it or not, and we'll discuss it.'"

That was Muriel's experience in her divorce case. "My lawyer treated me like I was a child, a middle-aged child who had been sheltered and taken care of by my ex-husband and would still be if I would just calm down and not get him any angrier at me," she said. Muriel had attempted to prepare herself for the experience by speaking to women's groups, collecting information on questions she should ask and issues to follow-up. The lawyer was not impressed. "He would just verbally pat me on the back and tell me not to worry, I didn't understand about these things. That was his general approach: If I would just calm down, my husband was a professional man and he would do the right thing, he was sure. But that was a total contradiction to what I had told him about the way my husband was acting."

Her lawyer's approach was more than annoying; it severely hampered her in the final settlement because he failed to argue strongly on her behalf. The presiding judge was also indifferent to her needs. Muriel asked that she be given enough money initially to go back to school to obtain her master's degree and teaching credential. "Then we would all be better off," she said. The judge, with no dissent from her lawyer, refused to make any provision for education. "He just said, 'You can work all day, go to school at night and juggle the kids somehow,'" Muriel said. In the settlement her husband got half of everything while she *and* three children had to share the rest. Now she is in debt to her brother for $35,000—much of it medical expenses for her son—while her ex-husband is worth several hundred thousand dollars.

Muriel's case is not unusual. The widely held assumption that women received favored treatment by the courts in family law matters is a myth. Studies have shown that the economic position of divorced men generally improves while that of divorced women deteriorates. "The Bureau of Census reports that the rise in divorce and separation rates is the most important factor in the dramatic increase over the last decade in the number of families headed by women—the only category of 'households' which has *increased* in poverty," said Schulman.[6] Studies show that less than half of divorced and separated mothers receive child support payments, and one survey of judges showed that even that support awarded was "usually not enough to furnish even *one-half* the actual cost of rearing a child."[7] In addition, says Laurie Woods, currently "alimony or wife support is granted only temporarily on the assumption the women will become self-supporting. The stark reality, however, is that jobs are simply not available."[8]

Some women resort to drastic actions after losing their financial security in a divorce. Phyllis [not her real name], a 48-year-old mother of four, was an upper-middle class housewife married to an attorney. After a divorce, she found herself strapped for money, unable to provide for her children. She began shoplifting—not for the children, she used her small salary and child support for them—but for herself, items like lipstick and hosiery. "She would never steal anything for the children," said a woman who knew Phyllis. "That was wrong." But somehow she felt she could steal for herself. A store owner finally caught her. She was arrested and jailed until a church organization came to her aid.

Child Custody

Women are at a disadvantage in custody battles as well. Following a general rule of fulfilling the "best interests of the children" more and more judges are employing economic criteria in their decisions, awarding custody of children to the parent with the greater economic resources. Usually that is the father. "It was formerly assumed that if one parent could provide a better material environment for the child, he or she could do so in the form of child support payments, to the custodial parent," said Laurie Woods, Vicki Been and Joanne Schulman, NCWFL lawyers.[9] "However several states have now expressly listed this as a factor the judge must consider in determining *custody*. In other states, judges are considering economic factors in deciding custody even when not specifically authorized to do so by statute."

The second criteria employed is the lifestyle of the parents. There judges often apply a double standard for men and women. The mother's fitness is tested against the "traditional" mother standard, while the father's standard is tested against the "traditional" father's standard, according to the NCWFL lawyers. That puts divorced and separated mothers in a Catch-22, by penalizing them for working outside the home, as well as for a lack of economic resources.

"Consequently," they said, "if a woman places 'undue' emphasis upon her career—a choice she is ironically under pressure to make in order to support her child and prevent loss of custody to the father with his high income—she nevertheless stands in jeopardy of losing custody of her child."[10]

The double standard holds true when weighing the moral standards of each parent. "It is permissible for fathers to have non-marital sexual relationships without jeopardizing custody rights," said the lawyers. "However, if a woman does so, she may well lose custody."[11] In one court case, both parents were having new sexual relationships. Fearful of jeopardizing custody of her children—the case was still in court—the woman stopped spending the night with her new fiance. The father lived with his woman friend, and slept with her in a one-room hotel room with the children present. He won custody.[12]

Battered Women

Just over 100 years ago, U.S. courts condoned wife-beating. In 1824 the Mississippi Supreme Court concluded that a "husband should be permitted to chastise his wife moderately in cases of great emergency without subjecting himself to vexatious prosecution for assault and battery, resulting in the discredit and shame of all parties concerned."[13] Other states invoked the "rule of thumb:" a husband could beat his wife as long as the stick was "no thicker than his thumb."[14]

Though the law no longer expressly upholds the right of a man to beat his wife, and most states have passed laws either to fund shelters for battered wives or to increase the role courts and police must play in protecting battered women, laws against wife-beating are not always vigorously enforced. Half of all married women will be physically abused by their husbands sometime during their marriage, studies show. Yet only two percent of men who beat their wives or live-in lovers are ever prosecuted.[15] Police departments and courts are simply reluctant to intervene in family disputes.

Moreover, battered women are at a severe disadvantage in custody battles if they seek divorce. For example, in considering evidence of the fitness of a parent many courts refuse to take into account a father's past record of beating his wife, as long as he did not also physically abuse the children. "Custody attorneys are all too familiar with 'but did he ever hit the children?' judicial response to wife-beating," said Joanne Schulman.[16] Courts also look upon a battered woman who frequently moves to flee her ex-husband as following an "unstable" lifestyle and therefore unfit as a parent. Her economic status as a "fit" parent is threatened if she loses her job because her ex-husband harassed her at work.[17]

TAKING CHARGE

Though the legal system frequently works against the interests of women, there are some ways women can take more control of the situation.

Information Problems

√ Make sure you and your husband have up-to-date wills, and that you know where they are.

√ Keep informed about—and participate in—your family's finances.

√ Learn what, and where, your husband's financial assets are—whether they be stocks and bonds, pensions, life insurance or a safe deposit box—and what his liabilities are, including taxes.

√ Ask questions. Read the documents and contracts he hands you to sign.

√ Maintain your own checking or savings account—at the very least for emergencies.

√ Familiarize yourself with the marriage laws in your state (i.e. do you live in a common law or community property state).

√ If you need a divorce, do not let your husband convince you that you should share an attorney; you will probably find yourself without an advocate.

√ Set up a network for attorney referrals at your local church or woman's club. Women who have gone through a divorce, landlord dispute or other legal actions are the best source for other women in search of a good attorney, or who to avoid.

Money Problems

√ Even if you do not have access to family funds, there are ways to pay for legal help. In some states (those with community property laws or provisions) you legally own half of your family's bank accounts. If you have a joint back account, says Rachofsky, you can get a blank check printed with your account number, then check the balance and write a check for half of it, because half of it is yours. (Ask your prospective attorney for advice on this.) Another way is simply to draw money out of a savings account that has your name on it. "Some lawyers," said Rachofsky, "upon proof that there are some bank accounts available, will ask the court for an attorney's fee contribution and they'll at least begin a case on the presumption that they'll get an order for payment from the court."

Most states do not have community property laws; thus property belongs to the person in whose name the assets are listed. A woman with no bank account of her own, and no joint account, faces a real bind if she needs legal help. Rachofsky suggests that, if possible, a woman in this situation seeking a divorce should contact the local Legal Services office, find out how long she must be separated to qualify for legal aid (generally about 30 days) and then move out and wait until she qualifies before taking action.

√ See if you qualify for federal legal aid (see chart in appendix). If so, contact the legal aid office in your neighborhood; a list of some offices appears in the appendix.

As noted before, the legal aid offices are suffering from severe budget cuts and may not be able to attend to your case for months. In that case, *obtain a letter from the legal aid office stating that you are qualified* for free legal help. Take that letter with you to the attorney to whom the legal aid office refers you; or to the local bar association, where you should ask for a reference to a private attorney who does *pro bono* work. The American Bar Association has stated that it will try to provide free legal help to compensate for the overload at legal aid offices. Many counties have free legal services: check your phonebook.

√ If you do not qualify for free legal aid and you cannot afford private attorneys, you may be able to get help from a woman's organization in the area. Ask the local bar association or the local National Organization for Women (NOW) office, for references. If your case has constitutional ramifications (involving civil liberties or social-political rights), you can contact the American Civil Liberties Union.

Do You Need An Attorney?

√ For many legal problems (primarily those involving disputes between two parties) you may want to use a professional mediator instead of a lawyer.

√ Small Claims Court is a good avenue in which to try to collect small amounts of damages (generally under $750, but check your local small claims court for its requirements) and you do not need a lawyer. In fact small claims courts were first started to minimize the need for attorneys. Only a small fee is required for filing. If you have the money, however, you may want to consult an attorney for advice on how best to use the small claims court in your area.

√ Do-it-yourself divorces are becoming a popular way to save money, but experts advise that you see a lawyer for an initial consultation and/or have a lawyer review the final settlement. You should only go this route if you think you are in a bargaining position equal to that of your husband.

Dealing With A Lawyer

√ *Be open and honest,* don't hold back information or distort the truth. If your attorney finds out later, in a courtroom or a bargaining conference, it will place your interests at a severe disadvantage.

√ *Ask questions* about your case and force your lawyer to explain the issues in terms you can understand. You have a right to know everything about your case, including your lawyer's strategy and time frame.

√ *Don't rely on your attorney for emotional help.* Your attorney should, of course, be supportive and understand your needs; but he or she is not a marriage counselor or a psychiatrist or anything but a lawyer. If you try to seek emotional support you risk damaging a respectful attorney-client relationship. This often occurs when women clients go to women attorneys. "Often the woman lawyer thinks that her women clients feel they are entitled to take more of her time than they would of a man's," wrote Cynthia Fuchs Epstein, a professor of sociology at Queens College. "Sometimes women clients even express shock on finding that 'talks' with women attorneys are professional interactions for which fees are charged. The wish to establish a personal relationship with the attorney creates unreasonable expectations for the amount of time and attention paid to the clients needs and problems."[18]

√ *Keep in touch* with your lawyer, offer to help gather the necessary information, and keep your attorney updated on new developments.

√ *Keep track of your attorney's progress.* Failure to return phone calls or letters and refusing to spend time with you may be a sign that your attorney is not putting sufficient time and effort into your case. Confront your lawyer if you think he or she is neglecting your case. If it is serious enough you should tell the lawyer that if the neglect continues, you will see another lawyer.

√ *Know your lawyer's fee structure.* He or she may charge you for that phone call you just made. Some common types of fees are: *retainer fee:* This is the money that an attorney wants up front (generally a small portion of the total fee) as a guarantee that in case you suddenly change your mind about needing legal help you won't leave a hardworking lawyer out in the cold. Once you have paid this fee, you have "retained" your attorney. It is credited toward the final bill, like a deposit. *flat fee:* You and your attorney may agree to a flat fee: say $500 to incorporate your business or $1,000 for your divorce, that will not change, even if your case is contested. *range fee:* The attorney may leave the final fee open—not knowing how difficult your case will be, whether it will be contested—and instead give you a range. (i.e. "It will be somewhere between $750 and $1,000 depending on. . .") *hourly fee:* An hourly fee is often charged when you just want legal research done. *contingent fee:* Your lawyer may agree that he or she won't charge you anything unless he or she wins the case, in which case he or she will take a percentage of what you win. This is a contingent fee. *percentage fee:* Percentage fees are often used in probate cases, when administering a deceased individual's estate, where the attorney takes a percentage of the estate.

You can save money by shopping around; you may find an attorney who charges less than the first one you contacted but is equally qualified. You can also try to negotiate a lower fee, by indicating that you are looking elsewhere. The important thing to keep in mind, though, is not to hire a lawyer of questionable qualifications just to save money. You may lose more in the end.

√ *Know who is actually handling your case.* Many law firms have paralegals, or law students or younger lawyer-associates working on cases, so your attorney may not actually personally be working on much of the case. Find out if this is the case and exactly what aspect of your case is being handled by someone else. "Be sure you make it clear to your attorney that any work done on your case by a law student or paralegal must be work that is suitable for such a person and that their work must be closely supervised and checked by your attorney," says Joseph C. McGuinn in his book, *Lawyers: A Clients Manual* (Prentice Hall, 1979). McGuinn's book contains important information on how to deal with a lawyer and should be read by anyone seeking legal help who is unfamiliar with the process.

√ *Keep a file, notepad and pocket calendar* so that you write down lawyer's instructions (e.g. getting hold of a particular paper), mark them on your calendar, and carry them out on time. With a file you can keep yourself organized and maintain a record of your costs.

Choosing A Lawyer

√ *Shop around.* Interview several lawyers, Rachofsky suggests, "remembering that a lawyer is performing a service and you have the right to get comparative bids so to speak, just like you do when looking for a plumber."

Use your consumer skills. Tell the lawyer, "no, I'm not here yet to retain you, but I want to get information." With that approach, says Rachofsky, a woman "will find out very quickly what lawyers are going to be tolerant of questions, what lawyers are going to be upfront about their billing, how they bill, when they expect payment and how much they expect. She'll understand very promptly if this lawyer is going to be tolerant of her personally; and if she'll get along with him or her."

In considering an attorney ask yourself these questions:

*Does s/he answer your questions willingly and explain the issues adequately?

*Does s/he seem willing to spend time with you?

*Is s/he anxious to help, without promising miracles?

*What kind of experience does s/he have with your kind of case?

*Does s/he express interest in your case or display a lackadaisical or condescending attitude toward you?

*What is his/her retainer fee on such a case (i.e. how much will you have to pay up front)? What does s/he estimate as the total cost? How does that compare with other attorneys' estimates?

√ Hire a specialist. If you want a divorce, for example, hire a family law attorney not someone who does divorces on the side. If you need legal help for a will, hire a probate attorney.

√ In divorce cases, do not hire a friend of the family or a relative; you need someone with an objective perspective. In a probate case, though, you may need someone who knows your family.

Getting Ready

Equip yourself with information before proceeding. You are not a lawyer and you should not try to be one. But you can familiarize yourself with concepts and terms and the particular laws in your state. Once you do that, the process will lose some of its mystery—you won't be intimidated and you will be more likely to get fair representation. There are plenty of handbooks on divorce and other legal issues available from the public library including:

Lawyers: A Client Manual, by Joseph McGinn (Prentice Hall, Inc. Englewood
    Cliffs, N.J., 1979)

Alone: Emotional, legal and financial help for the widowed or divorced woman,
    by Helen Antoniak, Nancy Scott and Nancy Worcester (Les Femmes Publications, Millbrae, C.A., 1979)

The Rights of Women. by Susan C. Ross (Sunrise Books, N.Y., 1973)

Handbook for Battered Women: How to use the law (1978, 49pp., $3.75) Available from the National Clearinghouse for Legal Services, Inc., 500 North Michigan Ave. Suite 1940, Chicago, IL. 60611

It is important to become familiar with the particular laws in your state: For that information, contact the local chapter of the National Organization for Women (NOW) or your local bar association.

Other organizations with valuable information include:

—The National Lawyer's Guild, 853 Broadway, New York, N.Y. (212) 260-1360.

—Women's Equity Action League (WEAL), 805 15th Street, NW #822, Washington, D.C. 20005.

—National Center on Women and Family Law, 799 Broadway #452, New York, N.Y. 10003.

—Women's Legal Defense Fund, 2000 P. Street NW, Washington, D.C.

—Children's Defense Fund, 1520 New Hampshire Ave. NW, Washington, D.C.

How To Complain About Your Lawyer

Taking charge also requires following up on a situation in which you feel you were cheated.

√ If your lawyer caused you financial harm, you can sue for damages. But the chances of winning are not good; and it is generally difficult to find an attorney who will take a fellow attorney to court.

√ The best way to handle the situation is to file a complaint with the local bar association; this won't always recover your money but it will help prevent the attorney from hurting someone else. You should file a complaint if you believe your lawyer acted unethically. Examples of unethical conduct include: neglecting a case; misinforming a client of a case's progress; and misusing a client's funds. Your complaint must focus on a specific case of *unethical conduct* or the bar association won't consider it. (A condescending attitude or failure to fully explain the issues unfortunately is not enough.)

To bring a complaint against a lawyer, find out the grievance procedure in the bar association where your lawyer's office is located. You will probably have to submit a *written* complaint. Make the complaint as specific as possible, including dates, names, documents, amount of money involved. If the complaint is eventually upheld by the bar association, the lawyer can be admonished, or in rare cases, disbarred. Call your local bar association for further information on filing a grievance.

FOOTNOTES

1. Brink, David, testimony before the Subcommittee on State, Justice, Commerce and Judiciary of the Senate Appropriations Committee, April, 28, 1982.
2. Riley, David, "The Mystique of Lawyers," in *Verdicts on Lawyers* (Mark Green, Ralph Nader, ed., Crowell Pub., NY, 1976) pp. 80–95.

3. Woods, Laurie, "The Challenge Facing Legal Services in the '80s," *Clearinghouse Review,* May, 1982.
4. Schulman, Joanne, "Poor Women and Family Law," National Center for Women and Family Law, Inc., 1982.
5. Riley, p. 90.
6. Schulman, p. 2.
7. Ibid, p. 1.
8. Woods, p. 27.
9. Woods, L.; Been, V.; Schulman, J., "The Use of Sex and Economic Discriminatory Criteria in Child Custody Awards," National Center on Women and Family Law, Inc., 1982.
10. Ibid.
11. Ibid.
12. Ibid.
13. *Bradley v. State of Miss.,* (Walker) 156, 158 (1824)
14. Prossner, N., *Handbook of the Laws of Tort,* 4th edition, 1971, p. 136.
15. Schulman, p. 3.
16. Ibid.
17. Ibid.
18. Epstein, Cynthia Fuchs, "Do You Expect More From a Woman Lawyer?" *MS.* Magazine, April, 1982, p. 41.

APPENDIX

Resources For Change

For further information or brochures and to share advertisements, ideas, suggestions and information, please contact:

Jean Kilbourne
51 Church Street
Boston, MA 02116

The media provide young women with few female images to emulate and provide few positive images of womanhood for people of either sex to respect .... Even though women are acquiring confidence, advanced degrees and technical skills, and although affirmative action laws are being enacted, the mass media tend to neutralize their effects. The constantly trivialized and objectified image of women not only undermines newly formed female confidence, but also subtly affects all aspects of life — economic, political, social and personal .... As media approaches reflect female capabilities, mass attitudes will change .... Future positive portrayals of women as talented, vibrant, self-sufficient people making decisions and controlling their own lives and destinies will produce more confident, competent women with increased potential.

Leslie Friedman

FEMINIST GROUPS

Support and get active in your local feminist groups, centers, and organizations.

Join or form a consciousness-raising group. For information, contact your local NOW chapter or Harriet Perl, Chair, National CR Committee, 1121 Hi Point St., Los Angeles, CA 90035. Send for *Guidelines to Feminist CR*, $6

Join or form a Media Reform Task Force in your local NOW chapter.

Support national feminist organizations working on this issue and start local chapters.

National Organization for Women (NOW), 425 13th St. NW, Washington, DC 20004. (NOW has task forces on many different issues)

Women Against Pornography, 579 Ninth Ave., New York, NY 10036 212-594-2801

Women Against Violence Against Women (WAVAW), 1727 N. Spring St., Los Angeles, CA 90019 213-936-6293 (Slide show for rent, newsletter)

Women Against Violence in Pornography and Media (WAVPM), Box 14614, San Francisco, CA 94114 415-552-2709 (Slide show, monthly newsletter, literature packet, media protest packet).

Women's Institute for Freedom of the Press, 3306 Ross Place NW, Washington, DC 20004 (*Media Report to Women*, monthly report on women and the communications media)

Support other national feminist organizations working on issues of special interest and concern to you, e.g., employment, politics, rape, battered women, women of color, reproductive freedom, health, etc. Contact Women's Action Alliance, 370 Lexington Ave., New York, NY 10017, a national clearinghouse which connects individuals and groups with the resources they need to eliminate sexism and sex discrimination.

Racism and sexism in America are not problems simply to be listed alongside other problems. They are part of the white male club's foundation .... It is essential to understand that I am suggesting that the club is the problem — not white males per se. It is more a question of social system than it is of biology. White males have options in relation to the club. They can actively defend and perpetuate it; they can react passively and conform to club pressures; or they can actively work to change the club. One cannot be passively anti-racist and anti-sexist. That option does not exist .... To be passive is to conform to the club and to support it.

Robert Terry

MEN'S RESOURCES AND GROUPS

Men can also join and support most feminist groups and can form consciousness-raising groups on their own.

Cincinnati Men's Network, 3618 Middleton Ave., Cincinnati, OH 45220

East Bay Men's Center, 2700 Bancroft Way, Berkeley, CA 94704 (publishes *Brother*, a monthly journal)

Emerge (A Men's Counseling Service on Domestic Violence), 25 Huntington Avenue, Boston, MA 02116 617-267-7690 (*To Have and To Hold*, a film about men who batter women)

Madison's Men's Center, Box 313, 306 N. Brooks, Madison, WI 53715 (publishes *M. Gentle Men for Gender Justice*, a nationwide journal)

Men's Programs Unit, Metrocenter YMCA, 908 4th Ave., Seattle, WA 98104 (*Facilitator's Manual for Men's CR and Support Groups* available for $3)

Men's Studies Collection, MIT Humanities Library, Cambridge, MA 02139 (Bibliography available)

Oasis (Organized Against Sexism and Institutionalized Stereotypes), c/o Jim Jackson, 33 Richdale Ave., Cambridge, MA 02140 617-864-9063 (*Stale Roles and Tight Buns: Advertising's Image of Men*, a slide show available for rent)

Being a Man: A Unit of Instructional Activities on Male Role Stereotyping by David Sadker, available from Superintendent of Documents, U.S. Government Printing Office, Washington, DC 20402 (order #017-080-01777-6)

The Male Sex Role: A Selected and Annotated Bibliography by Kathleen Grady, Robert Brannon, and Joseph Pleck, available free from National Clearinghouse on Mental Health, 5600 Fishers Lane, Rockville, MD 20857

What the whole community comes to believe in grasps the individual as in a vise.

William James

MEDIA AWARENESS AND PUBLIC INTEREST GROUPS

Action for Children's Television (ACT), 46 Austin St., Newtonville, MA 02160

American Council for Better Broadcasts, 120 East Wilson St., Madison, WI 53703 608-257-7712

American Council on Consumer Interests, 162 Stanley Hall, University of Missouri, Columbia, MO 65211

DOC (Doctors Ought to Care), 924 Webster St., Chicago, IL 60614

INFACT (Nestle Boycott), 3410 19th St., San Francisco, CA 04110

Media Action Research Center, Suite 1370, 475 Riverside Drive, New York, NY 10027 212-865-6690 (Publishes *Television Awareness Training*, an excellent collection of essays, information, and guidelines)

National Association for Better Broadcasting, 7918 Naylor Ave., Los Angeles, CA 90045 213-641-4903

National Association of Spanish Broadcasters, 2550 M St. NW, Suite 450, Washington, DC 20037 202-293-3873

National Black Media Coalition, 2413 Dowling St., Houston, TX 77004

National Citizens' Committee for Broadcasting, P.O. Box 12038, Washington, DC 20005 202-462-2520 (Publishes *access*, a biweekly magazine, and *Citizens' Media Directory*, an invaluable handbook of information about national and local media reform groups)

PTA TV Action Center, 700 N. Rush St., Chicago, IL 60611 (Maintains a national toll-free hotline to answer your questions about the TV industry — 1-800-323-5177)

Our society is today cultivating single vision, and the desensitization and the dehumanization that we feel all around us is a kind of sleep or death of awareness and conscience. We must revive in people a habit of double vision that can identify myths and values underlying society and can evaluate them from a perspective that transcends the limitations of that society.

William Fore

EDUCATIONAL ACTION

Support your local women's studies courses and programs and their teachers. Establish and support programs and courses teaching awareness of media, sexism and racism at all levels. For further information, contact:

American Association of University Women, 2401 Virginia Ave. NW, Washington, DC 22037 202-785-7700

Global Education Associates, 552 Park Ave., East Orange, NJ 07017

National Women's Studies Association, 4102 Foreign Language Building, University of Maryland, College Park, MD 20742 301-454-3757

Non-Sexist Child Development Project, Women's Action Alliance, Inc., 370 Lexington Ave., New York, NY 10017 (A national resource center for early childhood education)

Organization for Equal Education of the Sexes, Inc., 744 Carroll St., Brooklyn, NY 11215 (publishes *TABS: Aids for Ending Sexism in School*, a journal)

Project on Equal Education Rights (PEER) 1112 13th St. NW, Washington, DC 20005 202-332-7337 (Newsletter, resources, information on Title IX and on the influence of sexism on handicapped children)

Project on the Status and Education of Women, Association of American Colleges, 1818 R St. NW, Washington, DC 20009 202-387-7757 (Newsletter and resource papers on various issues)

Racism/Sexism Resource Center for Educators, 1841 Broadway, Suite 300, New York, NY 10023 (Fact sheets on institutional racism and sexism available for $1 each)

Resource Center on Sex Equity, 400 North Capitol St. NW, Suite 379, Washington, DC 20001 202-624-7757

Resource Center on Sex Roles in Education, National Foundation for the Improvement of Education, 1156 15th St. NW, Suite 918, Washington, DC 20005

Women's Educational Equity Communications Network, Far West Laboratory, 1855 Folsom St., San Francisco, CA 94103 415-565-3032

(A comprehensive, nationwide information service; send for *Sex Stereotyping in Instructional Materials and Television: Awareness Kit*)

SEE *READINGS AND OTHER MEDIA* FOR SUGGESTIONS FOR EDUCATIONAL MATERIALS

It seems to me that the cultural and economic liberation of women is inseparable from the creation of a society in which all people no longer have their lives stolen from them, and in which the conditions of their production and reproduction will no longer be distorted or held back by the subordination of sex, race or class.

Sheila Rowbotham

GOVERNMENT ACTION AND AGENCIES

Commission on the Status of Women, United Nations (UNESCO), New York, NY

Congressional Clearinghouse on Women's Rights, 722 House Office Building, Annex No. 1, Washington, DC 20515 (Write your Representative to be put on the mailing list)

ERA America, 1525 M St. NW, Suite 602, Washington, DC 20005

Federal Communications Commission (FCC), 1919 M St. NW, Washington, DC 20554

Federal Trade Commission (FTC), Washington, DC 20580

National Women's Political Caucus, 1411 K St. NW, Washington, DC 20005

U.S. Commission on Civil Rights, 1121 Vermont Ave NW, Washington DC 20425 (Send for *Window Dressing on the Set: Women and Minorities in Television* and *Sexism and Racism: Feminist Perspectives*)

Women's Equity Action League (WEAL), 805 15th St. NW, #822 Suite 200, Washington, DC 20005

Women USA, 76 Beaver St., New York, NY 10005 800-221-4945

To deny that the problem exists, in fact, is to deny the effectiveness of advertising. For what the critics are saying is that advertising, in selling a product, often sells a supplementary image as well. Sometimes, in woman-related advertising, that image is negative and depreciatory. Unfortunately, such images may be accepted as true to life by many men, women and children, especially when they reinforce stereotypes of a time gone by.

Seen in this light, advertising must be regarded as one of the forces molding society. Those who protest that advertising merely reflects society must reckon with the criticism that much of the current reflection of women in advertising is out of date. To the extent that this is true, advertising is neglecting its responsibility to be fair, accurate, and truthful, not only in the presentation of products and services, but also in the presentation of men and women.

The National Advertising Review Board

CORPORATE ACTION

Write to the advertisers c/o the magazines or the manufacturers. Send for WAVPM's *Write Back! Fight Back! Media Protest Packet* (listed under Feminist Groups). Also see "How to Send Revolution Through the Mail" by Marcia Rockwood, *MS*, January 1978, pp. 85-88.

Call local television stations or write to the network.

NBC, 30 Rockefeller Plaza, New York, NY 10020

CBS, 51 W. 52nd St., New York, NY 10019

ABC, 1330 Ave. of the Americas, New York, NY 10019

Remember to support positive images and enlightened members of the advertising industry — they need your help and encouragement.

National Advertising Division, Council of Better Business Bureaus, Inc. 845 Third Ave., New York, NY 10022 (Send for their 1975 report on *Advertising and Women* and information on their Children's Advertising Review Unit)

Task Force on Sexist Stereotyping, San Francisco Women in Advertising, 900 Chestnut St., San Francisco, CA 94109

READINGS AND OTHER MEDIA

Support feminist bookstores, presses, and journals. For an annotated list, see *Women's Movement Media: A Source Guide* by Cynthia Harrison, New York: R. R. Bowker, 1975.

Some suggested resources are:

Aegis: Magazine on Ending Violence Against Women, Box 21033, Washington, DC 20009

The Feminist Press, Box 334, Old Westbury, NY 11568
516-997-7660

KNOW, Inc., Box 86031, Pittsburgh, PA 15221 (Feminist publishing and distribution collective; numerous reprints of articles)

Journal of Communication, Annenberg School of Communications, University of Pennsylvania, Philadelphia, PA 19104

Media Monitor: Images of Women, (vol. 1, Winter 1978), Box 1020, Pearl River, NY 10965 (Extensive listing of curriculum resources)

Media Report to Women, Women's institute for Freedom of the Press, 3306 Ross Place NW, Washington, DC 20008 (Monthly report on women and the communications media)

WIN News (Women's International Network), 187 Grant St., Lexington, MA 02173 (A world-wide communication system)

Women's Studies Abstracts, P.O. Box 1, Rush, NY 14543

Women Today, Today News Service, Inc., National Press Building, Washington, DC 20045

ON SEX ROLE STEREOTYPING AND THE IMAGE OF WOMEN IN THE MEDIA:

The following list is by no means comprehensive but includes some readings of particular interest or merit. Please let me know your additional suggestions and recommendations.

Action for Children's Television, Sex-Roles Portrayed on Television, Fall, 1978 (A bibliography available from ACT, 46 Austin St., Newtonville, MA 12160), also *Television and Teens: The Experts Look at the Issues*, Reading, MA, Addison-Wesley Publishing Co., 1982

Bartos, Rena, "What Every Marketer Should Know About Women," *Harvard Business Review*, May 1978.

Butler, Matilda, *Sex Stereotyping in Instructional Materials and Television: Awareness Kit* (Available from WEECN; see Educational Action)

Butler, Matilda and William Paisley, *Women and the Mass Media: Sourcebook for Research and Action*, New York: Human Sciences Press, 1980.

Commission on the Status of Women, United Nations (UNESCO), New York, *Influence of the Mass Communication Media on Attitudes Toward the Roles of Women and Men in Present-Day Society*, Report #E/CN.6/601, 13 August, 1976

Friedman, Leslie, *Sex Role Stereotyping in the Mass Media: An Annotated Bibliography*, New York: Garland Publishing, 1977

Goffman, Erving, *Gender Advertisements*, Cambridge: Harvard University Press, 1978.

Interfaith Center on Corporate Responsibility, *Images of Women in Advertising*, 1977. Copies of this excellent pamphlet are available for $2 from the Interfaith Center, 475 Riverside Drive, Room 566, New York, NY 10027

Kilbourne, Jean, *The Changing Images of Females and Males in Television Commercials: Plus Ça Change, Plus C'est La Même Chose* (Doctoral dissertation, Boston University, 1980, available through University Microfilms International, P.O. Box 1764, Ann Arbor, MI 48106 800-521-3042) and "Images of Women in TV Commercials," *TV Book*, New York: Workman Publishing Co., 1977

Lederer, Laura, Ed., *Take Back the Night: Women on Pornography*, New York: William Morrow & Co., Inc., 1981

Miller, Jean Baker, *Toward a New Psychology of Women*, Boston: Beacon Press, 1976.

National Commission on the Observance of International Women's Year, *To Form a More Perfect Union . . . . Justice for American Women*, and *Media: A Workshop Guide*, 1976. Available from Office of Public Information, IWY Commission, Department of State, Washington, DC 20520

Rowbotham, Sheila, *Woman's Consciousness, Man's World*, Baltimore, MD.: Penguin Books, 1973

Schaef, Anne Wilson, *Women's Reality*, Minneapolis: Winston Press, 1981

Tavris, Carol and Carole Offir, *The Longest War: Sex Differences in Perspective*, New York: Harcourt Brace Jovanovich Inc., 1977

Tuchman, Gaye, Arlene Kaplan Daniels and James Benet, editors, *Hearth and Home: Images of Women in the Mass Media*, New York: Oxford University Press, 1978

ON SEXISM, RACISM, AND CLASSISM:

Fact sheets on institutional racism and sexism available from Racism/Sexism Resource Center for Educators, 1841 Broadway, Suite 300, New York, NY 10023

Breaking the Silence: Seven Courses in Women's Studies. A course guide for women whose access to education and employment has been limited because of race, sex or class discrimination. Explores the effects of sex role stereotyping on the lives of Third World, poor, working-class and institutionalized women. Order from EDC/WEEAP, 55 Chapel St., Newton, MA 800-225-3088

Memmi, Albert, *The Colonizer and the Colonized*, Boston: Beacon Press, 1965

New Perspectives: A Bibliography of Racial, Ethnic, and Feminist Resources, 1977 (Available from Pennsylvania Department of Education, Box 911, Harrisburg, PA 17126)

Rubin, Lillian Breslow, *Worlds of Pain: Life in the Working-Class Family*, New York: Basic Books, 1976

Schniedewind, Nancy, *Confronting Racism and Sexism: A Practical Handbook for Educators*. Available for $5 from Commonground Press, 155 Plains St., New Paltz, NY 12561

Sennet, Richard and Jonathan Cobb, *The Hidden Injuries of Class*, New York: Vintage, 1973

U.S. Commission on Civil Rights, Washington, DC 20425, *Window Dressing on the Set: Women and Minorities in Television*, 1978. Also *Sexism and Racism: Feminist Perspectives* (Civil Rights Digest, Volume 6, Number 3, Spring 1974)

As emblems for our collective unconscious and as the ironic end-result of our constant financial interaction, commercials may be America's most significant product.

Jonathan Price

ON ADVERTISING AND CORPORATE POWER:

Atwan, Robert, Donald McQuade and John Wright, *Edsels, Luckies & Frigidaires: Advertising the American Way*, New York: Dell, 1979

Barnouw, Erik, *The Sponsor*, New York: Oxford University Press, 1978

Berger, John, *Ways of Seeing*, New York: Penguin Books, 1972

Boorstin, Daniel, *The Image: A Guide to Pseudo-Events in America*, New York: Harper & Row, 1961

Dowie, Mark, et al., "The Corporate Crime of the Century," *Mother Jones*, November 1979 (Reprints available for $1 plus 55 cents postage from *Mother Jones*, 625 Third St., San Francisco, CA 94107; also available: *Raising Hell: A Citizen's Guide to the Fine Art of Investigation*)

Ewen, Stuart, *Captains of Consciousness: Advertising and the Social Roots of the Consumer Culture*, New York: McGraw-Hill, 1977

Goldsen, Rose, "Why Television Advertising is Deceptive and Unfair," *Et cetera*, Winter, 1978, pp. 354-375

Green, Mark and Robert Massie, Jr., *The Big Business Reader: Essays on Corporate America*, New York: Pilgrim Press, 1980

Jones, Stephen A., *Subliminal Advertising in American Broadcast Media*, New Haven, Conn: Yale Legislative Services, Yale Law School, 1978

Key, Wilson Bryan, *Media Sexploitation*, New Jersey: Prentice-Hall, 1976, and *Subliminal Seduction*, Prentice-Hall, 1972

Leymore, Varda Langholz, *Hidden Myth: Structure and Symbolism in Advertising*, New York: Basic Books, 1975

Price, Jonathan, *The Best Thing on TV: Commercials*, New York: Penguin Books, 1978

Williamson, Judith, *Decoding Advertisements: Ideology and Meaning in Advertising*, London: Marion Boyars Publishers, Ltd., 1978

The reduction of sexuality to a dirty joke and of people to objects is the real obscenity of the culture. Although the sexual sell, overt and subliminal, is at a fever pitch in most commercials, there is at the same time a notable absence of sex as an important and profound human activity. Sex in commercials is narcissistic and autoerotic and exists apart from relationships. Identical models parade alone through the commercials, caressing their own soft skin, stroking and hugging their bodies, shaking their long silky manes, sensually bathing and applying powders and lotions, and then admiring themselves at length in the mirror. Commercials depict a world in which there is pervasive sexual innuendo but no love, and in which passion is reserved for products.

Jean Kilbourne

FILMS AND SLIDE SHOWS:

Several excellent slide shows are available from WAVAW (1727 N. Spring St., Los Angeles, CA 90019), WAVPM (Box 14614, San Francisco, CA 94114), and Women on Words and Images (Box 2163, Princeton, NJ 08540)

Catalogue of Films on Women and/or Sex Roles. Women's Resources and Research Center, University of California, Davis, CA

Controlling Interest: The World of the Multinational Corporation, a 45-minute film by California Newsreel (630 Natoma Street, San Francisco, CA 94103 415-621-6196)

Images of Males and Females in Elementary School Textbooks, a slide tape by Lenore Weitzman and Diane Rizzo (Available from the Feminist Press, Box 334, Old Westbury, NY 11568)

Killing Us Softly: Advertising's Image of Women, a 16mm, 29-minute, color film based on Jean Kilbourne's slide presentation, produced and distributed by Cambridge Documentary Films, Inc., Box 385, Cambridge, MA 02139 (617-354-3677). Other films about social issues also available.

Positive Images: A Guide to Non-Sexist Films for Young People, available for $5 from Booklegger Press, 555 29th St., San Francisco, CA 94131

Stale Roles and Tight Buns: Advertising's Image of Men, a slide show available from Oasis (See Men's Resources and Groups)

Humanity has been held to a limited and distorted view of itself — from its interpretation of the most intimate of personal emotions to its grandest vision of human possibilities — precisely by virtue of its subordination of women .... A community of purposeful and sympathetic women directed to their self-determined goals is a new phenomenon. It has created an atmosphere and milieu that brings a whole new quality to life. It advances and fosters both attempts at knowledge and a personal conviction about the content and the methods of getting at knowledge. It creates a new sense of connection between knowledge, work, and personal life. All this has begun to happen for women.

Jean Baker Miller

The values that have been labeled "feminine" — love, compassion, cooperation, patience — are very badly needed in giving birth to and nurturing a new era of greater peace and justice in human society. It would be unfortunate if they were forsaken by women because they seem dysfunctional to competition in a "masculine" world. Now, more than ever, these are the values that need to be asserted by men and women in creating a new world order.

Patricia Mische

For information about **Killing Us Softly: Advertising's Image of Women**, a film based on **The Naked Truth**, please contact:

Cambridge Documentary Films
P.O. Box 385
Cambridge, MA 02139 (617-354-3677)

For information about **The Naked Truth: Advertising's Image of Women** and/or
Under the Influence: The Pushing of Alcohol via Advertising, illusted lectures by Jean Kilbourne, please contact:

Lordly & Dame
51 Church Street
Boston, MA 02116 (617-482-3593)

Credit Cards:
Auto Repair Protection

People use credit cards for different reasons. For some, credit is a necessity; for others, a convenience. But did you ever think about using a credit card as a protection against faulty or unnecessary auto repairs? Using a credit card instead of cash can save the day for a consumer who is having problems with an auto mechanic.

Suppose you take your car to the mechanic because of a noise in the power steering. The shop does a rack-and-pinion overhaul. You pay $180 with your credit card and drive home. The next afternoon, the noise is back. Another mechanic looks at the car and finds that the real problem was fluid leaking from the power steering pump. That will cost another $125 to repair.

A Negotiating Tool

What happens if the first mechanic refuses to make good on his mistake? If you had paid the bill with cash, you would be out $180 and might have to file suit to recover your money. If you paid by check, it would probably be too late to stop payment. Payment with a credit card not only gives you extra time, but is also an effective tool for negotiating with the mechanic.

You Can Refuse To Pay

According to Federal law, if you have a problem with goods or services purchased with your credit card, you have the same legal rights in dealing with the credit card issuer as you have with the auto mechanic. In other words, because you have the right to withhold payment from the auto mechanic for sloppy or incorrect repairs, you also have the right to refuse to pay the credit card company. Of course, you may withhold no more than the amount of the repair in dispute.

In order to use this important right, you must first try to work things out with the auto mechanic. Also, unless the card issuer owns or operates the repair shop (this might be true if your car is repaired at a gas station and you use a gas credit card), two other conditions must be met:

* The auto mechanic's shop must be in your home state or, if not in your state, within 100 miles of your current address.

* The cost of repairs must be over $50.

You can hold onto your money until the dispute is settled or resolved in court. The credit card company cannot make you pay interest or other penalty charges on the amount you are withholding until that time.

If you decide not to pay, send a letter to both the credit card company and the auto mechanic. Include the date of repair, the credit card used, your account number, why the service was unsatisfactory, and what you want in settlement of your dispute. It is a good idea to send the letter by certified mail with a return receipt requested.

This law was designed to protect you. Using it will put you in a good bargaining position with both time and money on your side.

Proceed With Caution

Many disputes will be settled at this point, with one side or both sides compromising to reach a settlement. Some will not be.

Sometimes the credit card company or the auto mechanic will take action to put a "bad mark" on your credit record because you did not pay your bill. You may not be reported as delinquent, but a creditor can report that you are disputing a charge. For this reason, you should know your rights under the Fair Credit Reporting Act.

This Act permits you to learn what information is in your credit file and to challenge any information you feel is incorrect. If the credit bureau can not prove the information is true, they have to remove it. You also have the right to have your side of the story added to your file.

The mechanic may also feel strongly enough to go to court to collect his bill. If this happens, you will probably want to talk to a lawyer to make sure you are on solid legal ground.

Using a credit card will not solve all your auto repair problems. But it is a tool to use in tough negotiations. And auto repair complaints are among society's toughest.

Complaints or requests for more information about your credit rights should be sent to the Federal Trade Commission, Credit Practices Division, Washington, D.C. 20580.

FEDERAL TRADE COMMISSION

WASHINGTON. D. C. 20580

OFFICIAL BUSINESS
PENALTY FOR PRIVATE USE. $300

POSTAGE AND FEES PAID
U.S. FEDERAL
TRADE COMMISSION

Women-Controlled Health Centers and Women-Controlled Advocacy Groups

ALASKA
Women's Resource Center
602 W. 10th
Anchorage, AK 99501
907-278-9047

ARKANSAS
Mari Spehar Health Education Project
Deep End
Box 545, 902 West Maple
Fayetteville, AR 72701
501-442-8041

Women's Center-Health Collective
207 N. Razorback Rd.
Fayetteville, AR 72701
501-443-2000

CALIFORNIA
Association for Childbirth at Home, International
P.O. Box 1219
Cerritos, CA 90701
213-865-5123

Berkeley Women's Health Collective
2908 Ellsworth
Berkeley, CA 94705
415-843-1437

Buena Vista Women's Services
2000 Van Ness
San Francisco, CA 94109

Chico Feminist Women's Health Center
330 Flume St.
Chico, CA 95926
916-891-1911

Coalition for the Medical Rights of Women
3543 18th St.
San Francisco, CA 94110
415-621-8030

Everywoman's Clinic
2600 Park Ave., Suite 106 & 102
Concord, CA 94520
415-825-7900

Fat Underground
P.O. Box 5621
Santa Monica, CA 90405

Feminist Health Program
AFSC
2160 Lake St.
San Francisco, CA 94121

Feminist Women's Health Center of Orange County
429 Sycamore

Feminist Women's Health Center
1112 Crenshaw Blvd.
Los Angeles, CA 90019
213-936-6293

Haight-Ashbury Women's Clinic
558 Clayton St.
San Francisco, CA 94117

Marin Women's Health Center
1618 Mission Ave.
San Rafael, CA 94901
415-456-2171

Network Against Psychiatric Assault/Women Against Psychiatric Assault
(NAPA/WAPA)
2150 Market St.
San Francisco, CA 94114

Oakland Feminist Women's Health Center
2930 McClure St
Oakland, CA 94609

Our Health Center
270 Grant
Palo Alto, CA 94306

Santa Cruz Women's Health Center
250 Locust St.
Santa Cruz, CA 95060
408-427-3500

San Francisco Women's Health Center
3789 24th St.
San Francisco, CA 94114
415-282-6999

Task Force on Older Women
National Organization for Women
3800 Harrison St.
Oakland, CA 94611

T.H.E. Clinic for Women, Inc.
2950 South Western Ave.
Los Angeles, CA 90018

Westside Women's Clinic
1711 Ocean Park Blvd.
Santa Monica, CA 90405
213-450-2191

Womancare
424 Pennsylvania Ave.
San Diego, CA 92103

Woman Against Violence in Pornography and Media
Box 14614
San Francisco, CA 94114

Women's Community Clinic
696 E. Santa Clara St.
San Jose, CA 95112

Women's Health Care Specialist Training Project
Northcountry Clinic
592 14th St.
Arcata, CA 95521

COLORADO
HERS
1744 Vine St.
Denver, CO 80210

Women's Health Service Clinic
1703 N. Weber St.
Colorado Springs, CO 80907
303-471-9492 or 303-471-8196

CONNECTICUT
Connecticut Women's Health Connection
c/o Karen Peteros
Box 49
Mansfield Depot, CT 06251

Women's Health Services
19 Edwards St.
New Haven, CT 06511

DISTRICT OF COLUMBIA
Abortion Rights Movement of Women's Liberation
1212 Pennsylvania Ave., SE
Washington, D.C. 20003

Campaign to End Discrimination Against
Pregnant Women
1126 16th St., NW
Washington, D.C. 20036

Health Task Force
c/o Womanspace
Box 3, Marvin Center
George Washington University
800 21st St., NW
Washington, D.C. 20052

National Women's Health Network
2025 I St., NW, Suite 105
Washington, D.C. 20006
202-543-9222

Women and Health Roundtable
Federation of Organizations for Professional
Women
2000 P St., NW
Washington, D.C. 20036

Women's Growth and Therapy Center
1425 Montague St., NW
Washington, D.C. 20001

Women's Health Collective
Washington Free Clinic
1556 Wisconsin Ave., NW
Washington, D.C. 20007
202-965-5476

Women's Health Project
D.C. Public Interest Research Group
1722 Irving St.
Washington, D.C. 20010

FLORIDA
Alternative Birth Center
1232 Laura St.
Jacksonville, FL 32206

Birthplace
635 NE First St.
Gainesville, FL 32601

Feminist Women's Health Center
1017 Thomasville Rd.
Tallahassee, FL 32303
904-224-9600

Gainesville Women's Health Center
805 SW 4th Ave.
Gainesville, FL 32601
904-377-5055 or 904-377-5551 (24-hr. hotline)

HELP (Health Education Learning Program)
Box 514
Cocoa Beach, FL 32931

Women Acting Together to Combat Harrassment
(WATCH)
c/o FWHC
1017 Thomasville Rd.
Tallahassee, FL 32303
904-224-9600

Tampa Women's Health Center
3004 Fletcher
Tampa, FL 33612
813-977-6176

GEORGIA
Feminist Women's Health Center
580 14th St., NW
Atlanta, GA 30318
404-874-7551

HAWAII
Women's Health Center of Hawaii
319 Paoa Kalani Ave
Honolulu, HI 96815

IDAHO
Magic Valley Rape Crisis Center
680 Clico St.
Hansen, ID 83334

ILLINOIS
Chicago Women's Health Center
2757 North Seminary
Chicago, IL 60614
312-935-6126

Chicago Women's Health Task Force
P.O. Box 7892
Chicago, IL 60680

Emma Goldman Women's Clinic
1628 A West Belmont
Chicago, IL 60657
313-528-4310

Evanston Women's Liberation Union Health Group
2214 Ridge
Evanston, IL 60202
312-475-4480

Health Evaluation and Referral Service (H.E.R.S.)
2757 North Seminary
Chicago, IL 60614
312-248-0166

La Leche League International, Inc.
9616 Minneapolis Ave.
Franklin Park, IL 60131
312-455-7730

Resource Center on Women and Health Care
1601 Parkview Ave.
Rockford, IL 61101

INDIANA
Indianapolis Women's Center Health Group
5626 E. 16th St., #32
Indianapolis, IN 46218
317-353-9371

IOWA
Cedar Rapids Clinic for Women
86 1/2 16th Ave., SW
Cedar Rapids, IA 52404

Emma Goldman Clinic for Women
715 North Dodge
Iowa City, IA 52240
319-337-2111

Hera
436 S. Johnson St.
Iowa City, IA 52240

Well-Woman Clinic
1125 W. 3rd St.
Cedar Falls, IA 50613

MAINE
Portland Women's Health Council
P.O. Box 8335
Portland, ME 04102

MARYLAND
Breast Cancer Advisory Center
P.O. Box 422
Kensington, MD 20795
301-949-2530

H.O.M.E. (Home Oriented Maternity Experience)
511 New York Ave.
Takoma Park, MD 20012
301-585-5832 or 301-656-6797

MASSACHUSETTS
Abortion Action Coalition
Box 2727
Boston, MA 02208

Alliance Against Sexual Coercion
P.O. Box 1
Cambridge, MA 02139
617-661-4090

BirthDay
Box 388
Cambridge, MA 02138

Boston Women's Health Book Collective
P.O. Box 192
W. Somerville, MA 02144
617-924-0271

CESA (Committee to End Sterilization Abuse)
Box 2727
Boston, MA 02208

C/SEC (Caesarian/Support, Education,
and Counseling)
132 Adams St., Room 6
Newton, MA 02158

COPE (Coping with the Overall Pregnancy
Experience)
37 Clarendon St.
Boston, MA 02116

D.E.S. Action Project
Box 117
Brookline, MA 02146

Elizabeth Stone House
128 Minden St.
Jamaica Plain, MA 02130
617-524-9872

Everywoman's Center
Health Project
University of Massachusetts
509 Goodell Hall
Amherst, MA 01003
413-545-0883

Framingham Women's Health Project
73 Union Ave.
Framingham, MA 01701

Homebirth
Boston University Station
Box 355
Boston, MA 02215

Marlborough Women's Health Services
P.O. Box 160
Marlborough, MA 01752

New Bedford Women's Health Services
15 Chestnut St.
New Bedford, MA 02740

Origins, Inc. (The Salem Women's Health
Collective)
169 Boston St.
Salem, MA 01970
617-745-5873

Resolve, Inc.
P.O. Box 474
Belmont, MA 02178
617-484-2424

Women, Inc.
570 Warren Ave.
Dorchester, MA 02122

Women's Community Health Center, Inc.
639 Massachusetts Ave., #210
Cambridge, MA 02139
617-547-2302

Women's Health Center
CAC of Cape Cod and Islands
Mary Dunn Rd., Box 954
Hyannis, MA 02601

Women's Health Clinic
Box 613
Provincetown, MA 02657
617-487-3220

Women's Health Program
c/o Martha Mason
Box 949
Edgartown, MA 02539

MICHIGAN
Ann Arbor Women's Health Collective
Community Health Center
2201 Hemlock Ct.
Ann Arbor, MI 48104

Feminist Women's Health Center
Women's Choice Clinic
15251 W. Eight Mile
Detroit, MI 48235
313-341-5666

NOW Health Task Force
Muskegon Ottowa NOW
P.O. Box 3964
Muskegon Heights, MI 49444

Women's Health and Information Project
Box 110, Warriner Hall
Central Michigan University
Mt. Pleasant, MI 48858
517774-3151

MINNESOTA
Elizabeth Blackwell Women's Health Center
3 E. 38th St.
Minneapolis, MN 55409
612-335-7669

National Communications Network for the
Elimination of Violence Against Women
4520 44th Ave. So.
Minneapolis, MN 55406
612-827-2841

Women of All Red Nations (WARN)
c/o St. Paul Urban Indian Health Board Clinic
643 Virginia St.
St. Paul, MN 55103

MISSISSIPPI
Women's Health Collective
c/o Barbara Prichard
5428 N. Venetian Way
Jackson, MS 39211

MISSOURI
St. Louis Women's Health Collective
Women's Resource Center
Box 1182
St. Louis, MO 63130

Women's Clinic
c/o People's Clinic
6010 Kingsbury
St. Louis, MO 63112

Women's Self-Help Center
27 N. Newstead Ave.
St. Louis, MO 63108

MONTANA
Blue Mountain Women's Clinic
218 E. Front St., Rm. 106
Missoula, MT 59801

NEW HAMPSHIRE
New Hampshire Feminist Health Center
38 South Main St.
Concord, NH 03301
603-224-3251

NEW JERSEY
Livingston Self-Help Group
Women's Center
Livingston College
Rutgers University
New Brunswick, NJ 08903

National Midwives Association
Box 163
Princeton, NJ 08540
609-799-1942

Together, Inc. (women and prescription drugs)
7 State St.
Glassboro, NJ 08028
609-881-4040

NEW MEXICO
Albuquerque Women's Health Center
106 Girard SE, Suite 114C
Albuquerque, NM 87106

Southwest Maternity Center
504 Luna Blvd., NW
Albuquerque, NM 87102
505-243-5584

Women's Health Services
316 E. Marcy St.
Santa Fe, NM 87501
505-988-2660

NEW YORK

Binghamton Women's Health Care Project
c/o Women's Center
66 Chenango St.
Binghamton, NY 13901

CARASA (Coalition for Abortion Rights and Against
Sterilization Abuse)
Box 124, Cathedral Station
New York, NY 10025

CESA (Committee to End Sterilization Abuse)
Box A244, Cooper Station
New York, NY 10003

D.E.S. Action
P.O. Box 1977
Plainview, NY 11803

The Feminist Alliance
Health Project
Rockland Community College
75 College Rd.
Suffern, NY 10901

Feminist Health Works
487-A Hudson St.
New York, NY 10014

Health House
555 N. Country Rd.
St. James, NY 11780

HealthRight, Inc.
41 Union Sq., Room 206-209
New York, NY 10003

Lay Non-Medical Midwives for Natural Homebirth
1364 East 7th St.
Brooklyn, NY 11230

Maternity Center Association
(free-standing birth center)
48 East 92nd St.
New York, NY 10028
212-369-7300

Rochester Women's Health Collective
3 Arlington St.
Rochester, NY 14607
716-461-2567

St. Marks Clinic Women's Health Collective
44 St. Marks Pl.
New York, NY 10003

Women's Health Alliance of Long Island, Inc.
P.O. Box 645
Westbury, NY 11590

Women's Health Care Center
101 N. Geneva St.
Ithaca, NY 14850

NORTH CAROLINA

Women's Health Counseling Service, Inc.
Switchboard
112 N. Graham St.
Chapel Hill, NC 27514

OHIO

Cleveland NOW Health Care Task Force
2648 Euclid Heights Blvd.
Cleveland, OH 44106

Self-Help Group
c/o Linda Goubeaux
37 1/2 East Frambes
Columbus, OH 43201

WomanSpace
1528 Euclid
Cleveland, OH 44115
216-696-3100

Women Against Rape
Box 02084
Columbus, OH 43202

OKLAHOMA

Oklahoma Women's Health Coalition
c/o Ann Mulloy-Ashmore
12225 Candytuft Ln.
Oklahoma City, OK 73132

OREGON

Ashland Women's Health Center
295 E. Main St.
Ashland, OR 97520

Birth Center Lucinia
207 W. 10th Ave.
Eugene, OR 97401

Southeast Women's Health Clinic
4160 SE Division
Portland, OR 97202

PENNSYLVANIA

CHOICE (Concern for Health Options, Information,
Care, and Education)
1501 Cherry St.
Philadelphia, PA 19102
215-567-7932 or 215-567-2904 (hotline)

Elizabeth Blackwell Health Center for Women
112 S. 16th St.
Philadelphia, PA 19102
215563-7577

Pennsylvania Women's Center
112 Logan Hall
University of Pennsylvania
Philadelphia, PA 19104

Philadelphia Women's Health Collective
5030 Newhall St.
Philadelphia, PA 19144

Women's Health Alliance
Women's Resource Center
108 W. Beaver Ave.
State College, PA 16801

Women's Health Concerns Program
112 S. 16th St., Suite 1012
Philadelphia, PA 19102

RHODE ISLAND

Rhode Island Rape Crisis Center
324 Broad St.
c/o YWCA
Central Falls, RI 02863

Rhode Island Women's Health Collective
P.O. Box 1313
Providence, RI 02903

SOUTH DAKOTA
Women's Health Collective
c/o Lorelei Means
General Delivery
Porcupine, SD 57772

TENNESSEE
Health Group--YWCA
200 Monroe Ave.
Memphis, TN 38107

TEXAS
Austin Women's Health Center
1902 Interregional Hgwy.
Austin, TX 78741

Houston Women's Health Collective
c/o Nancy Kern
1201 Welch, #2
Houston, TX 77006

Rosie Jimenez Fund
711 San Antonio St.
Austin, TX 78701
512-654-8662
· Provides direct subsidies for poor women unable
to obtain legal abortions due to Medicaid
cutbacks for abortion.

Women's Center of Dallas Health Group
2001 McKinney, #300
Dallas, TX 75201
214-651-9795

VERMONT
Women's Clinic
The Green Mountain Health Center
36 High St.
Brattleboro, VT 05301
802-257-1135

LUCRECE
c/o Health Information
Box 263
Johnson, VT 05656

Self-Help Group of Central Vermont
Box 283
Montpelier, VT 05602

Southern Vermont Women's Health Center
187 North Main St.
Rutland, VT 05701
802-775-1946

Vermont Women's Health Center
P.O. Box 29
Burlington, VT 05401

WHISTLE (Women's Hormone Information Service)
The Creamery Educational Foundation
Box 367
Shelburne, VT 05482

VIRGINIA
Tidewater Rape Information Services, Inc
P.O. Box 9900
Norfolk, VA 23505
804-622-4300

WASHINGTON
Abortion--Birth Control Referral Service
4224 University Way, NE
Seattle, WA 98105
206-634-3460

Aradia Women's Health Center
1827 12th Ave.
Seattle, WA 98122

Blackwell Women's Health Resource Center
203 W. Holly, M/12
Bellingham, WA 98225
206-734-8592

Birth Support Group
2228 Overhulse, NW
Olympia, WA 98502

Fremont Women's Clinic
6817 Greenwood Ave., N.
Seattle, WA 98103
206-782-5788

Women in Midstream
(midlife concerns, including menopause)
University of Washington YWCA
4224 University Way, NE
Seattle, WA 98105
206-632-4747

Women's Clinic at Open Door
5012 Roosevelt Way, NE
Seattle, WA 98105
206-524-7404

WEST VIRGINIA
Women's Health Center of West Virginia, Inc
3418 Staunton Ave., SE
Charleston, WV 25304
304-344-9834

WISCONSIN
Bread and Roses Women's Health Center
238 W. Wisconsin Ave., #700
Milwaukee, WI 53203

Feminist Health Care Organizing Group
Box 469
Madison, WI 53701

Women's Health Information Group
c/o Gay Radosevich
Rte. 1, Box 134
Prairie Farm, WI 54762

NEW from the
NATIONAL WOMEN'S HEALTH NETWORK

Health Resource Guides

The Most Up-To-Date Information On:

- **Menopause**
- **Hysterectomy**
- **Breast Cancer**
- **Childbirth**
- **DES**
- **Self-Help**
- **Birth Control**
- **Abortion**
- **Sterilization**

"Everything you need to know from the patient's point of view." — Barbara Seaman

"It's all here a national directory of health groups and centers, key resource people, books, magazines, and the latest medical information." — Phyllis Chesler, Ph.D.

CUT ALONG DOTTED LINE

ORDER FORM

MAKE CHECKS PAYABLE TO:
National Women's Health Network
224 Seventh St., SE
Washington, D.C. 20003

Please (✓) your order:

Please send me___books.
Enclosed is my check for $___

Name _____
Address _____
City_____State_____ Zip_____

	Member $4.00/copy	Non-member $5.00/copy
Menopause	_____	_____
Hysterectomy	_____	_____
Breast Cancer	_____	_____
Childbirth	_____	_____
DES	_____	_____
Self-Help	_____	_____
Birth Control	_____	_____
Abortion	_____	_____
Sterilization	_____	_____
Complete Set (9 books)	_____ ($30.00)	_____ ($36.00)

SUGGESTED READINGS TO LEARN MORE ABOUT YOUR HEALTH

*Our Bodies, Ourselves, the Boston Women's Health Collective (Simon and Schuster, New York) 1973

*Womancare: A Gynecological Guide to Your Body, by Lynda Madaras and Jane Patterson, M.D., F.A.C.O.G. (A new release: Avon Trade Paperback, $9.95)

*Take Care of Yourself: A Consumer's Guide to Medical Care, by Donald M. Vickery, M.D. and James F. Fries, M.D. (Addison-Wesley Publishing Co., Reading, Mass., paperback $9.95) 1981

*The People's Right to Good Health: A Guide to Consumer Health Rights and their Enforcement, by Terry Mizrahi Madison (National Clearinghouse for Legal Services, 500 North Michigan Ave., Suite 1940, Chicago, Ill., 60611) 1978

*Pill That Don't Work, by Sidney M. Wolfe, M.D., Christopher M. Coley and the Health Research Group (Health Research Group, 2000 P St. NW, Washington D.C., 20036, $6.00) 1980

*Stopping Valium, by Eve Bargmann, M.D., Sidney Wolfe, M.D., Joan Levin, and the Public Citizen Health Research Group, (Health Research Group, 2000 P St. NW, #708, Washington, D.C. 20036, $3.00) 1982

Reprinted from *Women: A Developmental Perspective;* Proceedings of a research conference sponsored by the National Institute of Child Health and Human Development in cooperation with the National Institute of Mental Health and the National Institute on Aging, November 20–21, 1980, National Institutes of Health, Bethesda, Maryland.

The Natural Capacity for Health in Women

Estelle R. Ramey, Ph.D.

When William Shakespeare wrote: "Frailty, thy name is woman," he didn't know about actuarial tables or the genetic advantages of the XX configuration. Like the Apostle Paul before him, Shakespeare was merely affirming accepted wisdom that women were the "weaker sex." It needed only Freud's proclamation that "anatomy is destiny" to give scientific blessing to the dogma that women were puny, hysterical propagators of the species. The essential counterpart to this is that men are the stronger sex--muscular, unemotional, and uncomplaining.

This mutually destructive pastiche of religious, social, and medical nonsense still acts to keep men, as well as women, from realizing their full potential for physical and mental health. Even in the 18th century it was observed that women tended to outlive men, yet very few efforts have been made by scientists since then to identify the biological advantages of females or the specific disadvantages that accrue to maleness. The obvious utility of such knowledge in extending male life expectancy has been virtually ignored by the male community of life scientists.

When the average American is asked to explain the noticeable imbalance between old men and old women in our society, the usual answer is that men work harder than women. About 8 years ago when my colleague Peter Ramwell and I began to investigate the sex differences underlying the development of certain cardiovascular lesions, we found a striking paucity of research data in the literature.

This volume will deal with the health problems of women, but it is impossible to understand the etiology, history, and prognosis of these problems without understanding the attitudes of physicians to what constitutes a healthy woman or a healthy man. It is well established that women visit health care practitioners more frequently than men (1). They do this not only for their own health problems, but also traditionally as the responsible parent in matters of child health. There are probably two major consequences of these frequent contacts between women and doctors:

a. Familiarity does indeed breed contempt, and some doctors evidently have viewed complaints as less serious than male complaints. The spin-off from this may be that psychotropic drugs are used far more frequently in the treatment of women.

Of all the prescriptions for psychotropic drugs in 1970, over 85 percent of the amphetamines, 68 percent of the tranquilizers and 60 percent of the barbiturates were prescribed for women (2). The efficacy of such medications in treating the social origins of the complaints that bring these women to physicians is questionable, and the safety of such medications should be of concern.

b. It may be, however, that women because of their habit of seeking help from the medical community, also benefit from earlier diagnosis of potentially life-threatening diseases. Men are taught that weakness of any kind is emasculating and are more reluctant to report disturbing symptoms. Men get less diazepam (Valium) but they also get later evaluation of serious ailments. It is clear that this distorted perception of female weakness and male strength damages the health of both sexes.

BIOLOGIC VIABILITY

As a first step in establishing the current status of women's health and health care in this country, we ought to look at the fundamental biologic viability with which women are endowed and then at the effect that the underestimation of that viability has had on women's physical and mental health.

In the human species the only fundamental advantage that males have is at conception. The estimates are that about 130-150 males are conceived for every 100 females (3), but the male fetal wastage is so much higher than the female that at birth the ratio is down to about 104-107 males to 100 females (4). Deaths in the first month of postnatal life are about 15/1000 for boys and about 11/1000 for girls (5). Furthermore, of about 190 neonatal abnormalities observed, close to three-fourths occurred mainly in males, while 25 percent were found chiefly in females (6). The explanation for these striking sex differences in early morbidity and mortality probably relates to the lack of gene redundancy on the Y chromosome which results in a greater number of expressed recessive traits on the X chromosome. Further, there may be greater immunological sensitization of the mother by male fetuses than by females (7). The net effect is not only to restrict the numbers of boys born, but also to increase the chances of health problems in the male at every stage of life. For example, the female has greater immunological responsiveness throughout the life span. This seems to be related in part to the number of Y chromosomes present in each cell because the levels of immunoglobulin are even higher in those females with the XXX configuration (8). In addition, estrogens after puberty increase immunoresponsiveness (9).

In the years between birth and puberty the disability and death rates for boys continue to be higher than for girls because social conditioning adds to biology to encourage more risky behavior in boys and more protected behavior in girls. The accident rate for boys and men remains higher throughout the lifespan. At puberty, the secretion of gonadal hormones introduces a second major biologic advantage in the female. In our laboratory we have been investigating the effects of testosterone, estrogens, and progestins on cardiovascular responses in animal species (10,11,12,13,14). The background to our research is as follows:

a. It is known that women in every age group have a significantly lower incidence than men of fatal arteriosclerotic heart disease, myocardial infarcts, transient coronary ischemia, and bronchopulmonary disease.

b. The prostaglandin system has been indicated as a major factor in many processes which regulate blood clotting, smooth muscle contraction, and myocardial contractility. Thromboxane acts to increase both platelet aggregability and myocardial contractility, while prostacyclin decreases these responses.

c. Since many physiological sex differences are mediated in large part by the gonadal steroids, the question we are trying to answer is "What is the relationship of the sex hormones to prostaglandin metabolism in the genesis of cardiovascular disease?"

We studied the effect of the prostaglandin metabolite, arachidonic acid, in vivo and in vitro on platelet aggregation and vascular reactivity in males and females, castrates and intact. In addition, we administered exogenous gonadal steroids to all these animal models and determined the effect on these cardiovascular parameters. In brief, we found that testosterone markedly increases arachidonate-induced platelet aggregability and thrombus formation with a concomitant increase in mortality rates. Testosterone also sensitizes blood vessel strips to the constrictor effects of the endoperoxides released during stress. The estrogens and progestins reduce these damaging responses in males but have little effect in females. Testosterone, however, increases mortality rates after arachidonate infusion in both males and females. These data together with reports that testosterone increases the LDL/HDL ratio (15) by acting to increase hepatic production of LDL by the liver, provide further insight into the high vulnerability of men to ischemic heart disease and its relationship to the gonadal hormones.

Even in circumstances of similar elevations in blood pressure, blood cholesterol and body lipids, females have a lower mortality rate than males. The importance of such data is that they present a possible avenue for the pharmacological intervention at different steps in the prostaglandin cascade so as to produce a more beneficial ratio of prostacyclin to thromboxane and thus reduce the risk of ischemic heart disease and stroke. An initial step has been taken with the use of aspirin in stroke victims (16). Aspirin, however, at the doses used appears to be effective only in men. More work is needed to find better prophylactic agents for both men and women. But first it must be recognized that the male hormone, for all its admirable effects on muscle mass and reproductive vigor, may also exact a toll from the cardiovascular system. It points up the possible dangers in giving female athletes androgenic steroids to increase muscle mass and speed. Giving exogenous androgens to males may place them at even greater risk.

The specific biochemical differences between normal women and men have not been adequately characterized. In the rather rare instances where such differences have been reported, a curious value judgment is often made. For example, depression is a mental disorder which appears to be more common in women than in men. It has been suggested that monoamine oxidase activity (MAO) is in some way related to this tension and depression (17). It has also been found that MAO activity changes during the menstrual cycle and is highest premenstrually. One conclusion from these coincident events has been that women have a higher incidence of depression because they develop high levels of MAO in a cyclic fashion. Further analysis of other data reveals that for most of the menstrual cycle, MAO activity is lower than that found in normal males, and that at the peak of MAO activity premenstrually the MAO activity is equal to the level found chronically in males (18). One can only conclude from such data that women should have less depression than men because most of the time their levels of MAO are below the ambient male levels. Obviously, depression has its etiology in a much more complex matrix of biological and social factors.

This is reminiscent of the frequent reports that women in the premenstrual or menstrual phase of the cycle have an increased incidence of suicides, violent crimes, and accidents (19). What is not mentioned in such reports is that men consistently have much higher rates of suicides, violent crimes, and accidents than women ever have. The study of women's biology can thus be used as a weapon against women. In fact, the health of the American woman is better than it has ever been. The life expectancy of a woman born in 1977 is 77.1 years, an average of 7.8 years longer than men (20). Nevertheless, given the biologic strengths of women, we are a long way from achieving optimum conditions for the expression of those strengths. More research is needed in every aspect of the changing health needs of the young, middle-aged, and old women.

The greatest self-imposed health hazard for women in the coming decade is sharply defined. Smoking stands alone as the major controllable threat to health (21). It potentiates other risk factors such as air pollution, occupational insults, and hormonal therapy. It is a hazard not only to the woman, but to the unborn child she may be carrying. Between the ages of 17-19 more women are new smokers than men. From 1965 the percentage of men smoking has dropped sharply from 51 percent to 36.9 percent in 1978, while the decrease for women has only been from 33 percent to 29.9 percent. Furthermore, these smokers are adversely affecting lung function in non-smokers in their vicinity (22). Any discussion of women's health must place the highest priorty on eliminating smoking as a risk factor. Otherwise, gains in other areas will be vitiated by the concomitant losses due to smoking. When the Surgeon General of the United States reports that the incidence of lung cancer in women will exceed the incidence of breast cancer by 1982, it is past time to attack this problem more vigorously. We know how to control lung cancer. The etiology of breast cancer remains obscure.

OTHER FACTORS

Women's health, like men's health, has a strong component of nonindigenous factors such as occupation, economic status, and the ability to control life situations. Given the natural biologic strengths of women, it is a tragic irony that the structure of our health care and research systems may be vitiating those strengths. Women represent more than half of the adult population and have the special needs of childbearing, yet it is estimated that only about 1.5 percent of the total NIH budget supports research on the reproductive biology of women (23). Even less goes into the special health care needs of older women despite the increasing numbers of such women in our hospitals, clinics, and nursing homes. Research in osteoporosis has not been heavily funded, even though in addition to the tragic disabling of otherwise healthy older women, it exacts a heavy economic cost from the whole society. (Some of this probably reflects the male domination of science. Increasing numbers of women are becoming physicians and research scientists, but the overwhelming preeminence of men in the decision-making cadres has not changed significantly.)

In 1979 women represented only 20 percent of those who had achieved a GS rating of 13 or above in the NIH structure, and only 7 percent at

the level of GS 16 or above (24). In 1969, 13.0 percent of medical
school faculties were women. In 1978 this had risen to only 15.1
percent (25). Only about 2 percent of department heads in the basic
sciences or the clinical sciences are women (26). This paucity of
women as directors and initiators of research projects must have an
effect on the selection of areas to be investigated. Priorities and
choices in the selection of research projects are no more exempt from
bias or emotion than any other choices in life. The disfiguring radical
mastectomy, for example, was retained as almost the only treatment, for
breast cancer long after data from many sources indicated that it was
no better than less traumatic surgery. Male surgeons didn't want to
mutilate patients. They wanted to save their lives, but inevitably
they were less sensitive than women to the consequences of this
assault on the woman's self-image. It is just one example of the
great need to have both women and men involved in every phase of
medical care and medical research.

Other examples may be found in birthing procedures which are convenient
for the doctor and potentially damaging to the mother and child, the
increased use of cesarean sections and hysterectomies. In 1975 there
were an estimated 781,000 hysterectomies in the United States, making
it one of the most common major surgical procedures. Moreover, the
increase in hysterectomies was approximately 30 percent between 1970
and 1975 (27). It is fortunate that women are so well endowed geneti-
cally; otherwise they would be hard put at times to survive.

All of these problems and many others unique to women are exacerbated by
the poverty and discrimination experienced by women from minority groups:
black, Hispanic, Asian-Pacific, and American Indian. Infant mortality
rates are a reflection of a complex pattern of cultural deprivation. In
1977 the infant mortality rate of blacks in the United States, for
example, was more than one and a half times that of whites (28) even
though medical care is available to black women. On the other hand,
the equally high infant mortality rate of American Indian women is
associated with an absolute deficiency of medical care facilities
for nonreservation rural Indians as well as for Indians on reservations
in remote areas of the country. Life expectancy for minority women is
lower than for white women by more than 7 years. There are obvious
reasons for this. Cervical cancer, diabetes, and hypertension have a
higher incidence of morbidity and mortality in black women. Alcoholism
is increasing in all women, but it is especially high in American Indian
women.

Migrant workers have even greater problems in the delivery of health
care. Most of these workers are Hispanic, and the women in these groups
suffer from the lack of adequate prenatal and maternal care as well as
the absence of all other health maintenance facilities. Contraceptive
information is not geared to barriers in the Hispanic culture and
religion, and women receive little education or counseling to overcome
such societal taboos. The absence of Hispanic women health professionals
contributes to these difficulties. Hispanic women are even more poorly
represented on PHS Health Advisory Committees and health care training
institutions than other minority women.

The disabling social conditions of minority women are associated with a
high incidence of mental illness but resources for treatment are grossly
inadequate. Bilingual health care specialists are virtually nonexistent

in many areas. This is especially damaging to the health care of Hispanic, Asian-Pacific, and Indian women whose cultural constraints, together with difficulties verbalizing symptomatology, exacerbate their distress and interfere with treatment. This lack also results in an ignorance of optimal nutritional and hygienic needs of the whole family and, most critically, of growing children and adolescents. In 1979, of women at risk of unintended pregnancy, only 63 percent of low- and marginal-income women, and only 56 percent of 15-19 year olds received medically supervised family planning services (29). Minority women represent a large fraction of this underserved group, and their teenage pregnancy rate is producing at least another generation of women who will be unable to climb out of an economic hole. The lack of public funding for procedures to terminate un-wanted pregnancies has its greatest impact on this group.

Thus we have the conundrum of women: highly endowed with natural resistance to environmental insults and degenerative diseases, who are made ill by neglect and misuse by virtue of their relatively power-less social status. It is ironic that these same women are now being warned that if they move into roles of power and achievement they will kill themselves. The very opposite effect actually occurs.

Now that more women are coming into the labor market there have been many reports (30) that the working woman will probably experience more heart attacks and other diseases common to men. Two recent studies suggest that this is not the case. Haynes' work shows that women in executive jobs do not show a higher incidence of heart disease (31). Only those women in clerical or low status jobs with poor support systems at home were found to be more vulnerable to cardiovascular disease.

Johnson did a more generalized study on age-adjusted life-expectancy data, and found that women are actually living longer despite their participa-tion in the work force (32). A report from the Metropolitan Life Insurance Company confirms these data in another way (33). They did a prospective study of the women listed in Who's Who in America starting with the listings in the mid-60's. The results in 1980 may be startling to those who think that the achievers in this society are destroyed by their own ambition and hard competitiveness. In fact, it is a lot better for your health to be successful and rich than to be poor and a failure. The women achievers had a 29 percent better life expectancy than their peer group in society. The Insurance Company had found exactly the same results earlier when they studied the men listed in Who's Who. The awesome burdens of responsibility which, incidentally, are also rewarded awesomely seem to be better tolerated than the stress of vulnerability and uncertainty.

Even underprivileged and economically deprived women outlive their male counterparts, however, and this contributes to a major social disloca-tion. The old women in this country represent the largest single group living below the poverty line set by the government. Their lack of economic independence during their earlier years leads to total dependency on social agencies in their later years. The health of older women is far below what it might be if they had the means to find adequate housing, food and health care. Thus, the early death of men and the underutiliza-tion of women in well-paying jobs during their youthful years place an enormous financial burden on a society which insisted on counterproductive role playing for both men and women.

In our pursuit of women's health, success will depend on the recognition of the relationship of women's health to increasing research, new modes of health care delivery, and a recognition of the health-defeating aspects of social stereotyping. We must also recognize, however, that healthy women can only be produced in a world that accepts the enormous physical and mental viability of women, and uses those attributes in every aspect of social planning. There is no doubt that this will at the same time contribute to the increased survival of the "stronger sex."

REFERENCES

1. Naierman, N.: Sex Discrimination in Health and Human Development Services. ABT Assoc. Inc., DHEW Office of Civil Rights, Contract No. HEW-100-78-0137, 1979.

2. Balter, M.: Extent and character of amphetamine use. In: Obesity: Causes, Consequences, and Treatment, Louis Lasagna (Ed.), Medcom, New York, New York, 1974.

3. Rasmuson, N.: Men--the weaker sex? Impact of Science on Society 21, 43, 1971.

4. Peterson, W.: Population (2nd Ed.), The Macmillan Co., New York, 1968.

5. Naeye, R.L., Burt, L.S., Wright, D.L., Blanc, W.M., and Tatter, D.: Neonatal mortality, the male disadvantage. Pediatrics 48, 902, 1971.

6. Singer, J.E., Westphal, M., and Niswander, K.R.: Sex differences in the incidence of neonatal abnormalities and abnormal performance in early childhood. Child Development 39, 103, 1968.

7. Renkonnen, K.O. and Makela, L.R.: Factors affecting human sex ratio. Nature 308, 1962.

8. Rhodes, K., Markam, R.L., Maxwell, P.W., and Monk-Jones, N.E.: Immunoglobulins and the X-chromosome. Brit. Med. J. 3, 439, 1969.

9. Steinberg, A.D., Melex, K.A., Raveche, E.S., Reeves, J.P., Boegel, W.A., Smathers, P.A., Taurog, J.D., Weinlein, L., and Duvic, M.: Approach to the study of the role of sex hormones in autoimmunity. Arthritis and Rheumatism 11, 1170, 1979.

10. Uzunoya, A.D., Ramey, E.R., and Ramwell, P.W.: Gonadal hormones and the pathogenesis of occulsive arterial thrombosis. Am. J. Physiol. 234, 454, 1978.

11. Baker, P.J., Ramey, E.R., and Ramwell, P.W.: Androgen-mediated sex differences in cardiovascular responses in rates. Am. J. Physiol. 235, H242, 1978.

12. Maggi, F., Tyrell, N., Maddox, Y., Ramey, E.R., and Ramwell, P.W.: Prostaglandin synthetase activity in vascular tissue of male and female rats. Prostaglandins 19, 985, 1980.

13. Loevey, E., Ramey, E.R., Maddox, Y., and Ramwell, P.W.: Effect of fasting and sex steroids on arachidonate uptake into rat platelets. Adv. Prost. Throm. Res. 8, 1277, 1980.

14. Pomerantz, K., Maddox, Y., Maggi, F.M., Ramey, E.R., and Ramwell, P.W.: Sex and hormonal modification of 6-keto-PGF_{1a} release by rat aorta. Life Sciences 27, 1233, 1980.

15. Ockner, R.K., Burnett, D.A., Lysenko, N., and Manning, J.A.: Sex differences in long chain fatty acid utilization and fatty acid binding protein concentration in rat liver. J. Clin. Invest. 64, 172, 1979.

138

16. The Canadian Cooperative Study Group: A randomized trial of aspirin and sulfinpyrazone in threatened stroke. New England Journal of Medicine 3, 777, 1968.

17. Grant, E.C.G. and Pryse-Davis, J.: Effects of oral contraceptives on depressive mood changes and on endometrial monoamine oxidase and phosphatases. British Medical Journal 3, 777, 1968.

18. Briggs, M. and Briggs, M.: Relationship between monoamine oxidase activity and sex hormone concentration in human blood plasma. Journal of Reproduct. Fertil. 29, 447, 1972.

19. Parlee, M.B.: The premenstrual syndrome. Psychological Bulletin 80, 454, 1973.

20. U.S. Department of Health, Education, and Welfare: Health United States 1979, DHEW Publication No. (PHS) 80-1232, Washington, D.C., U.S. Government Printing Office, 1980.

21. Office on Smoking and Health, Office of the Assistant Secretary for Health: The Health Consequences of Smoking for Women, A Report of the Surgeon General, Washington, D.C., U.S. Government Printing Office, 1980.

22. White, J.R. and Froeb, H.F.: Small airways dysfunction in non-smokers chronically exposed to tobacco smoke. New England Journal of Medicine 303, 392, 1980.

23. United States Department of Health and Human Services, National Institutes of Health, National Institute of Child Health and Human Development: An Evaluation and Assessment of the State of the Science, Report of the study group on fertility and infertility, NIH Publication No. 82-2304, U.S. Government Printing Office, Washington, D.C., October 1981.

24. United States Department of Health and Human Services: Affirmative Action Plan and Federal Equal Opportunity Recruitment Program FY 1980-1981, U.S. Government Printing Office, Washington, D.C., 1981.

25. Association of American Medical Colleges: Trends in Medical School Faculty Characteristics, New Faculty and Continuing Faculty, 1968-1978, Washington, D.C., 1980.

26. Association of American Medical Colleges: Directory of American Medical Education, 1980, Washington, D.C., 1981.

27. Walker, A.M. and Jick, H.: Temporal and regional variation in hysterectomy rates in the United States, 1970-1975. American Journal of Epidemiology 110, 41, 1979.

28. United States Department of Health, Education, and Welfare: Health United States, 1979, DHEW Publication No. (PHS) 80-1232, U.S. Government Printing Office, Washington, D.C., 1980.

29. Torres, A., Forrest, J.D., and Eisman, S.: Family planning services in the United States, 1978-1979. Family Planning Perspectives 13, 132, 1981.

30. Waldron, I.: Why do women live longer than men? J. Human Stress 2, 2, 1976.

31. Haynes, S.G. and Feinleib, M.: Women, work, and coronary heart disease. Prospective findings from the Framingham Heart Study. A. J. Pub. Health 70, 133, 1980.

32. Johnson, A.: Recent trends in sex mortality differentials in the United States. J. Human Stress 3, 22, 1977.

33. Metropolitan Life Insurance Company: Statistical Bulletin 60, 3, 1979.

From "Voices For Women," 1980 Report of the President's Advisory Committee for Women, 200 Constitution Ave., NW, Washington, D.C. 20210

Chapter IV

HEALTH

The health care system in this country is replete with evidence of inadequate provision for the health needs of women. Women require more health care than men because they are the child bearers and live longer, yet many services to meet their health care needs are unaffordable, uninsurable, or inadequate. We can mention some of the more glaring examples. Public monies for medical research include very little (less than 2 percent) for reproductive problems of women—certainly one of the Nation's major health care problems in view of the epidemic of teenage pregnancies. Women also are the victims in a large percentage of unnecessary surgeries, usually hysterectomies and mastectomies.

A major factor that makes possible such discrimination against women in health care is lack of female participation in decisions at the policymaking level. Males dominate in legislative bodies and in agency policymaking positions. Male-physician domination is gross in the current scheme for health planning represented by HSA's and P.L. 93-641. Males dominate in the administration of health care delivery facilities in this country.

Ernestine Small, R.N.
Greensboro, N.C.
President-Elect of the North Carolina Nurses Association

OVERVIEW

The health of U.S. women is better than it ever has been before. The life expectancy for a woman born in 1977 is 77.1 years.[1] Women are physiologically strong—living on the average of 7.8 years longer than men.[2]

Many of the leading health problems of women are the same as those faced by men. Accidents, cardiovascular disease, and cancer are leading causes of death for both women and men. However, certain problems have been identified as having a particularly significant impact on the health of women, and it is these problems which have been addressed by the President's Advisory Committee for Women.

Advancements in the areas of women's health have come very slowly. The special needs of women targeted by the PACFW are, for the most part, the same as those targeted by each preceding Advisory Committee. The recommendations made by previous Committees have been re-emphasized because of the lack of progress on many of the long-standing problems described in their reports. Examples are numerous.

Since 1970 the number of women entering the health professions as doctors and dentists has been increasing rapidly; however, the percentage appointed to policymaking positions remains small, thereby maintaining a male-dominated health field. Individual physicians are gradually becoming more sensitive to the needs of women, but sexist attitudes within the profession are still prevalent.

In response to the concerns voiced by women about the impersonal and isolated nature of obstetrical practices, "birthing centers" are being established throughout the Nation. These centers, which involve the entire family in home-like surroundings, have yet to become a standard option in all hospitals. Although women have voiced alarm about the rising rates of Caesarean deliveries, the rise continues. While the disfiguring Halsted radical mastectomy is no longer being used as the standard procedure for breast cancer, women with breast cancer are not always informed about the various options of therapy available

to them. A safe, inexpensive contraceptive agent has yet to be developed.

Women continue to represent a disproportionate number of the mentally ill because society's sexist attitudes, which have a negative impact on the mental well-being of women, have not been effectively addressed. In spite of the fact that special treatment needs of women who abuse drugs or alcohol have been identified, few treatment programs are designed to meet those needs.

In some areas the problems have become worse. With increasing numbers of sexually active adolescents, the serious consequences of adolescent pregnancy for both the mother and child are more apparent. At the other end of the life spectrum, with life expectancy increasing and with women outliving men, the health problems of old age will be experienced by more women.

Smoking, a health problem not previously addressed by preceding Advisory Committees, was targeted by PACFW as an issue of particular significance to women. For some years smoking has been seen as a man's health problem. It was believed that women were immune to the damaging effects of smoking. Research has conclusively shown this not to be the case. In fact, it is predicted that within 3 years deaths from lung cancer in women will surpass those from breast cancer. During the past decade men have become aware of the hazards of smoking and the percentage of men who smoke has decreased dramatically while the percentage of women who smoke has decreased little. In fact, at ages 17 through 19 more young women smoke than do young men.[3]

[1] *Health, United States, 1979;* Office of Health Research, Statistics, and Technology, National Center for Health Statistics, DHEW Publication No. (PHS) 80-1232, p. 138.

[2] *Vital Statistics of the United States,* Volume II, Section 5; Lifetables; National Center for Health Statistics, 1977.

[3] *The Health Consequences of Smoking for Women: A Report of the Surgeon General,* DHEW (PHS), Office of the Assistant Secretary for Health, Office on Smoking and Health, Jan. 1980.

It is depressing that the progress made in the areas of women's health has been so slow—there remains much do be done in the future. With more young women entering the health professions and with greater awareness and participation of women as utilizers of health care, there is hope that progress in the future will come about more rapidly.

Minority Women

Although there is greater awareness of the special health problems of minority women, these problems have yet to be adequately met. The health care needs of minority women have never been comprehensively studied. Infant mortality rates for Blacks and American Indians/Alaska Natives (7.6/1,000 and 7.3/1,000 live births, respectively) are double those for the white population (3.6/1,000). Maternal mortality is over three times greater than for whites. Life expectancy for Black women is lower than that for white women (68.3 years versus 75.5 years in 1975). The incidence of cervical cancer and of diabetes is higher in nonwhite than white women. Hypertension occurs more frequently in Black women than white women.

The influx of refugees from Southeast Asia is expected to have an adverse impact on the health status of Asian/Pacific American women. Both Asian/Pacific American women and Hispanic women share the need for bilingual services in health care facilities. All minority women face additional stresses in their lives because of racism. These stresses, compounding those due to sexism faced by all women, threaten the mental well-being of minority women.

The Delivery of Health Care

"All too often, women feel they never had a choice: their physician dictated what their method would be, discounting the women's feelings and concerns while assuming a condescending, paternalistic view."

Elaine Barney
Director of the Women's
Health Counseling Service
Raleigh, N.C.

The majority of the utilizers of the health care system are women. Women have more visits to physicians and higher rates of surgery than men. They require numerous reproductive health services. Since women live on the average longer than men, the chronic problems of old age are primarily experienced by older women.

The field of health, however, has a long tradition of being male-dominated. The detrimental effects of this domination on the care women receive can be seen in a number of ways:

• Prevailing sex stereotyping attitudes of the providers have a negative impact on care rendered. For example, male physicians tend to do more extensive workups for the complaints of male patients than for identical complaints of female patients.

• The direction of money spent on research has often not optimally met the health needs of women. An example is that more funds are channeled into research involving oral contraceptives instead of the barrier methods which involve less personal risk to women.

• The health care services rendered have not been sensitive to the needs of women. In 1976 less than 3 percent of alcohol treatment facilities funded by the National Institute on Alcohol Abuse and Alcoholism were designed for women. Appropriate use of surgical procedures on women has been questioned. In 1977 hysterectomy was the third most frequently performed surgical procedure, exceeded only by biopsies and D&C's.

Health insurance is more likely to be a problem for women than men, and as Congress deliberates national health insurance during the decade of the 80's, consideration must be given to the special needs of women.

Catherine Fogel, an R.N. from Chapel Hill, N.C., stressed the "involvement of the client in a collaborative role in all aspects of her health care." Speaking in the area of birth control, Elaine Barney, Director of the Women's Health Counseling Service in North Carolina, stated that "too often, women feel they never had a choice: their physician dictated what their method would be, discounting the women's feelings and concerns while assuming a condescending, paternalistic view of a woman's role as patient, not as a consumer of health care."

Testimony was heard from women of many minority groups relating how the delivery of health care was not meeting their needs. Cheryl Beasley, an R.N. and member of the Lumbee tribe, stated that, "the Indian woman in North Carolina is in a double bind when seeking health services. She experiences the health problems and lack of appropriate health services experienced by all American women. In addition, the Indian woman must suffer the health problems of those who do not match the picture of the American dream. As a member of an ethnic minority, she must cope with poor access to health care; then when care is accessible, it is fragmented and given by those who do not understand her needs as a woman or her role in the Indian family."

Alice Sanchez from Lafayette, Colorado, brought up the need for bilingual personnel in health care facilities. In Raleigh, N.C., Vickie McCullen, representing the Migrant and Seasonal Farm Workers Association, spoke of the migrant women's "low participation in (the) limited available programs which are already overloaded with 'locals' and cannot or will not accept the migrants who are 'outsiders'."

Federal Initiatives

The Privacy Act of 1974 grants individuals access to records maintained by Federal agencies, including medical records on the individuals. Pending legislation proposed by the administration would extend the individuals' access to hospital records, including in-patient and out-patient records. Several States already have laws allowing patients access to their medical records.

In FY'79 the Federal Food and Drug Administration, with the support of the White House Office of Consumer Affairs, proposed comprehensive patient labeling for drugs.

In FY'79 the HEW Steering Committee on Women's Issues called for an increase in the number of female representatives on advisory committees for obstetrical and gynecological devices.

Several national health insurance proposals have been submitted to Congress for consideration. One of these proposals was developed by the Carter administration.

PACFW RECOMMENDATION

Intensive efforts should be made by the Equal Employment Opportunity Commission (EEOC) to obtain regulations leading to equal pay for work of equal value, and should interpret Title VII to include equal pay for work of social value. By increasing women's incomes, most health care delivery problems can be decreased.

Women as Health Professionals

Historically, women have been the healers, but since the beginning of modern medicine they have practiced from the less influential health professions. They have been vastly underrepresented at the level of physicians, dentists, and pharmacists. This situation began changing during the 1970's when the number of women entering American medical schools dramatically increased from 1,256 in 1970-71 to 4,149 in 1977-78.[4] At the same time the percentage of women in academic positions has not markedly improved. In 1978 there were 15.2 percent women on the faculties of medical schools compared with 13.3 percent 10 years earlier.[5] In 1973-74, 5.9 percent of assistant deans, 3 percent of

associate deans and 0 percent of full deans were women. Likewise, 0.6 percent of department chairpersons in the basic sciences and 1.7 percent of department chairpersons in the clinical sciences were women.[6] Increasing the number of women in academic positions is important because the Nation's health policy-makers generally come from the academic ranks. At the National Institutes of Health as of September 1979 there were 152 women among the 492 active members of advisory committees. Representing minority women

[5] Wilson, Marjorie P., "The Status of Women in Medicine: Background Data," presented at a Johns Hopkins University conference, *Woman, M.D.,* Oct. 1979.

[6] Witte, Marlys H.; Arem, Arnold J.; and Holguin, Miguel; "Women Physicians in the U.S. Medical Schools: A Preliminary Report," *Journal of the American Medical Women's Association* 31:5, May 1976, p. 211.

[4] Wallace, Helen M., "Women in Medicine," *Journal of the American Medical Women's Association* 35:8, Aug./Sept. 1980, p. 201.

were 21 Black women, 9 Hispanic women, 7 American Indian women and 6 Asian/Pacific American women.[7]

The progress which began during the 1970's is only now becoming reality as the women who began their training during that period of time

Percentage of Women in Selected Health Professions

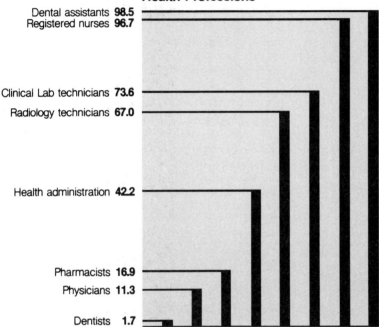

Dental assistants	**98.5**
Registered nurses	**96.7**
Clinical Lab technicians	**73.6**
Radiology technicians	**67.0**
Health administration	**42.2**
Pharmacists	**16.9**
Physicians	**11.3**
Dentists	**1.7**

are now emerging as health care providers. It is encouraging to see more women entering those health professions that dictate health policy. These young women are the key to reaching the goal of women directing health policy to meet the needs of women.

Ernestine Small, speaking on behalf of the North Carolina Nurses Association, emphasized the need for women in policymaking positions. She stated, "A major factor that makes possible such discrimination against women in health care is lack of female participation in decisions at the policymaking levels."

Gayle Briggs, Chair of the Committee on Sexism for the Colorado Division of Mental Health, related that "there are no women directors of mental health centers or clinics in the Colorado Mental Health system" and that "there are few women in the higher levels of mental health management—it appears that the number of women in top level positions in the mental health system is decreasing."

In addressing the concerns of nurses, Gail Hallas, an R.N. from Florida, described "grave unrest among women in the nursing profession." She said that "there is an extremely high employment turnover rate of nurses within health care facilities. Many reports are up to 80 percent annually. This is caused by poor working conditions, overwhelming job dissatisfaction, low wages, and long hours (double shifts and ten-day stretches are not uncommon)."

Federal Initiatives

Research findings show that one of the barriers to women entering the nontraditional health professions is their frequent deficiency in math and science. Women and girls tend to avoid these subjects for fear of failure and also through biased counseling. The Department of Education is committed to overcoming such bias and stereotyping of girls and women in its education programs and is encouraging States to develop projects which will address the problem of math and science anxieties.

Sections 799a and 845 of the Public Health Service Act prohibit discrimination on the basis of sex in the admission of students to health training schools or centers.

Women are serving in the following policymaking positions in the Department of Health and Human Services: Deputy Assistant Secretary for Planning and Evaluation/Health; Deputy Assistant Secretary of Health Policy, Research, and Statistics; Chief Nurse Officer; and Director of National Center for Health Statistics.

[7] *Appointment of Women and Minorities to Advisory Committees,* Monthly Report, Sept. 1-30, 1979, prepared by ADAMHA-CMO, October 3, 1979.

As of March 31, 1980, women were serving on the following agency health committees:

Agency	Total Number of Committees	Members Serving	Women Serving
Alcohol, Drug Abuse, and Mental Health Administration	36	511	165
Center for Disease Control	3	42	9
Food and Drug Administration	30	356	101
Health Resources Administration	5	68	26
Health Services Administration	5	38	14
National Institutes of Health	139	2001	440

PACFW RECOMMENDATION

It is essential that women fill policymaking positions in the governing institutions. The appointment of women to visible professional roles in universities and professional schools is a vital step in the recruitment of young women. Affirmative action laws must be enforced.

Health Education

In recent years Americans have become more aware of the importance of preventive health practices. As increasing numbers of life-threatening infectious diseases are brought under control, it has become clear that many of us will die of chronic diseases. As the chart indicates, 75 percent of all deaths in this country are due to degenerative disease such as heart disease, stroke and cancer.[8]

Although the causes of chronic diseases are complex, research is beginning to reveal those risk factors which can be reduced through preventive measures.

Effective preventive efforts must begin early in life. As more women enter the work force,

[8] *Healthy People: The Surgeon General's Report on Health Promotion and Disease Prevention,* DHEW (PHS) Publication No. 79-55071, 1979, pp. 1-2.

children spend more time in child care centers. These centers have the opportunity to reinforce good eating, exercise, and hygiene habits that can set the pattern for a healthy lifestyle. As children enter school, the need grows for awareness and understanding of good health practices, but with the "back-to-basics" movement, subjects like health are frequently neglected. Children often do not receive health instruction from teachers trained specifically in health education. Food served in school lunch programs can be used to demonstrate the proper usage of salt, sugar, and fat in the diet. Good exercise programs must be stressed for girls as well as boys. Beyond the school years, in the work place exercise programs and facilities, which in the past have not always been made available to women employees, have an important role in preventive health. Continuing health education can show adults how to lead a healthy lifestyle and how to

"To fulfill a collaborative role in all aspects of her health care, education is mandatory."
Catherine Fogel, R.N.
Raleigh, N.C.

participate knowledgeably in their own health care. Greater knowledge of health can help parents pass along good health habits to their children. Only then will we break the vicious cycle whereby uninformed children become uninformed adults who then raise uninformed children.

The philosophy of health education was expressed by Bonnie Davis, Extension Home Economics Agent in North Carolina. Speaking particularly about nutrition she stated, "it is important to help people help themselves. It corresponds to the old proverb: 'If you give a man a fish you feed him for a day; if you teach him how to fish, you feed him for life'." Davis further related that "poor food habits are not practiced solely by the poor, but improved food habits and nutrition often can help lift the poor up the economic ladder."

The need for health education was emphasized by many other testifiers. "More awareness on the part of women of preventive measures" was stressed by Robin Krivanek, representing the Florida Gulf Health Systems Agency. Elaine Barney, Director of the Women's Health Counseling Service in North Carolina, noted that women have a "lack of knowledge or misinformation about the method of birth control." Vickie McCullen from the Migrant and Seasonal Farmworkers Association described the need for nutritional education among migrant women. In order for a woman "to

fulfill a collaborative role in all aspects of her health care," said Catherine Fogel, an R.N. from N.C., "education is mandatory."

Tom Gilmore, Deputy Secretary of the North Carolina Department of Human Resources, called for "health education programs to be stepped up all across this country."

Federal Initiatives

In April 1979 the Office of Comprehensive School Health was established in an answer to Congress' directive for the Office of Education to work with the Public Health Service to increase efforts in health promotion and disease prevention. This newly created office is acting as an advocate and coordinator of comprehensive school health.

In 1978 the Elementary and Secondary Education Act, Title III, Part I (P.L. 95-561) authorized $10 million to establish and support programs of health education in elementary and secondary schools but no dollars were appropriated.

PACFW RECOMMENDATION
Funds should be appropriated for health education through the Elementary and Secondary Education Act of 1978 (P.L. 95-561).

Smoking

Smoking may well prove to be the major health problem facing women in the 1980's. While the hazards associated with smoking in men have been widely recognized, the prevailing myth has been that women are somehow immune to the damaging effects of smoking. In stark contradiction to that assumption stand the findings of a recent report of the Surgeon General, *The Health Consequences of Smoking for Women*. Released January 1980, this report has brought to national attention these facts: Cigarette smoking is associated with cancer of the lung, larynx, oral cavity, esophagus, bladder, and kidney in women.

In one-fourth of all cancer deaths among women, cigarette smoking is a contributing factor.

Women who smoke are 2.5-5 times more likely to develop lung cancer than women who do not smoke.

Within 3 years, more women are predicted to die from lung cancer than from breast cancer.

Chronic bronchitis, emphysema, chronic sinusitis, peptic ulcer disease, and arteriosclerotic heart disease all are common in women who smoke.

The incidence of coronary heart disease is twice as high for women smokers, and the risk of death from stroke (due to intracranial hemorrhage) is 3 times greater.

Women who smoke heavily and use oral contraceptives at the same time face 20 times the risk of myocardial infarction (heart attack) than do nonsmoking women.

Pregnant women who smoke give birth to infants of lower birth weight. (The greater the amount smoked during pregnancy, the greater is the reduction in birth weight. When a woman stops smoking early during pregnancy, however, the risk of low birth weight is reduced.)

The incidence of "sudden infant death syndrome" is more common in babies whose mothers smoked during pregnancy.

Since 1965 the percentage of men who smoke has decreased dramatically—down from 51.1 to 36.9 percent in 1978. Among women the decrease has been far smaller, dropping from 33.3 to 29.9 percent. Of great concern is the fact that by ages 17 to 19, more young women smoke than do young men.

The decision to smoke may be a personal one, yet, a recent study conducted at the University of California at San Diego demonstrated that the lung functions of nonsmokers are adversely affected by environments containing smoke from coworkers.[9] A growing body of research lends support to the conclusion of the Surgeon General's Report: "The reduction of cigarette smoking is the keystone in our nation's long-term strategy to promote a healthy lifestyle for women and men of all races and ethnic groups."

Federal Initiatives

In response to the Surgeon General's Report, the Department of Health and Human Services has begun a campaign to educate women about the health hazards of smoking. The campaign, carried out by the Office of Smoking and Health, has particular emphasis on reaching pregnant women, minority women, and adolescent girls. Approximately half of the $500,000 budgeted for public service advertising will be used for educational efforts targeting women.

In addition, the Office of Smoking and Health is involved in planning for creation of a national Women and Smoking Network. This Network would coordinate the information activities of the Federal Government and the voluntary health sector, and be liaison with health professionals.

"The reduction of cigarette smoking is the keystone in our nation's long-term strategy to promote a healthy lifestyle for women and men of all races and ethnic groups."

The Surgeon General
The Health Consequences
of Smoking for Women

[9] White and Groeb, "Small-Airways Dysfunction in Non-Smokers Chronically Exposed to Tobacco Smoke," *New England Journal of Medicine*, March 27, 1980.

PACFW RECOMMENDATION

The leading controllable cause of rising morbidity and mortality in adult American women is smoking. No techniques are available to alter the incidence of breast cancer, but lung cancer in women was a rare disease until the current era and can be controlled by eliminating smoking. The Office of Smoking and Health is understaffed, underhoused and underfunded. It is not a priority item in the national health programs. The PACFW recommends greatly increased funding for the Office of Smoking and Health, with targeted funds for increased outreach to educational institutions, churches, television stations, and publishers of magazines and comic books to create a different image of the adolescent smoker.

Mental Health

"Society still sees a woman as helpless, dependent, and passive. Women are seen as less powerful people. Women also learn to view themselves in that role."
Gayle Briggs
Denver, Colo.

U.S. women are faced with many stresses in their lives that threaten their mental well-being. Women entering the work force have faced sexism which has kept them powerless in lower paying jobs. Women heading single-parent families are forced to work to support their families while at the same time caring for their children and home. Finding adequate child care at a price they can afford is an added stress. Women who are not forced to work but choose to often are plagued with feelings of guilt when their responsibilities as mothers conflict with the demands of their careers. Due to divorce or death of husbands, many middle-aged and older women find themselves alone and independent for the first time in their lives—a change that is deeply stressful.

Minority women have additional stresses in their lives. They experience conflicting identities between themselves as members of an ethnic group with its set of values and themselves as U.S. citizens with the values of the larger society. The recent refugee women suffer from being uprooted and having to adjust to a different society.

One of the major mental health problems faced by women is that of depression. There are 17 women hospitalized because of depression to every 100 men, and 238 women receive outpatient treatment for depression to every 100 men.[10] The powerlessness experienced by women and the traditional "feminine" behavior (helplessness and dependency) encouraged by society are contributing factors of depression. Once women seek treatment, they find the same sexist attitudes in the health professionals who serve them. Therapy influenced by traditional "feminine" ideals and encouraging traditional "feminine" roles contributes to the despair of the woman seeking help. The overprescription of psychotropic drugs further complicates the situation.

"The special needs of women are not adequately being met," emphasized Gayle Briggs of Lakewood, Colorado. "The pressures for a woman of living in a sexist culture add a special dimension to women's mental health problems. Sexism and victimization of women are

[10] *Summary—Report of the Special Populations Subpanel on Mental Health of Women*, submitted to the President's Advisory Commission on Mental Health, Feb. 1978.

increasingly exposed. Society still sees a woman as helpless, dependent, and passive. Women are seen as less powerful people. Women also learn to view themselves in that role. The lower self-esteem of women as a group has been well documented."

Dr. Martha Bernal of Denver spoke about the additional stresses Hispanic women face as minority women. Gerontologist Patricia Walters from Tampa addressed the stresses faced by older women. She revealed that many older women who find themselves divorced or widowed "have never seen themselves as separate beings, never had an identity or learned to care for themselves without anyone's help."

Anne Fishel, a psychiatric nurse from Chapel Hill, N.C., related that "employment has been shown to have clearly positive effects on women's health; however, the triple responsibility of work, child-rearing and household management place women under great stress and future health will be further impaired unless adequate social supports are established, and soon!" She recommended that "passage of ERA, implementation of affirmative action plans and a reduction in the extent to which jobs are segregated by sex would raise the earning potential of millions of women. The resultant increase in income would reduce the impact of life stress and raise the self-concept

of women on a scale not possible through remedial psychotherapies."

Federal Initiatives
During 1977 President Carter established a Commission on Mental Health to review the mental health needs of the U.S. population and make recommendations on how these needs might be best met. A special populations subpanel studied the special needs of women. This subpanel reported "since there is no scientific evidence to suggest that women are innately more vulnerable to mental illness, we conclude that our usual social institutions have a differential and more stressful impact on women. Compounding these ordinary events are extraordinary experiences to which women are also subjected, such as rape, marital violence and incest." The subpanel went on further to say that "any carefully conceived national strategy for the prevention of mental illness and the promotion of mental health must have as one of its basic goals eradication of sexism and racism in the larger society."

PACFW RECOMMENDATION
The National Institute of Mental Health should increase its research and training programs in the area of depression in women.

Substance Abuse

Substance abuse among women is of deep concern. It is estimated that 2 million women are dependent on prescription drugs. In 1975 more than 229 million prescriptions for psychotropic drugs were filled. Of these prescriptions, 80 percent of the amphetamines, 67 percent of the tranquilizers, and 60 percent of the barbiturates/sedatives were for women.[11] Sex stereotyping

[11] *Report of the Special Populations Subpanel on Mental Health of Women,* submitted to the President's Advisory Commission on Mental Health, Feb. 1978.

attitudes held by physicians are considered to play a role in the over-prescription of psychotropic drugs to women.

There is no accurate data as to the number of women who are alcoholics. Alcoholism in women tends to be a hidden problem because of the social stigma associated with a woman alcoholic. In certain segments of the population (for example, American Indians) alcoholism is a particularly grave problem. If a pregnant woman drinks heavily (more than two drinks a day) her infant may develop the Fetal Alcohol

Syndrome and may be born dependent upon alcohol.

When a woman dependent on drugs or alcohol seeks treatment, she is faced by significant barriers. Only a limited number of facilities accept women and few programs are sensitive to the special needs of women. These needs include: provision for child care, therapy for the children, involvement of the family in the woman's therapy, non-sexist attitudes on the part of the health professionals, job-training and support networks for the future.

During the Raleigh hearing the plight of women who are seeking help for their substance abuse was vividly described by an anonymous 28-year-old married white woman who was formerly addicted to drugs. In her testimony, presented by a friend, she stated, "I found that drug programs typically reflected society's male hierarchy; few women had an active role and few women participated. When we did participate, we faced several unique challenges in addition to the difficult task of becoming drug-free. Since drug programs reflected society's structure, sexism was rampant. On admission, women's health needs were neglected, women with children were almost automatically eliminated from residential care, and finally, women faced destructive stereotyping. It was an assumption that we as female drug abusers suffered from poor relationships with our fathers, feared men, mistrusted women, and were sexually promiscuous. Therapy concentrated on these problems. Little consideration was given to my self-esteem, consciousness raising, educational skills development, or to spending time with older women.

"My therapy usually focused on helping me to find my long-lost femininity and regain my chastity. Vocational and educational services were rarely encouraged or offered. Once I completed therapy, my chances of becoming employed were rare. I might have been drug-free but was still unskilled and uneducated.

"During my treatment in that drug abuse treatment program, I was depersonalized and desexualized in terms of dress and hairstyle and then assigned the traditional woman's tasks of kitchen duty and cleaning detail while the men had their stereotypical duties of yard work and maintenance. It was quite a mixed message.

"I found that drug programs typically reflected society's male hierarchy."

Anonymous woman who was formerly addicted to drugs. Raleigh, N.C.

"We women were encouraged to look feminine but not whorish. We were told to find the right man who would take care of us. In other words, we were told to go back to being the stereotypical woman with no options, which for many of us had created the problems leading to drug abuse in the first place. Teaching women to cope better in their feminine stereotypical roles without options is no treatment program. Women often left treatment free of drug addiction, but still a second class citizen. The problems became even greater upon release..."

In Denver, Arlene Wimmer, Muriel Ashmore, and Rose Robe testified about the tragedy alcoholism has brought to American Indian women and their families. Robe described the "low self-esteem, depression, apathy and loss of identity" in the American Indian substance abuser, and Wimmer asked what alternatives do these women have. Ashmore called for "programs that will treat alcoholism and give them back an identity in their culture."

Federal Initiatives

In FY '79 the National Institute on Alcohol Abuse and Alcoholism funded programs especially for women. This marked the beginning of programs to test better methods of treating alcohol abuse in women.

A major HHS initiative is the Fetal Alcohol Syndrome Program, a public education program providing information regarding the effects of a mother's drinking habits on her unborn child. Currently funded research will provide data on the extent and causes of alcoholism in women and the relationship of specific consumption patterns to women's biomedical and psychological problems.

NIAAA is preparing a paper entitled "Pioneering Efforts in Treating Problem Drinking Women." It addresses the findings of the first seventeen NIAAA programs.

PACFW RECOMMENDATION

More women need to be trained in the mental health care delivery program. More non-health personnel should be trained in specific programs at NIH to deal with substance abuse and depression in women. Funding should be made available to lay organizations such as Alcoholics Anonymous to establish additional programs in under-served areas with minority populations.

Older Women

Demographic studies in the United States indicate that the elderly (defined as those 65 years or older) constitute the most rapidly increasing segment of the population.[12] Because women outlive men by an average of 7.8 years, the majority of older Americans are female; thus the health problems of old age tend to be older women's issues.[13] These problems tend to be of a chronic nature requiring extensive therapy. Poor nutrition, dental trouble, and cancer are problems faced by all elderly. Other problems affect only older women (i.e. cervical cancer) or are much more prevalent in women than in men (i.e. breast cancer and osteoporosis). By age 90, 80 percent of women will have osteoporosis and 20 percent will have suffered a hip fracture.[14] Because so many older women are widowed (approximately two-thirds) and are more likely than men to live alone, mental health is often a problem—particularly loneliness and depression. Many health problems are intensified by poverty, and half of the elderly have annual incomes of $3,000 or less.[15] The lack of or inaccessibility of transportation makes it difficult for many to use the health services available. Substandard housing is another frequently encountered problem.

While only 5 percent of all elderly are institutionalized, only 1.1 percent of Medicare funds are spent on home health services.[16]

Access to these services is a most pressing need. Services such as meals-on-wheels, cleaning and cooking, and health care would allow older people the chance to stay at home amid familiar, comfortable surroundings and avoid unnecessary institutionalization.

"Older women in the U.S. are in 'triple jeopardy,'" said gerontologist, Dr. Edith Sherman from Denver, Colorado. "They are underprivileged and 'at risk' on these separate scores. First as females, with a long history of inequitable treatment and differential opportunities. Second—as 'aged' members within the female gender who suffer multiple and inflated disabilities as a consequence of being 'old' compared to their male counterparts. Third—as the 'poor' or 'poverty' category within the older population in proportions and to an extent not warranted by their actual numbers and ratios to the generalized 'poor'."

Judith Travis, an R.N. representing the Visiting Nurse Association of Hillsborough County, Florida, added that "improvements in the delivery of medical care, with a concomitant increase in life-sustaining medications and treatments, have done much to prolong life. The question before us now is how to improve the quality of these lives which we have prolonged. Life expectancy has increased tremendously so that we now have a category of elderly aged seventy-five and above. During the latter years of one's life change becomes exceedingly difficult. The comfortable, familiar surroundings of home are of vital importance. There is a humane and cost-effective mechanism available through which many of our elderly citizens can remain in their own homes. The

[12] White House Conference on Aging.

[13] *Vital Statistics for the U.S.;* Vol. II, Section 5; National Center for Health Statistics, 1977.

[14] Schiff, Isaac and Ryan, Kenneth J.; "Benefits of Estrogen Replacement", Boston Hospital for Women, Harvard Medical School, NIH Consensus Conference Paper.

[15] *The Older Woman: Continuities and Discontinuities,* Report of the National Institute on Aging and the National Institute of Mental Health Workshop, September 1978, p. 1.

[16] *Roundtable Report,* Volume IV, No. 4, Women and Health Roundtable, A Project of the Federation of Organizations for Professional Women, Feb. 1979.

"The question before us now is how to improve the quality of these lives which we have prolonged."
Judith Travis, R.N.
Visiting Nurse Assn.
Tampa, Fla.

"Older women in the U.S. are in 'triple' jeopardy."
Dr. Edith Sherman
Gerontologist
Denver, Colo.

Deaths for Selected Causes as a Percent of All Deaths: United States, Selected Years, 1900–1977

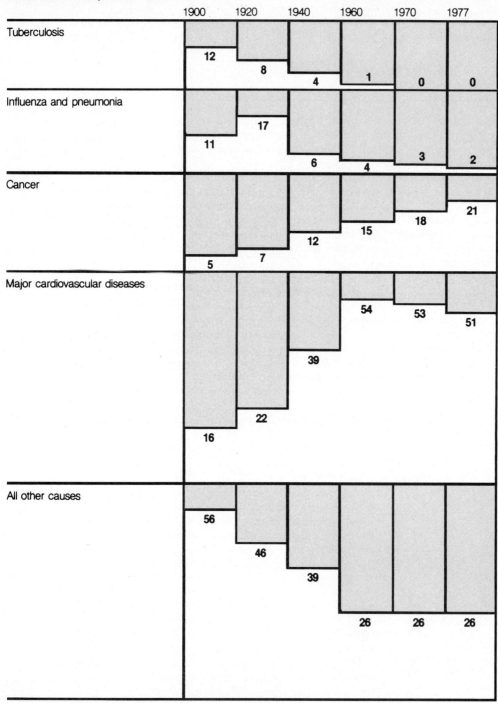

NOTE: 1977 data are provisional; data for all other years are final.

Source: National Center for Health Statistics, Division of Vital Statistics

problem now is how to improve the barriers that are being erected which prevent this from happening."

Another concern voiced by Virgie Cone, Director of the Area Agency on Aging for District III—Florida, is the cost of medical services. "Medicaid to help those with low incomes has problems," she stated. "Reimbursement delays and minimal service coverage cause physicians to be reluctant to accept Medicaid patients."

Federal Initiatives

The Long Term Care Task Force (established by the Under Secretary of HEW) is looking at the inequities in the Medicaid program. The Task Force has a particular interest in the provision of the Medicaid program which provides support for nursing home care but will not pay for health care services in the sick individual's home. Such care would facilitate independent living and postpone or prevent the need for nursing home care. The Task Force is proposing an amendment which would provide medical funds for home health service.

The Title XX Program of the Social Security Act provides and helps to coordinate a comprehensive range of in-home and community based social services. States have identified five target groups, one of which is the elderly, although women are not singled out as special beneficiaries. The estimated expenditure for home-based services in 1979 was $570 million. These services included: Homemaker Services, Home Management Services, Home Health Services, and Chore Services.

The Title XX Program of the Social Security Act authorizes States to provide transportation to and from service providers or community resources and facilities, including medical and health facilities.

The Nurse Training Amendments of 1979 provided for the inclusion of geriatric training programs under Section 820, Special Project Grants and Contracts. Twenty-seven grants totaling $2 million have been awarded to medical, nursing, and allied health professions schools.

PACFW RECOMMENDATION

Title XX of the Social Security Act should be expanded for homemaker services, home management services, and home health services for older women.

Contraception

Being able to control fertility has had a positive effect on the lives of U.S. women. The health of women and their infants is improved when women choose to have children at the optimal time in life (20-35 years of age), space the births, and limit the size of their families. In addition, women can then choose to participate in the work force. Greater numbers of women are practicing contraception; however, not all women have access to family planning services. Estimates are that 4.5 million low and marginal income women, in addition to 1.7 million teenagers, are not receiving family planning services that they need.[17]

Women can choose among a variety of birth control methods but not one is ideal. Birth control pills and intrauterine devices generally offer better protection from pregnancy than the barrier methods but are associated with greater risk to the health of women. Because of the

[17] *Family Planning;* prepared by the Alan Guttmacher Institute; 1220 19th Street, N.W., Washington, D.C.; April 1980; p. 4.

155

adverse side effects of birth control pills, more women are choosing the safer barrier methods. While 64 million prescriptions for birth control pills were filled in 1975 by retail pharmacists, only 49 million were filled in 1978.[18] In comparison to the number of options available for women, the condom and sterilization are the only currently available male methods of contraception. During fiscal year 1978, $6,011,000 was spent on female contraceptive development with only $966,000 being spent on male contraceptive development.[19]

"To date, there is not one method of birth control that is safe, 100 percent reliable in user effectiveness, easy to use, inexpensive and under the control of the woman herself," emphasized Elaine Barney of North Carolina. "How sad an indictment: we live in a society which spends billions on research into outer space and can put people on the moon; we spend billions to subsidize auto industries and other economic interests; yet women are faced with a limited choice of birth control methods that are not entirely safe nor entirely effective."

Alix Perry of Florida stressed that "women who are now emerging as full individuals seeking autonomy for their own aspirations are recognizing the fact that complete independence rests on two basic capabilities. The ability to be self-supporting and the ability to control one's fertility. And these two capabilities are inalterably intertwined. Without the ability to avoid pregnancy and childbearing, educational plans are disrupted, marketplace experience curtailed and too often inappropriate marriages hastily consummated." She went on further to state that "contraceptive services and counseling by adequately trained and sensitive individuals is a need that must be met for all ages regardless of ability to pay for services."

Federal Initiatives

The primary objective of the HHS' family planning services, supported through a variety of programs, is to provide family planning and related reproductive health services to all low-income adult women and to sexually active adolescents.

[18] Colen, B.D.; "Use of Birth Control Pill Down Sharply Nationwide," *The Washington Post*, Nov. 3, 1979.

[19] Op. Cit., *Roundtable Report*, Vol. III, No. 2.

Regulations for Title X of the Public Health Service Act, the chief source of funding for family planning services, require that priority be given to serving low-income individuals. In addition, P.L. 91-572, the Family Planning Services and Population Research Act of 1970, indicates that incomes of individuals desiring services are to be considered as a factor in awarding family planning service grants and contracts.

As a result of initiatives launched by the Federal Government, a diverse group of clinics, located in all parts of the country and administered by a variety of public and private agencies, have been established in the last decade and now provide services to more than 4 million persons each year. The clinics also provide low- and marginal-income women with basic health screening services they might not otherwise receive. On-going HHS efforts to improve the availability and quality of the services include:
- Information and education programs;
- Innovative approaches to service delivery;
- Research to improve the quality of care in all organized family planning programs;
- Technical assistance to local clinics, centers, and other health agencies.

Alleged abuses associated with federally funded sterilizations prompted HEW to issue its April 18, 1974, regulations. These were revised in 1978, and new regulations were published and became effective March 8, 1979. They seek to limit funding to sterilizations which are voluntarily requested. Major features of the new regulations include a longer (30-day) waiting period; increased physician responsibility for assuring informed consent; restrictions on the Federal funding of hysterectomies; and a prohibition on the Federal funding of sterilizations of persons under 21, mentally incompetent persons, and institutionalized individuals.

HEW established a Task Force on Diethyl stilbestrol (DES) which met over a period of several months and submitted its report to the Secretary. The report deals with women who were given DES as a preventive for miscarriage, and with the effect of DES on the offspring of these women. It makes recommendations for necessary research.

Health and Human Services through Title X of the Public Health Services Act, the chief source of funding for family planning, should increase its outreach through State and local agencies to provide information on acceptable contraceptive methods and provide the funding for local community participation in family planning education and provision of services.

Adolescent Pregnancy

t is estimated that 11 million (4 million females and 7 million males) teenagers are sexually active. Approximately one-tenth of adolescent women become pregnant each year —resulting in about 1.1 million pregnancies.[20]

[20] Tietze, Christopher; "Teenage Pregnancies: Looking Ahead to 1984"; *Family Planning Perspectives* 10:4; July/Aug. 1978; p. 205.

Number of births per 1,000 females aged 15-19, selected countries, 1970s

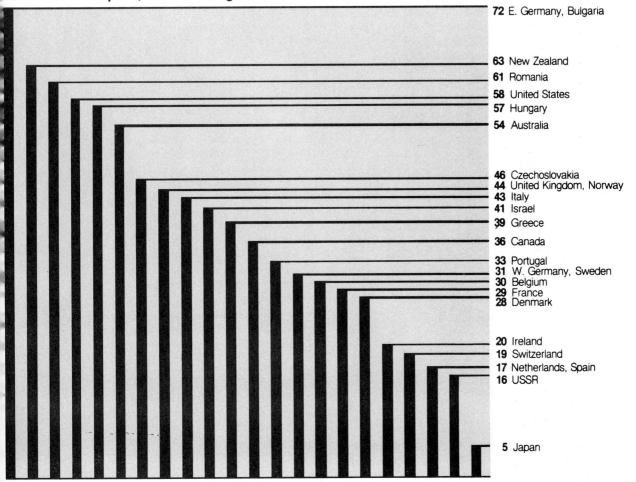

72	E. Germany, Bulgaria
63	New Zealand
61	Romania
58	United States
57	Hungary
54	Australia
46	Czechoslovakia
44	United Kingdom, Norway
43	Italy
41	Israel
39	Greece
36	Canada
33	Portugal
31	W. Germany, Sweden
30	Belgium
29	France
28	Denmark
20	Ireland
19	Switzerland
17	Netherlands, Spain
16	USSR
5	Japan

Adolescent pregnancy has serious consequences for the adolescent woman and the children she may bear. The death rate from complications of pregnancy, labor, and delivery is 60 percent higher for adolescents who are younger than 15, and 13 percent higher for those 15-19 than for women 20-24.[21] Toxemia, anemia, and premature births are other complications more frequently encountered in the pregnant adolescent. Studies suggest that these complications are related more to the quality of care obtained by the pregnant adolescent rather than to her youth—adolescents are less likely to seek prenatal care than older women.[22] Infants born to adolescents are more likely to die in the first year of life.

The National Center for Education Statistics has found that only a third of public schools offer sex education or family life programs, although most people of this country appear to favor sex education.[23] Studies on the impact of sex education classes on the students' knowledge have shown that participation increases knowledge of sexuality and can bring about more tolerant attitudes toward the practices of others while at the same time not affecting the students' own personal moral standards.[24] Sarah Shuptrine, Director of Health and Human Services for South Carolina, spoke of the urgency of the problem of adolescent pregnancy: "I appear before you today to request your assistance in bringing about a national commitment to address the growing concern of teenage pregnancy, which all too often results in human suffering, social and economic deprivation, and infant mortality and morbidity... These young mothers and their infants face grave health risks."

The tragedy of "children caring for children" was again emphasized by Dr. Robert Knuppel,

Director of Maternal-Fetal Medicine at the University of South Florida School of Medicine, when he described an adolescent mother who "washed her new infant in Lysol."

To address adolescent pregnancy, Alix Perry, President of N.O.W. in Broward County, Florida, suggested that "Sex education in the public schools is the place to begin. From the fourth grade through the twelfth, young boys and girls must have access to accurate information. Not only about their body functions and reproductive systems, but about feelings toward themselves and others, about dating and codes of conduct, of life plans—and of timeframes for all of these."

Federal Initiatives

The administration strongly supported legislation to make available resources designed to prevent unwanted pregnancy, especially among those 17 and under, and to provide badly needed health education and social services to pregnant adolescents. The legislation was included in Title VI, VII, and VIII of the Health Services and Centers Amendments and became Public Law 95-626 on November 12, 1978.

The Office of Adolescent Pregnancy Programs, established by the above law, administers the Adolescent Pregnancy Prevention and Care Program and coordinates all HHS programs concerned with various aspects of adolescent pregnancy. Priorities of the office are:

- to develop and expand services to prevent initial and repeat pregnancies among adolescents;
- to encourage linkages among public and private community organizations providing services for pregnant adolescents and adolescent parents;
- to assist pregnant adolescents and adolescent parents to become productive, independent contributors to family and community life.

PACFW RECOMMENDATION

Given the epidemic proportions of teenage pregnancies in the United States, the President should establish a high level commission in the Office of Family Planning to review, evaluate, and coordinate the currently funded programs and executive agencies that deal with the

[21] *Adolescent Fertility*, prepared by the Alan Guttmacher Institute, April 1980, p. 1.

[22] Baldwin, Wendy; "Adolescent Pregnancy and Childbearing Rates, Trends and Research Findings from the Center for Population Research"; National Institute of Child Health and Development, Oct. 1979; p. 3.

[23] *The Condition of Education*, National Center for Education Statistics, DHEW, USGPO, 1979.

[24] Kirby, Alter and Scales, *An Analysis of U.S. Sex Education Programs and Evaluation Methods*, CDC-2021-79-DK-FR, July 1979.

problems of teenage pregnancies. Some of these programs presently include the Youth Employment Development Act Program in the Department of Labor, Teenage Pregnancy Program at the Women's Bureau, Sex Education Program in the Department of Education, Child Development at the Department of Health and Human Services, the Office of Family Planning, and Title VII, Office of Adolescent Pregnancy. One of the functions of this Commission would be to insure comprehensive community input to the solution of this increasing problem.

Abortion

In the United States during 1978, 28.9 percent of all pregnancies, excluding those which were interrupted by miscarriage, were terminated with abortion. The abortions were more frequently obtained by women who were: living in urban areas (more than 90 percent), in their first trimester (more than 90 percent), unmarried (approximately 75 percent), and adolescents (approximately 33 percent).[25]

Deaths resulting from legally induced abortions were 1.4/100,000 abortions during 1977 [26] (compared with 11/100,000 deaths from pregnancy and childbirth).[27] Deaths reported in association with illegally performed abortions gradually declined from 1972 to 1976 but rose in 1977. The number of reported deaths is considered to reflect the total number of illegal abortions performed. The decline in deaths through 1976 was felt to correlate with the increased availability of legal abortions following the 1973 Supreme Court ruling which affirmed the women's right to choose to have an abortion. The rise in deaths in 1977 corresponded to restriction of Medicaid funding for abortion imposed by the Hyde Amendment to the Labor-HEW appropriations bill. The restrictions on Federal funding of abortions place the heaviest burden on poor women and their families; however, the cost to society is high for each unwanted birth to women receiving public assistance.

Natalie Cohen, speaking on behalf of North Carolina Coalition for Choice, emphasized that "there is a very strong correlation between a woman's physical and mental well-being and how she perceives herself as a person. And there is a very strong correlation between how a woman views herself and her ability to control and direct her own destiny. And the single and most vital right that a woman should have is the right to control her own fertility.

All other issues of equality take second place to this fundamental one. Government has no right to interfere with such a crucial decision as to whether or not a woman decides to have

[25] Rich, Spencer; "Legal Abortions Seen in 30 Percent of Pregnancies." *The Washington Post;* Jan. 9, 1980; p. A10.

[26] *Center for Disease Control Abortion Surveillance 1977,* USDHEW, Public Health Service; issued Sept. 1979, p. 1.

[27] *Abortion,* prepared by the Alan Guttmacher Institute, A Special Affiliate of Planned Parenthood Federation of America, Washington, DC, April 1980.

a child." She went on further to add "abortion is a legal right. Justice demands that this right be made available to all women regardless of their income level."

Concern was voiced, however, by Margaret Baker of Tampa, Florida, about abortion clinics. "A few months ago fetal material, syringes, and other garbage from plastic bags were found by children (who were incidentally playing with the syringes). This was near a Florida West Coast abortion clinic. More recently two Jacksonville nurses discovered dismembered babies with identifiable parts outside an abortion clinic."

Federal Initiatives

In 1977 the original Hyde Amendment prohibited Federal funding of abortions unless the life of the woman was threatened by carrying the fetus to term. The amendment has since then been modified to allow funding in cases of promptly reported rape and incest. In June 1980 the Supreme Court upheld Congress' right to restrict, almost to exclusion, payments for abortions funded by Medicaid.

Abortion related activities monitored by the Center for Disease Control include:

- the health effects of restricted Federal funding for abortion;
- health impact of restricted public funds for abortion;
- quality of abortion services;
- the role of providers;
- septic complications associated with illegally induced abortion.

PACFW RECOMMENDATION

All legally available services for curtailing unwanted or medically dangerous pregnancies should not be denied to any woman who is unable to pay for those services.*

* Because of the nature of this issue the dissenting votes of Committee members Erma Bombeck and Mary Helen Madden should be noted.

Obstetrical Practices

With the greater utilization of prenatal services and with the technological advances in obstetrical practices, mothers and infants are doing better than ever before. Maternal mortality is at a low of 11/100,000 (1976) [28] and infant mortality is at a low of 14/1,000 live births (1977).[29] However, in comparison with other industrial nations, the United States is lagging behind. Good prenatal care beginning in the first trimester of pregnancy is one of the keys to reducing morbidity and mortality. There are certain segments of the population (low-income women, adolescents and migrant women) who do not have adequate accessibility to such care.

[28] Ibid.
[29] Healthy People: The Surgeon General's Report on Health Promotion and Disease Prevention, 1979, Public Health Service, DHEW (PHS) Publication No. 79-55071; p. 3-1.

There have been many positive changes in obstetrical practices during the past decade. Birthing centers, which include the family in a home-like atmosphere but provide emergency facilities when needed, are being established throughout the Nation. In response to recent studies demonstrating the importance of maternal-infant bonding, rooming-in of infants with their mothers has been encouraged. Research has shown breast milk to be superior to formula feeding, and more women are choosing to breast feed their babies.

In some areas, research and technology have raised new concerns. Fetal monitoring, a process by which the infant's status during labor is followed by electronic or ultrasonic means, has become a frequent procedure. Women's advocacy groups have questioned whether monitoring is being used appropriately. Another area of concern is the three-fold increase in Caesarean births in this country and that women and infants may be exposed unnecessarily to the risks of Caesarean delivery.[30]

"Although 80 percent of all pregnancies are uncomplicated, pregnant clients have special needs which are poorly addressed by traditional health care systems," reported Catherine Fogel of North Carolina. "Approximately 20 percent of all expectant mothers will experience problem associated with pregnancy. More than 7 percent of all live births are low birth weight infants—those infants more apt to be the product of a high risk pregnancy and more apt to have problems later in life.... The majority of health care services currently available to pregnant women focus on the medical management of these physical conditions, particularly existing pathology. Interventions are aimed at prevention of specific obstetrical complications. Little attention is given to other aspects of the woman as a person nor is wholistic or comprehensive health care seen as a priority."

Many testifiers emphasized the underserved populations. Juanita Leon, speaking on behalf of the Colorado Migrant Council, related that "migrant women work throughout their pregnancies and receive little, if any, prenatal care before delivery or are receiving prenatal care late in their pregnancy which puts them in the category of being very high risk." Cheryl Beasley of the Lumbee tribe pointed out the discrepancy between the rate of neonatal deaths of North Carolina Indians (8/1,000 survivors) to that of the N.C. white population (3.8/1,000 survivors).

[30] Bottoms, Sidney F.; Mortimer G. Rosen; and Robert J. Sokol; "Current Concepts—The Increase in the Caesarean Birth Rate;" *The New England Journal of Medicine* 302:10; March 6, 1980; p. 559.

Infant Mortality Rates: Selected Countries, 1975
Rate per 1,000 live births

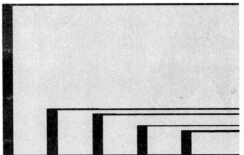

57 Chile

17 United States
16 England and Wales
11 Japan
9 Sweden

NOTE: The most recent year of data for Chile is 1971.
Sources: United States, National Center for Health Statistics, Division of Vital Statistics; other countries, United Nations.

Federal Initiatives
The National Institutes of Health has sponsored consensus conferences dealing with obstetrical issues. During the conference on "Antenatal Diagnosis" in March 1979, the recommendation was made that "the use of electronic fetal monitoring (EFM) should be strongly considered in high risk patients." The participants found "no evidence at present that electronic monitoring reduces mortality or morbidity in low risk patients." The most recent consensus conference pertaining to obstetrical problems dealt with Caesarean deliveries.[31]

HEW funded a study evaluating Caesarean sections in the United States. The report identifies principal factors leading to the increasing number of Caesarean sections and makes recommendations for relevant action by the Department.

PACFW RECOMMENDATION
The single most important reason that the infant mortality rates in the United States are higher than in other western countries is that low income, rural, and minority women do not get that necessary allocation of funds for prenatal care and delivery. We recommend that a reallocation of funds from the National Institute of Child Health and Development be made to such high-risk and underserved populations.

[31] Consensus, NIH Consensus Development Conference Summaries, Vol. 2, 1979.

Breast Cancer

Breast cancer is currently the leading cause of death from cancer in women. Approximately 1 out of every 11 women will develop breast cancer during their lifetime. During 1980 it is estimated that 109,000 new cases of breast cancer will be

[32] Cancer Facts and Figures, 1980; American Cancer Society; 777 Third Ave., N.Y., N.Y. 10027, pp. 16-17.

diagnosed and 36,000 deaths from breast cancer will occur.[32] Early detection of breast cancer is being stressed in an effort to improve the prognosis of the disease. Breast self-examination has been encouraged in order for women to discover breast cancer earlier and get help faster. Physicians now have new techniques, such as mammography, xeroradiography and thermography, to detect early breast cancer.

Cancer Deaths By Site and Sex
1980 Estimates

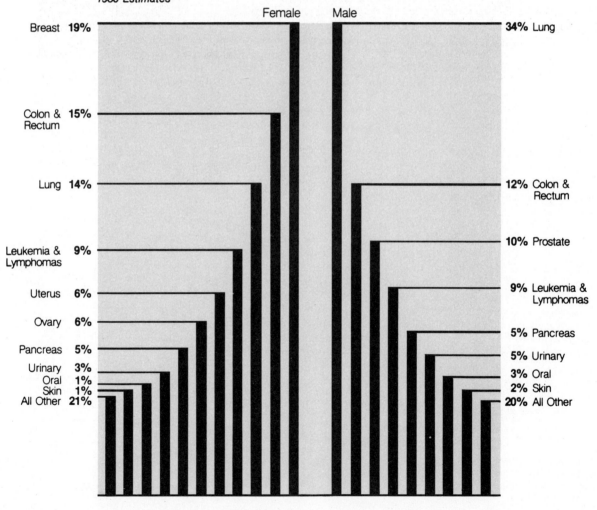

	Female	Male	
Breast **19%**			**34%** Lung
Colon & Rectum **15%**			**12%** Colon & Rectum
Lung **14%**			**10%** Prostate
Leukemia & Lymphomas **9%**			**9%** Leukemia & Lymphomas
Uterus **6%**			**5%** Pancreas
Ovary **6%**			**5%** Urinary
Pancreas **5%**			**3%** Oral
Urinary **3%**			**2%** Skin
Oral **1%**			**20%** All Other
Skin **1%**			
All Other **21%**			

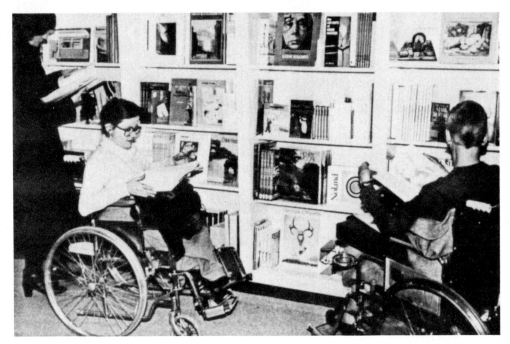

Risk factors have been identified that aid the physician in determining which women are more likely to develop breast cancer and require closer screening.

When breast cancer is suspected, a diagnostic biopsy should be done as a separate procedure before any further therapy is carried out. The woman with breast cancer can then participate in the choice of therapy for her cancer. There are several options available for breast cancer treatment once the extent of the disease is known. Treatment modalities include: surgery, chemotherapy, hormonal therapy, and radiation therapy. For years the Halsted radical mastectomy was the standard surgical procedure; however, in 1979 a National Institutes of Health Consensus Conference on the treatment of breast cancer concluded that the total mastectomy (which is less debilitating and disfiguring) "should be recognized as the current treatment standard."[33] At the time of surgery, it is important for samples of breast cancer tissue to be taken for estrogen-receptor analysis. Recent studies have shown that the presence or absence of estrogen-receptors is an important factor in selecting the type of therapy.

In spite of the research performed and the new techniques for diagnosis and therapeutic modalities being developed, the survival rates from breast cancer have not markedly improved. The 5-year survival rate increased from 53 percent of all cases diagnosed during the 1940's to 65 percent of all cases diagnosed during the 1970's.[34]

Federal Initiatives
The following recent National Institutes of Health Consensus Conferences have dealt with the treatment of breast cancer:
Sept. 1977—Breast Cancer Screening
June 1979—Treatment of Primary Breast Cancer: Management of Local Disease
June 1979—Steroid Receptors in Breast Cancer
July 1980—Adjuvant Chemotherapy of Breast Cancer

PACFW RECOMMENDATION
Since breast cancer is the leading cause of death from cancer in women, the budget of the National Cancer Institute should reflect this.

[33] Op. Cit., Consensus.

[34] Op. Cit., Cancer Facts and Figures, 1980.

ISSUES AFFECTING TARGET POPULATIONS

There are special populations of women who face additional health problems beyond those faced by all U.S. women. In the past there have been little accurate data on the health status of these women. Generally, the health of non-white women is poorer than the health of white women. Minority women face added stress on their mental well-being because they do not fit society's stereotyped image of the dream woman and because of conflicting identity as members of an ethnic group and as members of a larger society.

Many minority women, disabled women, and migrant women testified during the three PACFW hearings about the lack of sensitivity shown by health professionals to their special health needs and the inaccessibility to health services to meet these needs.

American Indian/Alaska Native Women

The health status of American Indian women in general has been poorer than that of white women. The infant mortality rates are higher, and alcoholism is of deep concern. In addition, urban Indian women are faced with the lack of accessible health care facilities.

PACFW RECOMMENDATION

Full funding for the Indian Health Care Improvement Act should be authorized.

Asian/Pacific American Women

Little data are available on the health status of Asian/Pacific American women. The influx of new immigrants, who have significantly poorer health status, is expected to have an adverse impact on the health status of Asian/Pacific American women in the future. Of great concern to Asian/Pacific American women is the mental stress they experience that results from cultural and social isolation and particularly their absence from decisionmaking positions.

PACFW RECOMMENDATION

Systematic studies should be funded by the National Institute of Mental Health to document the unique mental health problems faced by Asian/Pacific American women and the effects of acculturation and cultural change on the mental health of these women.

Black Women

Black women generally have a poorer health status than white women. They have a higher incidence of hypertension, cervical cancer, and diabetes. Black infant and maternal mortality is higher and life expectancy lower than that for the white population.

PACFW RECOMMENDATION

A reallocation of funds from the National Institute of Child Health and Development

should be made to high-risk and underserved populations.

Hispanic Women

Currently, there are little data on the health status of Hispanic women. However, a major concern of Hispanic women is the lack of bilingual services that are needed for delivery of health care. Preventive health care services for Hispanic women are critical for the future.

PACFW RECOMMENDATION

Life expectancy of minority women is significantly lower than that of white women. Bilingual professionals should be trained in dietary care, and bilingual educational materials should be published by the Institute on Aging.

Disabled Women

During the past, many disabled women have not been adequately informed about the effect of their disability on their reproductive system including their ability to bear children and appropriate options for contraception.

PACFW RECOMMENDATION

More research is needed to determine the special hazards related to specific disabilities in women, including prenatal care and delivery. Educational programs and the media should be encouraged to focus on the disabled woman's capabilities to carry and deliver normal children.

Migrant Women

The health of migrant women is jeopardized by the numerous occupational hazards (pesticides and herbicides, etc.) to which they are exposed, the lack of knowledge of good health practices, and the lack of accessible health facilities (especially prenatal services).

ADDITIONAL HEALTH RECOMMENDATIONS

Because of the complexity of the health issues, the President's Advisory Committee for Women felt that these further recommendations must be made.

Delivery of Health Care

- Retraining and relicensing of both male and female health professionals should include sensitization to specific needs of women.
- Increased funding should be made available to train police and hospital personnel in dealing with rape victims. More women should be added to rape prevention squads and all related professions.
- In medical schools receiving government aid, the curricula should be required to include programs on special needs of women in the following categories: rape, alcohol, drug abuse, and depression.
- Licensing examinations for foreign health professionals should include sensitization to the special needs of women.

Women as Health Professionals

- Women must be encouraged to pursue careers in the health and professions at every level—physicians, dentists, nurses and para-professionals. Guidance counselors in high schools and colleges should be sensitized in this area, and the training of new guidance counselors should reflect non-sexist attitudes.

Health Education

- Good nutrition should be demonstrated by example in school lunch programs.
- Parents, through organizations such as the Parent-Teacher Associations, should work with government agencies to implement programs at home.
- Health education training should be provided to child care providers and in-service workshops developed for teachers. Teachers and administrators need to be given the opportunity to acquire and develop skills for teaching in health areas. Schools should be encouraged to hire trained school health educators.

Smoking

- The Office of Smoking and Health should target minority women's groups who have the highest incidence of smoking for special programs to discourage women from starting or continuing a disastrous habit.
- Special educational programs should be directed toward the effects of smoking in areas other than cancer, such as heart disease, fetal damage and stroke.
- Additional studies should be funded to determine the effect on non-smokers of the toxic fumes generated by smokers in situations where presence of non-smokers is obligatory, such as in offices and factories.

Mental Health

• All health care professionals in the area of drug abuse and counseling should be required to participate in programs for continuing education with special emphasis on the genesis of mental health problems of women.

Substance Abuse

• Programs already established, such as the National Indian Council on Alcoholism, should be required to provide greatly increased services to female alcoholics. Regulations should mandate that an increased number of women members serve on the council.

• Educational programs on substance abuse should be funded that target ethnic, minority and low-income women. The aim of these programs should be to teach pregnant women that they should not take drugs or medications unless prescribed by a qualified physician.

Older Women

• Special educational programs in local communities should be developed to teach older women to care for their health maintenance with regard to specific health problems such as osteoporosis and nutritional deficiencies.

• The Nurse Training Program of 1979, which provides for the inclusion of geriatric learning programs under Section 820 of the Special Projects Grants and Contracts should be greatly expanded in all educational institutions.

• Present inequities of the Social Security benefits for women should be eliminated in order to aid older women in caring for their health needs.

Contraception

• Health and Human Services and the Department of Labor should increase training in local communities for male family planning education programs as well as for female programs.

• Health and Human Services should allocate research funds for male contraceptive devices as well as new female methods.

• Health and Human Services should insure that sterilization of low income and poorly educated women (especially those with language barriers) be stringently controlled. Federal funds should be denied to any health care delivery institution or agency where such standards for sterilization are not enforced.

Abortion

• Monitoring of all health care facilities where abortions are performed should be increased by local and Federal agencies. Title X regulations for health care delivery centers should be applied more vigorously to all facilities where abortions are performed.

Obstetrical Practices

• Health and Human Services should increase efforts to put more women on advisory councils and policymaking boards which advise on prenatal health care expenditures and establish criteria for hysteretomies, Caesarean deliveries and home deliveries.

• Increased funding should be made available by Health and Human Services for high quality midwifery programs in medical educational institutions.

• Under Health and Human Services a program should be set up to evaluate home deliveries in the United States with respect to infant and maternal morbidity and mortality as well as the credentials of the health care personnel involved in the deliveries. The result of such studies should be widely publicized.

• Qualified midwives should be given increased hospital privileges.

• Training programs should be established by Health and Human Services for bilingual paramedical personnel in obstetrical practices. Where possible, local women should be recruited for such training.

Breast Cancer

• The National Institutes of Health should sponsor a consensus conference to examine thoroughly the various modalities of treatmen· for breast cancer in order to determine what is the optimal therapy available (including opinions in surgery, radiation and chemo-therapy) and to delineate future research needs. The information derived from the conference should be widely distributed to the public and the medical profession.

Immediate
Release
1/23/79

Facts for Consumers
from the Federal Trade Commission
BUREAU OF CONSUMER PROTECTION · OFFICE OF CONSUMER EDUCATION · WASHINGTON, D.C. 20580

Cosigning a Loan

A Serious Business

What will you do if a friend or relative asks you to cosign a loan? Should you or shouldn't you? It's easy enough. You just sign your name on the dotted line.

You may think all you're doing is "backing up" a person who means a lot to you. If you do, you're wrong. Three out of four cosignors of finance company loans are asked to pay. So, your signature means a lot more than just a vote of confidence. Cosigning is a serious business.

If the borrower can't pay back the loan, the lender can hold you--as thecosignor--personally responsible for the debt. And the debt can include late charges and fees if your relative or friend is slow in payment. It can even include court costs and attorneys' fees, if the lender decides to sue to collect. You could end up owing a lot more than you thought.

If you don't pay, the lender can choose to sue you rather than sue the borrower. If the lender wins the case, he can take your wages and property.

Cosignors Often Pay

You might think it unlikely that you'll have to pay. However, the facts show cosignors are often asked to pay. For example, a survey submitted by the National Consumer Finance Association to the Federal Trade Commission shows that 74.6% of those who cosign finance company loans are asked to pay them.

That shouldn't surprise you. When you are asked to cosign, you are being asked to take a risk a professional lender won't take. Think about it. The lender wouldn't need a cosignor if the borrower were a safe risk.

If You Do Cosign

Cosignors don't get a dollar in return for the risk they take. And they frequently end up paying. However, there may be times when you may want to cosign. Perhaps you want to help a son or daughter with a first loan or a close friend who's in trouble on a loan and facing repossession or court action. If you do, here are a few things to consider:

1. Be sure you can afford to pay the loan. You may have to. If you are asked to pay and can't, you could be sued—or your credit rating could be severely damaged.

2. Try to get the lender to agree that you will only owe a fixed amount. (The lender doesn't have to do this but it's worth a try.) Agree to pay the principal balance on the loan, but try not to be responsible for late charges, court costs, and attorneys' fees. You could ask the lender to write a statement like this into the contract: "The cosignor will only be responsible for the principal balance on this loan at the time of default."

3. Make sure that you don't pledge your property to secure the loan. Do not agree to pledge your automobile or furniture.

4. Ask that the lender agree, in writing, to notify you if the borrower misses a payment. Notification should come before a late charge is added and always before the loan is "accelerated" (the whole loan is demanded and not just a back payment or two). This way you'll have time to find a solution or at least make back payments without having to come up with the whole amount of the loan.

5. Make sure you get copies of all the important papers signed by the borrower: the loan contract, the Truth-in-Lending Disclosure Statement, and any warranties for products purchased if it's a credit sale. These may come in handy if there is a dispute later between the borrower and the seller.

6. Finally, don't be pressured. Cosigning may not be a good idea. Take your time. Think about it. Make your own decision for your own peace of mind.

FEDERAL TRADE COMMISSION

WASHINGTON, D. C. 20580

———

OFFICIAL BUSINESS

PENALTY FOR PRIVATE USE, $300

POSTAGE AND FEES PAID
U. S. FEDERAL TRADE COMMISSION

Immediate
Release
6/12/79

Facts for Consumers
from the Federal Trade Commission

BUREAU OF CONSUMER PROTECTION • OFFICE OF CONSUMER EDUCATION • WASHINGTON, D.C. 20580

Utility Credit

The Federal Trade Commission sometimes receives this kind of letter from women:

"My husband and I always paid our phone, gas, and electric bills promptly. Then...suddenly...he was gone. When I tried to get utility service in my own name, each company wanted me to make a deposit ranging from $25 to $100. Isn't this discrimination?"

Answer: "It could be. But there are several sides to this issue that you ought to understand, in order to exercise your rights."

Utility Acct. Is a Credit Acct.

First, you should know that a utility account is a credit account. You get service now and you pay for it later--and that's credit. Second, you should know that utility companies--like department stores--keep a record of your good or bad payment patterns; this record is your utility credit history.

The Equal Credit Opportunity Act has some very specific rules about considering credit histories. Utility companies--like department stores and other creditors--must abide by these credit history rules.

Utility companies frequently require a consumer to make a deposit or to get a letter of guarantee from someone who will agree to pay the bill if the consumer doesn't. Under the law, requiring a deposit or letter of guarantee can be the same thing as denying credit.

It's generally all right for a utility company to ask for a deposit if you have a bad utility credit history or if you're a new customer and the utility company routinely requires all new customers to pay deposits. However, in some situations, it is illegal to require deposits.

Living With an Ex-Husband's Credit Record

A utility company might ask a newly widowed or divorced woman to pay a deposit simply because there is no record of her name on her husband's account. But if she requests an account in her name and tells the utility company she had previous service in the name of her husband, the utility company must consider his credit history as hers, also.

Then there's the other side of the coin. What if the husband's utility credit history was bad? Not only could they ask the wife to pay a deposit or get a letter of guarantee, they might also ask her to pay off her husband's old debts before her service is connected.

Because of the Equal Credit Opportunity Act, she has a chance to prove that her husband's bad credit history did not reflect her own willingness or ability to pay. For example, if she could prove she didn't live with him when the account was overdue, the company must take that into consideration. Maybe she never saw the bills or maybe she didn't know they were overdue but paid them as soon as she found out--all that must be considered, too. If she can convince the utility company she was not responsible for the past bad credit history, the company must lift its requirements. If she can't convince them, she'll have to pay a deposit or get a letter of guarantee. (She might even be asked to pay the unpaid bills on an account listed in his name, but that is a matter determined by state law and not by the Federal Equal Credit Opportunity Act.)

Pay "Under Protest," If You Have To

Whenever you're denied credit--including utility credit--you have the right to know the specific reason. Therefore, if you're asked to pay a deposit, ask them to give you the reason in writing before you pay it. If you can't wait for the hookup, pay the deposit under protest: Just write on your check, "Paid Under Protest" and enclose a note saying you think you shouldn't have to pay and why. If you pay willingly, you may be waiving your right to know the specific reason why.

Your spouse's utility credit history can only be considered on your account if your spouse is living with you or using your account. However, if you live in a community property state (Arizona, California, Idaho, Nevada, New York, Texas, and Washington), the utility company can ask questions about your spouse even if you're no longer living together.

Where to Write

If you feel you've received illegal treatment by your utility company, write the FTC, "Utility Credit," Washington, D.C. 20580. The Equal Credit Opportunity Act also allows individual consumers to take legal action against companies violating the law. You may want to discuss this possibility with an attorney.

Utilities are a necessity. But, unlike your relationship with most other creditors, you can't shop around for better utility credit terms. This makes it all the more important for consumers to demand fair treatment from the utility companies in their communities.

Equal Credit Opportunity

If you still think only of credit cards when you hear the word "credit," think again. Credit is used by millions of consumers for a variety of purposes: to finance educations, remodel homes, obtain small business loans, and pay for home mortgages.

A law passed by Congress ensures that all consumers will be given an equal chance to receive credit. The Equal Credit Opportunity Act says *it is illegal for creditors to discriminate against applicants on the basis of their sex, race, marital status, national origin, religion, age, or because they get public assistance income.* This doesn't mean all consumers who apply for credit will get it. Creditors can still use factors such as income, expenses, debts, and credit history to judge applicants.

The law protects you when dealing with any creditor who regularly extends credit, including: banks, small loan and finance companies, retail and department stores, credit card companies, and credit unions. Anyone participating in the decision to grant credit, such as a real estate broker who arranges financing, is covered by the law. Businesses applying for credit are protected by the law, too.

Consumers have equal rights in every phase of the credit application process. Here is a checklist of important rights to remember when you request credit:

When You Apply For Credit, A Creditor May Not...
- [ ] Discourage you from applying because of your sex, marital status, age, religion, race, national origin, or because you receive public assistance income.
- [ ] Ask you to reveal your sex, race, national origin, or religion. *A creditor may* ask you to voluntarily disclose this information if you are applying for a real estate loan. This information helps federal agencies enforce anti-discrimination laws. *A creditor may* ask what your residence or immigration status is.
- [ ] Ask whether you are divorced or widowed.
- [ ] Ask what your marital status is if you are applying for a separate, unsecured account. *A creditor may* ask you to reveal this information if you live in Arizona, California, Idaho, Louisiana, Nevada, New Mexico, Texas, and Washington—the "community property" states. In any state, *a creditor may* ask for this information if you apply for a joint account or any account secured by property.
- [ ] Ask you for information about your husband or wife. *A creditor may* ask about your spouse if: your spouse is applying with you; your spouse will be allowed to use the account; you are relying on your spouse's income or on alimony or child

FEDERAL TRADE COMMISSION/BUREAU OF CONSUMER PROTECTION

FT
BC

support income from a former spouse; or if you reside in a community property state (listed above).

- [ ] Ask about your plans for having or raising children.
- [ ] Ask if you receive alimony, child support, or separate maintenance payments. *A creditor may* ask for this information if you are first told that you don't have to reveal it if you won't rely on it to get credit. *A creditor may* ask if you have to *pay* alimony, child support, or separate maintenance payments.

When Deciding To Give You Credit, A Creditor May Not...

- [ ] Consider your sex, marital status, race, national origin, or religion.
- [ ] Consider whether you have a telephone listing in your name. *A creditor may* consider whether there is a phone in your home.
- [ ] Consider the race of the people who live in the neighborhood where you want to buy or improve a house with borrowed money.
- [ ] Consider your age, with certain exceptions:
  - if you are too young to sign contracts. Generally, this applies to those 18 and under.
  - if you are 62 or over, and the creditor will favor you because of your age.
  - if it is used to determine the meaning of other factors which are important to credit-worthiness. (For example, a creditor could use your age to see if your income might be reduced because you are about to retire.)
  - if it is used in a scoring system which favors applicants age 62 and over. A credit-scoring system assigns different points to your answers to application questions. (For example, owning a home might be worth 10 points, while renting might be worth 5.) The total number of points helps the creditor to decide if you are credit-worthy.

When Evaluating Your Income, A Creditor May Not...

- [ ] Refuse to consider reliable public assistance income in the same manner as other income.
- [ ] Discount income because of your sex or marital status. (For example, a creditor cannot count a man's salary at 100% and a woman's at 75%.) A creditor may not assume a woman of child-bearing age will stop work to have or raise children.
- [ ] Discount or refuse to consider income because it is derived from part-time employment or from pension, annuity, or retirement benefit programs.
- [ ] Refuse to consider consistently-received alimony, child support, or separate maintenance payments. *A creditor may* ask you for proof that this income has been received consistently.

You Also Have The Right...

- [ ] To have credit in your maiden name (Mary Smith), your first name and your husband's last name (Mary Jones), or your first name and a combined last name (Mary Smith-Jones).
- [ ] To get credit without a co-signer, if you meet the creditor's standards.
- [ ] To have a co-signer other than your husband or wife, if one is necessary.
- [ ] To keep your own accounts after you change your name, marital status, reach a certain age, or retire, unless the creditor has evidence that you are unable or unwilling to pay.
- [ ] To know whether your application was accepted or rejected within 30 days of filing it.
- [ ] To know *why* your application was rejected. The creditor must either immediately give you the specific reasons for your rejection or tell you of your right to learn the reasons if you ask them within 60 days. (Examples of reasons are: "Your income was too low," or "You haven't been employed at your job long enough." Examples of unacceptable reasons are: "You didn't meet our minimum standards," or "You didn't receive enough points on our credit-scoring system.") Indefinite and vague reasons are illegal—ask for specifics.

☐ To learn the specific reasons why you were offered less favorable terms than you applied for. (Examples of less favorable terms include higher finance charges or less money than you requested). This does not hold if you accept the less favorable terms.

☐ To know the specific reasons why your account was closed or why the terms of the account were made less favorable to you. This does not hold if these actions were taken because your account was delinquent or because you have not used the account for some time.

A Special Note to Women

A good credit history, or record of how you paid past bills, is often necessary to obtain credit. Unfortunately, this hurts many married, separated, divorced, and widowed women. There are two common reasons women do not have credit histories in their own names: they lost their credit histories when they married and changed their name, and creditors reported accounts shared by married couples in the husband's name only.

The law says that when creditors report histories to credit bureaus or to other creditors they must report information on accounts shared by married couples *in both names.* This is true only for accounts opened after June 1, 1977. If you and your spouse opened an account before that time, you should ask the creditor to use both names.

If you are married, divorced, separated, or widowed, you should make a special point to call or visit your local credit bureau(s) to ensure that all relevant information is in a file under *your own name.* To learn more about building your credit file, write for a free brochure, "Women and Credit Histories," from any of the FTC offices listed below.

What You Can Do If You Suspect Discrimination . . .

☐ Complain to the creditor. Make it known that you are aware of the law. The creditor may reverse the decision or detect an error.

☐ Many states have their own equal credit opportunity laws. Check with your state's Attorney General's office to see if the creditor violated state laws. Your state may decide to take the creditor to court.

☐ Bring a case in Federal district court. If you win, you can recover actual damages and be awarded a penalty. You can also recover reasonable attorney's fees and court costs. An attorney can advise you on how to proceed.

☐ Join with others to file a class action suit. You may recover punitive damages for the class of up to $500,000 or 1% of the creditor's net worth, whichever is less.

☐ Report violations to the appropriate government agency. If you are denied credit, the creditor must give you the name and address of the agency to contact. While the agencies do not resolve individual complaints, they do use consumer comments to decide which companies to investigate. A list of agencies appears at the end of this brochure.

Where To Send Complaints and Questions

If a retail store, department store, small loan and finance company, oil company, public utility company, state credit union, government lending program, or travel and expense credit card company is involved, contact the Federal Trade Commission office nearest you:

150 Causeway Street
Boston, Massachusetts 02114
(617) 223-6621

26 Federal Plaza
New York, New York 10278
(212) 264-1207

118 St. Clair Avenue
Cleveland, Ohio 44114
(216) 522-4207

1718 Peachtree Street NW
Atlanta, Georgia 30367
(404) 881-4836

55 East Monroe Street
Chicago, Illinois 60603
(312) 353-4423

1405 Curtis Street
Denver, Colorado 80202
(303) 837-2271

2001 Bryan Street
Dallas, Texas 75201
(214) 767-0032

11000 Wilshire Boulevard
Los Angeles, California 90024
(213) 824-7575

450 Golden Gate Avenue
San Francisco, California 94102
(415) 556-1270

915 Second Avenue
Seattle, Washington 98174
(206) 442-4655

Central Office:
6th Street & Pennsylvania Avenue NW
Washington, D.C. 20580
(202) 724-1139

- ☐ If your complaint concerns a *nationally-chartered bank* (National or N.A. will be part of the name), write to:
  Comptroller of the Currency
  Consumer Affairs Division, Washington, D.C. 20219
- ☐ If your complaint concerns a *state-chartered bank* that is a member of the Federal Reserve System, write to:
  Board of Governors of the Federal Reserve System
  Consumer Affairs Division, Washington, D.C. 20551
- ☐ If your complaint concerns a bank that is *state-chartered and insured by the Federal Deposit Insurance Corporation, but is not a member of the Federal Reserve System,* write to:
  FDIC
  Consumer Affairs Division, Washington, D.C. 20429
- ☐ If your complaint concerns a *federally-chartered or federally-insured savings and loan association,* write to:
  Federal Home Loan Bank Board
  Equal Credit Opportunity, Washington, D.C. 20552
- ☐ If your complaint concerns a *federally-chartered credit union,* write to:
  National Credit Union Administration
  Consumer Affairs Division, Washington, D.C. 20456
- ☐ Complaints against *all kinds of creditors* can be referred to:
  Department of Justice
  Civil Rights Division, Washington, D.C. 20530

Revised July 1982
Publication No. L-02-1

Federal Trade Commission
Washington, D.C. 20580

Official Business, Penalty
For Private Use: $300

Postage and Fees
Paid by the U.S.
Federal Trade Commission

Women and Credit Histories

- Mrs. Becker had been using her husband's department store charge card for several years. The charges were billed to her husband, but she took responsibility for paying the bills on time. Recently, she applied for her own credit card from the store and her application was denied. The reason? The store had no record of her bill-paying history on her husband's account.
- Louise Martin changed her name when she got divorced. Although she had several successful credit accounts in her married name, her applications for credit in her maiden name were repeatedly denied. Creditors told her: "We can't find a record of your credit history under the name you gave on your application form."
- Bess Fenton, a young single woman, recently moved to the West Coast to start a new job. She applied for her first credit card with a national oil company, but since she had no record with the local credit bureau, her application was denied. Her question: "If it takes credit to get credit, how do I begin?"

You may have faced similar problems when you have applied for credit. Each year, many women are denied credit because they cannot show how they have used it. A good credit history is the way most companies predict your future success in using credit. The record of your payments on credit cards, charge accounts, installment loans, and other credit accounts is how you get a "track record." It gives a creditor evidence that you are a good risk.

Know your rights under the law

Two federal laws give you specific rights that help protect your credit history and make it easier for you to obtain credit:

- The Equal Credit Opportunity Act (ECOA) prohibits a creditor from discriminating against you on the basis of sex or marital status in any aspect of a credit transaction. The ECOA also forbids discrimination on the basis of your race, color, age, national origin, religion, because you receive public assistance payments, or because you exercised rights under federal consumer credit protection laws.
- The Fair Credit Reporting Act (FCRA) protects consumer privacy and safeguards the accuracy of credit bureau reports.

Ask the credit bureau to help

Credit bureaus gather and sell credit information about consumers and are a principal source of information about your credit history. Creditors usually rely on credit bureau reports before issuing a line of credit. So it makes sense to ask your local credit bureaus (listed in the Yellow Pages) for your report. The bureau will report whatever it has on file, which might include what kinds of credit accounts you have, how you pay your bills, and whether you have ever filed for bankruptcy or were sued. This report may include other credit references that you can use in new credit applications to give a more complete picture of your financial situation.

Some credit references may not appear in your file simply because the creditor may not report the information to the credit bureau. Credit bureaus obtain most of their information from creditors who send them regular reports. Some creditors only report delinquent accounts; accounts with good payment histories may go unreported. Most national credit card companies report their accounts to credit bureaus, but many local creditors do not.

Fill an empty file

If creditors have failed to supply information to your credit file, or if you have never had credit in your own name, a "no file" report can cause your application to be rejected.

For example, when a woman is widowed, divorced, or simply wants credit in her own name, a credit bureau may report "no file" exists for her. She might have a great credit history, but all in her husband's name. A newly married woman may have the same problem if she changes her name. Old accounts held in her maiden name may not have been transferred to a file listed under her married name. For all practical purposes her credit history is lost.

For your own protection you should learn how to prevent credit history "evaporation." There are steps you can take to fill an empty file with your past credit history or to build the file with new information.

Build your credit file

☐ If you have never had credit, start building a good record now. A local bank or department store may approve your credit application even if you do not meet the standards of larger creditors. But do not apply for too many accounts at one time. Credit bureaus keep a record of each creditor who inquires about you. Some creditors may deny your application if they think you are trying to open too many new accounts too quickly.

☐ If you have had credit before under a different name or in a different location, make sure your local credit bureau has complete and accurate information about you in a file under your current name. Locate credit bureaus by looking in the Yellow Pages under headings such as "Credit" or "Credit Rating and Reporting Agencies." Then call each bureau to find out if they have a file on you. Most cities have two or three bureaus. Bureaus may charge a small fee for checking your file.

☐ If you have shared accounts with your husband or former husband, visit or call your local credit bureau. Be certain that you have a credit file in your own name that lists these accounts. If credit information was reported only in your husband's name or former husband's name, the credit bureau may be willing to add those references to your file. Ask. Keep in mind that a small fee may be charged for each item added.

☐ If you were married or divorced recently and changed your name, ask your creditors to change your name on your accounts. Once these accounts are in your new name, your complete credit history should be reported correctly to the credit bureau.

☐ Notify each creditor that you want accounts you share with your husband reported in both names. (You can use the form provided below as a sample.) Then wait a couple of months, visit the credit bureau, and ask if the accounts are being reported as requested.

Give your best credit references

List your best credit accounts, open and closed, on any credit application—including accounts you shared with your husband or former husband. Offer to assist the creditor in providing verification of your credit references when an account history does not appear in a credit bureau report. If you can show a credit history applied to you, even though it was in your husband's or former husband's name, the creditor must consider it. If any previous history was unfavorable and it does not accurately reflect your credit worthiness, explain this to the creditor.

Credit histories for married people

If you are married, but want to establish a credit history in your own name, simply write your creditors and request it. Creditors have an obligation to provide the history in both names when accounts are shared. As a sample of what you should say, you can use the following format.

Acme Department Store
Credit Division
1798 Third Street
Cincinnati, OH 70239

Dear Madam or Sir:

Under the Equal Credit Opportunity Act, I request that you report all credit information on this account in both names.

_____
ACCOUNT NUMBER

ACCOUNT NAMES: *PRINT OR TYPE*

FIRST	MIDDLE	LAST
FIRST	MIDDLE	LAST

STREET, NUMBER, APT.

CITY, STATE, ZIP

_____
SIGNATURE OF EITHER SPOUSE

Ask questions if your application is denied

The ECOA gives you the right to know the specific reasons for denial if you receive a notice that your application was denied. If the denial was based on a credit report, you are entitled to know the specific information in the credit report that led to the denial. After you receive this information from the creditor, you should visit or telephone the local credit bureau to find out what information was reported. The bureau cannot charge for disclosure if you ask to see your file within 30 days of being notified of a denial based on a credit report. You may ask the bureau to investigate any inaccurate or incomplete information and correct its records.

If you live in a community property state*, a creditor may consider your husband's credit history even if you are applying for your own account. You still should make certain that your local credit bureau has a separate credit file in your name.

For more information on this subject, call or write to Jean Noonan at (202) 724-1184, Division of Credit Practices, Federal Trade Commission, Washington, DC 20580.

---

*Community property states are Arizona, California, Idaho, Louisiana, Nevada, New Mexico, Texas, and Washington.

FTC offices where you can seek information are the following:

6th and Pennsylvania, N.W.
WASHINGTON, D.C. 20580
(202) 523-3598

150 Causeway Street
BOSTON, Massachusetts 02114
(617) 223-6621

26 Federal Plaza
NEW YORK, New York 10278
(212) 264-1207

118 St. Clair Avenue
CLEVELAND, Ohio 44114
(216) 522-4207

1718 Peachtree Street, N.W.
ATLANTA, Georgia 30367
(404) 881-4836

450 Golden Gate Avenue
SAN FRANCISCO, California 94102
(415) 556-1270

55 East Monroe Street
CHICAGO, Illinois 60603
(312) 353-4423

1405 Curtis Street
DENVER, Colorado 80202
(303) 837-2271

2001 Bryan Street
DALLAS, Texas 75201
(214) 767-0032

11000 Wilshire Boulevard
LOS ANGELES, California 90024
(213) 824-7575

915 Second Avenue
SEATTLE, Washington 98174
(206) 442-4655

GPO : 1982 O - 377-383 : QL 3

Fair Credit Reporting

If you've ever applied for a charge account, a personal loan, insurance, or a job, someone is probably keeping a file on you. This file might contain information on how you pay your bills, or whether you've been sued, arrested, or have filed for bankruptcy.

The companies that gather and sell this information are called "Consumer Reporting Agencies," or "CRA's." The most common type of CRA is the credit bureau. The information sold by CRA's to creditors, employers, insurers, and other businesses is called a "consumer report." This generally contains information about where you work and live and about your bill-paying habits.

In 1970, Congress passed the Fair Credit Reporting Act to give consumers specific rights in dealing with CRA's. The Act protects you by requiring credit bureaus to furnish correct and complete information to businesses to use in evaluating your applications for credit, insurance, or a job.

The Federal Trade Commission enforces the Fair Credit Reporting Act. Here are answers to some questions about consumer reports and CRA's:

How do I locate the CRA that has my file?
If your application was denied because of information supplied by a CRA, that agency's name and address must be supplied to you by the company you applied to. Otherwise, you can find the CRA that has your file by calling those listed in the Yellow Pages under "credit" or "credit rating and reporting." Since more than one CRA may have a file about you, call each one listed until you locate all agencies maintaining your file.

Do I have the right to know what the report says?
Yes, if you request it. The CRA is required to tell you about every piece of information in the report and, in most cases, the sources of that information. Medical information is exempt from this rule, but you can have your physician try to obtain it for you. The CRA is *not* required to give you a copy of the report, although more and more are doing so. You also have the right to be told the name of anyone who received a report on you in the past six months. (If your inquiry concerns a job application, you can get the names of those who received a report during the past two years.)

Is this information free?
Yes, if your application was denied because of information furnished by the CRA, and if you request it within 30 days of receiving the denial notice. If you don't meet these requirements, the CRA may charge a reasonable fee.

What can I do if the information is inaccurate or incomplete?
Notify the CRA. They're required to reinvestigate the items in question. If the new investigation reveals an error, a corrected version will be sent, on your request, to anyone who received your report in the past six months. (Job applicants can have corrected reports sent to anyone who received a copy during the past two years.)

What can I do if the CRA won't modify the report?
The new investigation may not resolve your dispute with the CRA. If this happens, have the CRA include your version or a summary of your version of the disputed information in your file and in future reports. At your request, the CRA will also show your version to anyone who recently received a copy of the old report. There is no charge for this service if it's requested within 30 days after you

FEDERAL TRADE COMMISSION/BUREAU OF CONSUMER PROTECTION

receive notice of your application denial. After that, there may be a reasonable charge.

Do I have to go in person to get the information?

No, you may also request information over the phone. But before the CRA will provide any information, you must establish your identity by completing forms they will send you. If you do wish to visit in person, you'll need to make an appointment.

Are reports prepared on insurance and job applicants different?

If a report is prepared on you in response to an insurance or job application, it may be an *investigative* consumer report. These are much more detailed than regular consumer reports. They often involve interviews with acquaintances about your lifestyle, character, and reputation. Unlike regular consumer reports, you'll be notified in writing when a company orders an investigative report about you. This notice will also explain your right to ask for additional information about the report from the company you applied to. If your application is rejected, however, you may prefer to obtain a *complete* disclosure by contacting the CRA, as outlined in this brochure. Note that the CRA does not have to reveal the sources of the investigative information.

How long can CRA's report unfavorable information?

Generally seven years. Adverse information can't be reported after that, with certain exceptions:

- ☐ bankruptcy information can be reported for 10 years;
- ☐ information reported because of an application for a job with a salary of more than $20,000 has no time limitation;
- ☐ information reported because of an application for more than $50,000 worth of credit or life insurance has no time limitation;
- ☐ information concerning a lawsuit or judgment against you can be reported for seven years or until the statute of limitations runs out, whichever is longer.

Can anyone get a copy of the report?

No, it's only given to those with a legitimate business need.

Are there other laws I should know about?

Yes, if you applied for and were denied credit, the Equal Credit Opportunity Act requires creditors to tell you the specific reasons for your denial. For example, the creditor must tell you whether the denial was because you have "no credit file" with a CRA or because the CRA says you have "delinquent obligations." This law also requires creditors to consider, upon request, additional information you might supply about your credit history.

You may wish to obtain the reason for denial from the creditor before you go to the credit bureau.

Do women have special problems with credit applications?

Married and formerly married women may encounter some common credit-related problems. For more information, write the FTC for a free brochure on "Women and Credit Histories" at the address listed below.

Where should I report violations of the law?

Although the FTC can't act as your lawyer in private disputes, information about your experiences and concerns is vital to the enforcement of the Fair Credit Reporting Act. Please send questions or complaints to the FTC, Washington, D.C. 20580.

Federal Trade Commission
Washington, D.C. 20580

Official Business, Penalty
For Private Use: $300

Postage and Fees
Paid by the U.S.
Federal Trade Commission

PENSION RIGHTS CENTER, 1346 CONNECTICUT AVENUE, N.W., ROOM 1019, WASHINGTON, D.C. 20036

The Pension Rights Center is preparing a series of fact sheets to help people understand pension laws and how to exercise their rights under those laws. This fact sheet focuses on the Employee Retirement Income Security Act of 1974. The fact sheet was written because few of the millions of people affected by this private pension reform law have any real idea of what the law does and does not do for them.

Pension Facts #1 focuses on basic pension rights and misconceptions, or myths, about the private pension law. It concentrates on the minimum requirements of the law and how they affect those private pension plans that promise to pay a specific dollar amount each month at retirement. Future fact sheets will deal with other kinds of private plans, as well as government plans.

Note: In reading this fact sheet you should keep in mind that pension plans can, and many do, have better provisions than the minimum required by law.

MYTHS & FACTS

MYTH #1

The pension law gives you a pension.

THE FACTS

You may get a pension as a result of the law but only if you meet certain conditions.

You can be *sure* of getting a pension as a result of the law only if, after 1976, you worked full-time for a company that contributes to a pension plan and you keep on working for that company for 10 or more years without stopping for any reason *and* you live until age 65.

You also have a good chance of getting a pension if you can answer YES to all of the questions in the following checklist:

☐ 1. Do you work for a private company, not a government agency?

☐ 2. Does your company contribute to a pension plan?

☐ 3. Are you at least 25 years old and have you worked 1 year?

☐ 4. Did you start work more than 5 years before your plan's "normal retirement age"?

☐ 5. Did you work after the date in 1976 when your plan was required to comply with the new law?

☐ 6. Do you regularly work more than half-time or more than half a year?

☐ 7. Have you worked at least 10 years?
   ☐ a. for your present employer, or employers if yours is an industry-wide plan that credits all work done in the industry? AND
   ☐ b. after the age of 22?

☐ 8. Has your employer contributed to your plan (or an earlier plan) for at least 10 years?

☐ 9. Have you worked for your company at least 3 years after 1970?

☐ 10. Was your work for the company continuous without a break in service—or—if you had a break in service, was it:

   ☐ a. before 1976 and not considered a break under the plan then in effect?

   ☐ b. after 1976 and less than 9 months?

   ☐ c. after 1976 and shorter than the period you worked before the break?

If you haven't yet worked 10 years for an employer (or employers) contributing to a plan, will you? **Government statistics show that 56% of full-time employees covered by private pension plans have been on their present job** *less than 10 years.*

If you have not worked 10 years and do not expect to do so, you may still get a pension if yours is one of the relatively few plans that have either chosen or been required by the government to provide partial benefits after fewer years. Remember, too, that plan provisions can always be better than the law requires.

NOTE: Plans are not required to *pay* **pensions until age 65.** You may find that you have to wait until age 65 to get your pension even though, in the past, the customary retirement age under your plan has always been less than 65.

MYTH #2

The pension you get as a result of the new law will give you an adequate income after you retire.

THE FACTS

If you will get a pension solely because of the requirements of the new law, chances are that your pension, even when added to social security payments, will not provide you with an adequate retirement income. **This is because the new law says nothing about the size of a pension. It simply requires that the pension "pie" be cut differently. Since more people will now get pieces of the pie, the pieces are likely to be smaller.**

Your pension is likely to be based only on the years you work under the plan.

Examples: If you work for 10 years under a plan that provides pension benefits equal to 1% of final pay for each year of service and your final salary is $10,000 a year, your pension at age 65 will be $1,000 a year or $83.33 a month.

If you work for 10 years under a plan that provides benefits equal to $10 a month for each year of service, your pension benefit will be $1,200 or $100 a month.

Your pension will probably be fixed as of the time you leave a plan, no matter how much your income or the cost of living goes up before you reach retirement age.

Your pension is likely to be reduced if you retire early. Typically there is a percentage reduction for each year you are retired before age 65. Some plans provide a second much bigger reduction for persons not working under the plan when they apply for their pension.

Your pension may be reduced even further if you are married.

Most plans provide a pension benefit in addition to social security **BUT** your social security payments may not be as much as you expect: **$3960 a year** is the average for nonmarried persons over age 65. The average payment received by couples is **$6756.**

You should also know that many plans provide for a social security "offset". Under these plans, pension benefits and social security payments are combined. If you are covered by this kind of plan, you may find that when you subtract the social security, your pension amounts to little or even nothing at all.

MYTH #3

Your husband or wife will get your pension when you die.

THE FACTS

Your husband or wife will not get *your* pension when you die. **The most that the law requires is that he or she get a surviving spouse benefit equal to one-half of your reduced pension and then only if you die after age 55 under certain circumstances.**

Death after retirement: If you die after retirement, your surviving spouse will receive the 50 percent benefit only if at the time you retired, your pension benefit was reduced to provide a surviving spouse benefit. The law provides that your pension will automatically be reduced unless you sign a paper before retirement saying you do not want your pension reduced.

Example: You are entitled to a $100 a month pension at age 65. Your wife is 62. You can sign a paper saying that you want to receive the $100 while you live, in which case your wife gets nothing if you die first, or you can have your pension reduced to $80 for your life so that, if you die first, your wife can get $40 for the rest of her life. Of course, if she dies first, you still get only the $80 a month.

Death before retirement: If your plan has early retirement provisions and you keep working after age 55, your surviving spouse will receive the 50 percent benefit only if you sign a paper agreeing to a reduction in your pension at retirement *and you do not die as a result of a heart attack, cancer or other "natural causes" within two years of signing the paper.*

IF YOU DIE BEFORE AGE 55, YOUR HUSBAND OR WIFE WILL GET NOTHING, NO MATTER HOW LONG YOU WORKED UNDER THE PLAN.

MYTH #4

Your plan is insured by the government so you can count on getting exactly what you've been promised by your pension plan.

THE FACTS

Many plans are insured so that if a company shuts down (or stops its pension plan for any other reason) and does not have enough money to pay the benefits promised, a government insurance corporation will step in to pay benefits. **But not all plans are insured and, even more important, not all benefits promised by insured plans will be paid.**

IS YOUR PLAN INSURED? Most plans are insured, but there are exceptions:

- Plans that do not meet all the requirements of the pension and tax laws are not insured.
- Plans that are paid for only by union dues are not insured.

- Plans with less than 25 employees set up by doctors, dentists, architects, lawyers, performing artists and other professionals are not insured.
- Plans set up by churches may not be insured.

ARE YOUR BENEFITS INSURED? Your *age 65 retirement pension* will be paid if, when your plan stopped, you had worked long enough to get a "vested" (legal) right to a pension and your pension is based on plan provisions that had been in effect for at least 5 years.

Your pension is not insured at all if at the time the plan stops you have not worked long enough to get a "vested" right to a pension. Since in most cases vesting occurs at 10 years, this means if your plan stops after you have worked 9 years and 11 months, you will get nothing, even though you'd planned to spend your lifetime working under the plan.

Your pension may not be fully insured if your plan has been improved within 5 years before the plan stops. Also, if your plan was set up by a union and more than one company and it gets into serious financial trouble, there is a chance that you could lose part of your pension.

Your *survivors benefit* and *early retirement age pensions* will only be paid up to certain specified minimum amounts REGARDLESS OF THE PROVISIONS OF YOUR PLAN even if your plan is insured. The insurance generally won't cover any pre-age 55 survivors benefits, any lump sum death benefits, or **survivors benefits equal to more than 50% of a retiree's reduced pension.** The insurance won't cover special early retirement benefits such as 30-and-out benefits.

PENSION RIGHTS

All participants in pension plans have these basic rights

YOU HAVE THE RIGHT . . .

To receive basic information about your plan in easily understandable language.

BOOKLET: *Plans must give employees booklets telling them what they have to do to get a pension and the dollar amount of the benefits paid by the plan.*

"If you have not received a booklet, or if the language in the booklet is not easy to understand, you should contact the nearest office of the United States Department of Labor.

Watch for misleading language in booklets. "Eligibility" provisions usually will tell you only whether you are covered by a plan *not* whether you are "eligible" to receive a pension. Ordinarily you have to be covered by a plan for a fairly long time before you are eligible to receive a pension, and then you will have to wait until retirement age to collect the pension.

IMPORTANT: Many booklets are including statements that say if there is a difference between the language in the booklet and the language in the full legal plan document on file at the main plan office, you canNOT rely on what the booklet says. Although these disclaimer statements would appear to be inconsistent with the intent of the new law, there has as yet been no ruling as to their legality.

BENEFIT INFORMATION: *While You Are Working Under a Plan: Your plan must tell you whether you are entitled to a pension and if so, how much you can expect to get, if you ask for this information in writing. You can ask for this information once a year.*

The language in the benefit statement may be confusing. If the statement tells you that you have an "accrued benefit" of a certain amount this does NOT mean that you have a right to get that amount. Only if you have worked long enough to get a "vested" or "nonforfeitable" benefit will you actually get your "accrued benefit."

If yours is a plan that did not keep records in the past, you may find that your benefit statement is based partly on estimates.

BENEFIT INFORMATION: *When You Stop Working Under a Plan: If you are entitled to a pension, the plan must give you a statement saying that you have a right to a pension and the amount to which you will be entitled. You will get a second copy of this statement when you apply for social security.*

The statement will show the amount you can expect to receive at "normal retirement age", usually age 65. It will not show how much that amount will be reduced if you retire before that age or if you are married.

Also it is up to you to go back to the company and apply for the pension when you reach retirement age.

INVESTMENT INFORMATION: *The money contributed to the pension plan comes out of your earnings. You have the right to be told where your money is being invested, how well it is being invested and by whom.*

You will get a summary of this information each year but to find out important details, such as exactly what companies your plan is investing in or to whom it has made loans, you will have to ask in writing for a copy of the full Annual Report. You may be charged copying costs but they must be reasonable. You should also know that current rules say that with a very few exceptions the plan only has to show investments held as of the last day of the plan year. If the plan doesn't want you to know about a questionable loan or stock purchase, it can simply get rid of it before the end of the year.

YOU HAVE THE RIGHT . . .

To have your pension money invested wisely and only in the interests of employees and their spouses.

If you think your pension money is being invested speculatively or used primarily to advance the interests of your company or union and not your interests, you should contact the United States Department of Labor immediately.

YOU HAVE THE RIGHT ...

Not to be fired to deprive you of your pension.

If you think you have been fired, or otherwise discriminated against, to deny you your pension, you have the right to go to court. You will, however, have the burden of proving that this, and not the reason given by the company or union, was the cause of your discharge.

YOU HAVE THE RIGHT ...

To go to court if your pension application is wrongfully denied.

If the plan decides not to give you a pension, it must give you a written statement of the reasons your claim was denied. You can then ask the plan to review that decision. If you are still unsatisfied, you can go to state or federal court and sue the plan.

You may find that it is both difficult and expensive to find a lawyer willing to take your case. Few lawyers take employee pension cases and it is completely up to the court to decide whether or not, if you win, the plan should pay your legal costs.

YOU HAVE THE RIGHT ...

To protest if your plan does not meet the requirements of the new law.

In order for your company to get tax benefits your plan must be approved by the Internal Revenue Service. At the time your plan is filed with the IRS all employees must be told that they have a right to comment on their plan. If you think that your plan may not meet the requirements of the new law you should first ask the IRS for a copy of your plan, read it and then either write directly to the IRS or ask the Labor Department to review your plan and comment.

The IRS must give you your plan, but can charge you copying costs. Be sure to ask just for your plan. One employee was told that copying costs would be $500 even though only $12 of that amount was for the plan, the rest was for lists of contributing employers.

PENSION RIGHTS CENTER

The Pension Rights Center is a nonprofit public interest group organized to protect and promote the rights of people who look to private pension plans for a secure retirement income. It is supported by grants and contributions and is in continuing need of funds in order to carry out its objectives. All donations to the Center are tax-deductible. To receive Pension Facts #2, *Women and the Facts*, or additional copies of this fact sheet send 25 cents and a self-addressed envelope for each copy to the Pension Rights Center, Room 1019, 1346 Connecticut Ave., N.W., Washington, D.C., 20036.

Other pension publications:

Retirement Income is a 24-page newsmagazine filled with up-to-date information on pension and social security matters—from the pitfalls that can deny you your pension to what Congress is doing about retirement income problems. Copies are available for $2.00 from the Pension Rights Center.

Often Asked Questions About the Employee Retirement Income Security Act of 1974 is one of several Labor Department publications describing the new law. All publications are available free of charge from the U.S. Department of Labor, Pension and Welfare Benefit Programs, Washington, D.C. 20216.

You and Your Pension by Ralph Nader and Kate Blackwell was written before the new law was passed but remains the most comprehensive and easily understood description of how the private pension system works. Copies are available for $1.00 through the Pension Rights Center.

PENSION RIGHTS CENTER
Room 1019
1346 Connecticut Avenue, N.W.
Washington, D.C. 20036

PENSION FACTS 2

PENSION RIGHTS CENTER, 1346 CONNECTICUT AVENUE, N.W., ROOM 1019, WASHINGTON, D.C. 20036

The Pension Rights Center is preparing a series of fact sheets to help people understand their rights under the Employee Retirement Income Security Act of 1974. Pension Facts #1 concentrated on common misconceptions about this new law. Its purpose was to explain what the law does and does not do.

Pension Facts #2 focuses on women, the group most disadvantaged by the private pension system. Its purpose is to provide information, before it is too late, so that millions of women will not have to ask "what happened" to the pension security they thought was theirs.

Note: These fact sheets do not deal with government plans. They cover only private pension plans, primarily those that promise a specific dollar amount each month at retirement, and the minimum standards those plans must meet. You should keep in mind that plans can and many do have better provisions than the law requires.

WOMEN AND THE FACTS

YOU NEED A PENSION

Social security and savings will not provide you with an adequate retirement income.

WILL YOU GET THE PENSION YOU NEED?

Before the new pension law only 2 percent of all widows received a benefit from their husbands' pension plans and only 10 percent of all women retiring from private companies received a pension. The new law has made some important changes but there are still many ways that women, both as wives and workers, will continue to lose out. Unless women understand retirement income realities and start acting to protect themselves, older women are likely to remain the single poorest group in our country. Look at your retirement situation without a pension. Social security and savings are the only other sources of income for most older women. Will they give you enough to live on?

> "Over 5 million women over the age of 65 live alone and half that number are living their last years below the official poverty level. Most of these women have not always been poor. What happened to them is not inevitable, but is rather the result of discrimination throughout their lives which strikes its cruelest blow at the end."
> —Congresswoman Patricia Schroeder

SOCIAL SECURITY AND SAVINGS

Social security benefits for the average couple are $4800 a year. Less than half of the couples have savings of $2000 or more. Is that enough? Government statistics show that such a couple needs $6,310 a year to maintain an intermediate standard of living. You must also realize that 85 percent of all wives outlive their husbands. If your husband dies, your social security will be reduced. Instead of a couple's benefit (his benefit plus a wife's benefit), you will get only his benefit or your own, whichever is greater. For women over 65 who are alone, social security payments average only $2676 a year. Half of these women have savings of less than $1000 to last the 17.5 years they are expected to live beyond age 65.

IF YOUR HUSBAND GETS A PENSION, it belongs to him, not to you.   See Page 2.

IF HE DIES, at best you will get a widows benefit. Under many circumstances you will get nothing at all.   See Page 2.

IF YOU DIVORCE, you lose all rights to any benefit from your ex-husband's pension plan.   See Page 4.

IF YOU HAVE A PENSION PLAN where you work, you may or **may not** get a pension when you retire. See Page 3.

IF YOU GET A PENSION, it may be less than you expect. See Page 3.

IF YOU HAVE NO PENSION PLAN where you work, you can set up your own "pension plan" See Page 4.

DO YOU DEPEND ON YOUR HUSBAND'S INCOME?

More than half of all wives do not work outside the home. If you are among them, chances are you depend entirely on your husband's earnings. Where will your income come from if he dies? You may find yourself in the situation in which Gloria DeSantes found herself after being a wife and mother for 30 years. When her husband died suddenly, she found herself at age 50, "too young" for social security and "too old" to get a job. Mr. DeSantes had told his wife that if anything happened to him his pension plan would provide for her. After all, he had worked more than 33 years for the company. What neither Mr. nor Mrs. DeSantes realized was that, even though *he* could be sure of getting a pension, that did not mean *she* would get anything. Mrs. DeSantes was told that her 52-year old husband had died too early. His plan provided benefits only to widows of employees who died after age 55. In her words, all the years her husband worked toward his pension went "down the drain." Be sure you know exactly what widows benefit provisions your husband's plan has.

WILL YOU GET A WIDOWS BENEFIT?

Before the new law, private pension plans did not have to offer benefits for widows. Those plans that did usually required the husband to sign a form and agree to take a reduction in his pension. Often the husband just never got around to signing the paper. Even though he had good intentions, his wife still got nothing when he died. The new law made some important changes if your husband is now covered by a private pension plan and has met his plan's requirements for a pension by the day of his death. From 1976 on, all plans must include provisions for the payment of widows benefits under some circumstances. The rules vary depending on when your husband dies.

IF YOUR HUSBAND DIES AFTER HE RETIRES, the general rule is that his pension will automatically be reduced at retirement to allow for a widows benefit. Therefore, if he does nothing, you will get a widows benefit if he dies. However, he can sign a form before he retires saying he does not want his pension reduced. The plan will then pay your husband his full pension during his lifetime but there will be no benefit for you if he dies. Because it is "his" pension, the decision is entirely his and he does not even have to tell you if he makes this choice.

If your husband wants to provide for you, the automatic provision works like this. Let's say your husband will receive a $100 a month pension at age 65 and you are 3 years younger than he is. In a typical plan if he does nothing, his pension will be automatically reduced to $80 a month for his lifetime. If he dies first, you will get half that amount or a $40 a month widows benefit. If you die first, he still gets only $80 a month. If you are much younger than your husband, his benefit will be reduced even more and your benefit will be half of that smaller amount, because you are expected to receive the widows benefit over a longer period of time.

There are some exceptions to the general rule. You will not get a widows benefit if you and your husband are not married for a full year before he starts getting his pension *and also* for a full year before he dies. Also, if your husband starts to receive his pension before the special "early survivor option" age which is often 55, there will be no benefit for you.

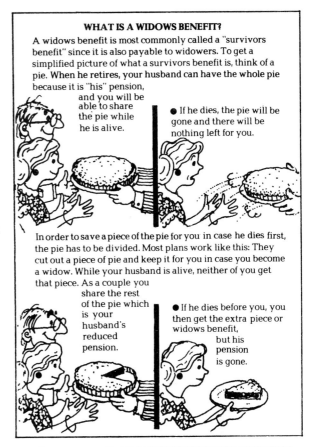

WHAT IS A WIDOWS BENEFIT?

A widows benefit is most commonly called a "survivors benefit" since it is also payable to widowers. To get a simplified picture of what a survivors benefit is, think of a pie. When he retires, your husband can have the whole pie because it is "his" pension, and you will be able to share the pie while he is alive.

● If he dies, the pie will be gone and there will be nothing left for you.

In order to save a piece of the pie for you in case he dies first, the pie has to be divided. Most plans work like this: They cut out a piece of pie and keep it for you in case you become a widow. While your husband is alive, neither of you get that piece. As a couple you share the rest of the pie which is your husband's reduced pension.

● If he dies before you, you then get the extra piece or widows benefit, but his pension is gone.

IF YOUR HUSBAND DIES WHILE HE IS STILL WORKING, the rules are harder to understand.

FIRST. For you to get a widows benefit if your husband dies while working, his plan must have a provision allowing him to take early retirement.

SECOND. If his plan allows for early retirement, your husband must have reached the special "early survivor option" age specified under his plan before he dies. This special age is the plan's early retirement age or 10 years before the plan's normal retirement age, which ever is **later.** *One woman wrote that her husband died after 40 years under his company's plan and 3 months before his 60th birthday. She got no widows benefit because the early retirement age under the plan was 60. Another woman whose 52-year old husband was killed in a car accident after 22½ years under his plan discovered that she didn't qualify for a widows benefit. Even though her husband had passed his plan's early retirement age, he was more than 10 years away from his plan's normal retirement age of 65. Under nearly all plans, you will not get a widows benefit if your husband dies before he is 55.*

THIRD. The provision for an early widows benefit is NOT AUTOMATIC. Your husband must sign a form agreeing to take a reduction in his early retirement pension in order to provide a widows benefit for you if he should die before he retires. If he does not sign the form, a widows benefit will not be paid. *(continued on page 4)*

DO YOU EARN YOUR OWN INCOME?

A pension can add substantially to retirement income. In 1975 women received private pensions averaging $1887 a year. Private pensions for men averaged $2725 a year.

WILL YOU GET A PENSION?

Not necessarily. You may get a pension and then again you may not.

FIRST, Ask yourself, do you work for a company or belong to a union that has a pension plan? Many women do not. Twice as many women as men have no pension coverage. One reason is that they tend to work in jobs that do not provide pensions. *For example, over half of all working women are employed in sales and service industries, the industries which have the fewest number of pension plans.*

SECOND, If your employer or union has a pension plan, are you covered? Plans do not always cover every category of worker. *For example, a factory that has a pension plan for its assembly line workers may not have a plan for its secretaries.*

THIRD, If you are covered by a pension plan, will you work long enough to get a pension? As result of the new law, most plans say you need ten years of work to get a pension. Will you stay on the job that long? *Government statistics show that more than half of all full-time workers covered by private pension plans have not been on their present jobs ten years. Half of the men have less than 9.2 years on the job and half of the women have less than 6.8 years.*

FOURTH, If you've worked enough years will all your years count? The new law says that plans don't have to give you credit for certain years you've worked. Not counting important years can cause both men and women to lose out, but the reality is that more often than not, women are the losers. The reason is not hard to find. The years that don't count include years before certain breaks-in-service, early years of employment, and some years of part-time, part-year, or seasonal work. Ignoring these years can greatly affect a woman's chances of earning a pension, especially if earning income is not a woman's only work. If she is also a wife and mother, her work patterns are likely to reflect her family's needs. *Think of the typical married woman. It is easy to see the impact of these rules. This typical woman works continuously for a number of years, then stops when her first child is born. She may go back to work when her children are ready for school, but often she works only part-time until her children are grown. When her family responsibilities lessen, she then goes back to full-time work. If she works for a company whose pension plan meets only the minimum standards required by the law, she is likely to find that many of the years she has worked do not count toward a pension.*

Years before breaks-in-service—Under the new law you may be able to count years worked before a break-in-service depending on how long you work before the break and how long you are away from work. You must get pension credit for years worked before a break if the period you are away from work is shorter than your period of employment before you stopped work and if your break

in service took place after the new law took effect. Unfortunately, if your break-in-service was before 1976, this rule doesn't apply. Your rule is what your plan said about breaks-in-service on the day your break started. Under many plans even a short time away from work was counted as a break and you lost pension credit for all the years you'd worked up to that time.

Early years of employment—Even with the improvements in the new law you may not be able to count the years you worked before age 22. Although plans can be better, many start giving you pension credit only after you reach age 22. If you began working right out of school, this rule can affect your chances of getting the ten years you need for a pension.

Years of part-time, part-year, or seasonal work—Under the new law you may be able to count periods of part-time, part-year, or seasonal work. The law now requires that plans count years in which you work at least 1000 hours. In most cases this means that you will get pension credit for any year in which you are regularly employed at least 20 hours a week or six months a year. If you are one of the more than 8 million women who are not working full-time, it is very important that you make sure that you are not losing pension credit by failing to work a few additional hours or days. You should also know that if you work less than 500 hours in a given year you can be considered to have a break-in-service for that year. However, if you work between 500 and 999 hours, even though you get no pension credit for the year, that year cannot be counted as a break.

IF YOU GET A PENSION, HOW MUCH WILL IT BE?

Although some plans pay a flat dollar amount for each year of service, most plans multiply the years you work under the plan times a percentage of your earnings.

YEARS—Just as not all years have to count in determining whether you will get a pension, not all years have to count in figuring the dollar amount of your pension and the years may not be the same. Plans don't have to give dollar value to years worked before you are 25, before some breaks-in-service, or before your first two years of continuous service. Also, if you work under a plan that in the past excluded categories of employees such as older or part-time workers, you may find that when your plan complies with the law, even though years worked before 1976 now count toward determining whether you have a right to a pension, they still do not count toward the dollar amount of that pension. *Mary Shaw went to work in a department store at age 46 after her family was grown. Now that she is ready to retire at 65, she has found that because her old plan didn't cover anyone who began work after age 45, she will get a pension figured not on 19 years, but only on the two years she has worked since the law went into effect.*

EARNINGS also affect most pensions. At present, for every dollar men earn, women average only 57 cents. Since women often have fewer years under a plan and their earnings are often low, it is not surprising that statistics show women's pensions average only half the amount of men's. Other things can also affect the amount of your pension.

- Your age when you apply for benefits. If you retire early, your pension will probably be cut a certain percent for each year you retire short of normal retirement age.
- If your plan combines your pension and social security benefits and your earnings are low, you may find the "pension" part of your benefit amounts to little or nothing. *Pat Ames found that after 27 years under an integrated plan her monthly "pension" was only $12.*
- You may not get your full pension if your plan ends without enough money to pay the pensions that have been promised. The law insures benefits only up to certain minimum levels.

IF YOUR HUSBAND DIES *(continued from page 2)*

FOURTH. Even if your husband's plan has early retirement provisions and even if your husband meets the age requirements and signs the form to provide the early widows benefit, the benefit may still not be paid. Plans do not have to pay out widows benefits if the husband dies of cancer, a heart attack or any other "natural" cause within 2 years of signing the agreement to provide for his wife.

FIFTH. None of these provisions apply if your husband is not working under the plan or is not receiving a pension at the time he dies. *Take this example: June Wyckoff's husband was 55 and had worked 34 years for the same company when he decided to change jobs. He could have collected an early retirement pension, but since the pension he would get at age 65 was twice as large, he decided to wait. What he didn't realize was that between the time he left the plan and the time he planned to apply for his pension there would be no opportunity to provide for his wife. When he died at age 64, she got nothing.*

> "Far from being the darling of the law, the homemaker is the most vulnerable woman in society with the least knowledge available to her of the reality of her legal status."
> —Former Congresswoman Martha Griffiths

IF YOU GET A WIDOWS BENEFIT, HOW MUCH WILL YOU GET?

Before the new law widows benefits were typically $50 a month. This amount is not likely to change very much. All that the law requires is that a widows benefit be equal to one-half of her husband's reduced pension.

However, there is always the possibility that your husband's plan may have more generous provisions than the minimum required by the law. For example, there are plans that don't require a reduction in a husband's benefit to provide for a widow. Some plans pay widows more than one-half of the husband's pension. A few plans give a widow the same benefit her husband was receiving at the time of his death. There are also a number of plans that provide death benefits to widows whose husbands died before retirement age. Although in many cases these benefits are only enough to cover funeral expenses, in others they can provide a monthly income for a number of years, usually no more than five. You may, of course, get life insurance, but insurance ordinarily does not provide a lifetime income. Typically it equals about two years of your husband's earnings and is meant to tide you over as you adjust to widowhood.

Under the new law your husband has certain important legal rights.

- **The right** to get a statement from his plan administrator once a year telling him whether he will get a pension and how much he would get at retirement age if he stopped working now.
- **The right** to get a statement from his plan administrator as he nears retirement telling him exactly the dollar value of (1) his full pension, (2) his pension reduced to provide a widows benefit for you and (3) the amount of the widows benefit. Be sure that your husband exercises his rights and that you have read these statements.

IF I AM DIVORCED?

There is now one divorce for every two marriages in this country. Although most divorces occur in the early years of marriage, recent estimates show that more than one woman in fifty will face divorce after the age of 45. This seriously affects pension security. Since your husband's pension belongs to him alone, you'll get no part of it if you divorce. At best you may get other property of roughly equal value, but in many cases you will get nothing at all. As for the possibility of a survivors benefit when your ex-husband dies, you are out of luck. Regulations issued under the new law state that to get a widows benefit you must be married at least one full year before your husband begins getting his pension AND also a full year before he dies.

CAN I PROVIDE FOR MYSELF?

The new pension law has a special provision if you work outside the home and you are not covered by a pension plan. You can set up an Individual Retirement Account (IRA) and save for your retirement. Basically these accounts allow you to take a tax deduction for amounts set aside in your own retirement fund. If you contribute to an IRA, you can deduct 15% of your income or $1500 (whichever is less) from your earnings each year before you pay income taxes. When you retire and begin collecting benefits, you pay taxes then, usually at a lower rate.

If your IRA is paid out in lifetime payments, you may find your monthly benefits are smaller than those of a man who has contributed the same amount. This will happen if your payments are based on life expectancy tables that assume women live longer than men and that your account has to be spread over a longer period of time.

If you are a homemaker, you are not eligible to set up an IRA because you do not earn income. A recent change in the tax laws may help if your husband is eligible for an IRA. He can set up separate IRAs, one for you and one for himself, and pay a maximum of $875 into each. He may also establish a joint IRA account, with limits of 15% of his income or $1750 per year, whichever is less. A future fact sheet will focus in detail on these accounts and on Keogh plans for the self-employed.

PENSION RIGHTS CENTER
The Pension Rights Center is a nonprofit public interest group organized to protect and promote the rights of people who look to private pension plans for a secure retirement income. It is supported by grants and contributions and is in continuing need of funds in order to carry out its objectives. All donations to the Center are tax-deductible. To receive copies of this and other fact sheets send 25 cents and a self-addressed stamped envelope for each copy to the Pension Rights Center, Room 1019, 1346 Connecticut Ave. N.W., Washington, D.C. 20036. Please state whether you are requesting Pension Facts #1: Pension Myths and Facts, or additional copies of this fact sheet.

DOWN WITH INSURANCE RATES

Buyer's Guide to Insurance

What the companies won't tell you.

National Insurance Consumer Organization
344 Commerce St., Alexandria, VA 22314

Buyer's Guide To Insurance

Many books have been written on the four kinds of personal insurance—auto, homeowners or renters, life and health insurance—discussed in this booklet. We can't say everything here, but we think most readers can save hundreds of dollars by using the ideas that follow.

If you want more information, check the public library for back issues of Consumer Reports. CR suggests which companies offer lower rates and provide better claims service.

Auto Insurance

There are four major coverages in a typical auto insurance policy: **bodily injury liability** (including personal injury protection in no-fault states), in case you injure someone; **property damage liability,** in case you damage someone else's car or other property; **collision,** in case you damage your own car; and **comprehensive,** in case your car is stolen, vandalized or otherwise damaged.

HOW TO SAVE MONEY:

If you don't need it; don't buy it. Every $1 in insurance premiums returns about 60¢ in claims; the remainder is overhead. So, if you're an average driver you can save about 40% (the overhead) by "self-insuring" those risks you can afford to assume.

Don't buy Collision. This is often the most expensive coverage. If your car isn't too valuable, Collision may not be worth it. If you itemize deductions on your Federal income tax, you should know that casualty losses exceeding $100 are deductible; many who own more expensive cars can avoid that 40% overhead and have Uncle Sam pay a portion of any loss by dropping Collision. The same logic applies to Comprehensive, but premiums are often less and the risk of total loss (due to theft) may be higher. One advantage to retaining Collision, however, is that if another driver damages your car in an amount that exceeds your Collision deductible, your company will try to collect for you.

NICO is a non-profit public interest membership organization. It helps consumers buy insurance wisely, serves as consumer advocate on public policy matters, and works for reform of unfair industry practices and marketplace abuses.

Robert Hunter, *President.*
Former Federal Insurance Administrator and a property/casualty actuary.
James Hunt, *Director.*
Former State Insurance Commissioner of Vermont and a life/health actuary.
Howard B. Clark, *Director.*
Former State Insurance Commissioner of South Carolina and an insurance lawyer.

Beginning in 1983, casualty losses in excess of $100 are deductible from income for Federal tax purposes only in an amount by which the sum of all such losses in the tax year exceeds 10% of Adjusted Gross Income. This severely limits the tax advantage we referred to. ------------------->

Increase deductibles. If you buy Collision, consider increasing the deductible from $100, say, to $250, which would save you almost 20%; or to $500, which would save you about 35%. Similar savings are available on Comprehensive. In no-fault states, a personal injury protection deductible may be available.

Don't buy incidental coverages. If you have adequate medical insurance, consider skipping Medical Payments coverage. Substitute Transportation and Towing and Labor are examples of coverages that offer little in the way of benefits, yet add to costs. Memberships in auto clubs sold by agents often are of little value.

Agents almost always sell insurance on commission. The more money you pay them, the more they make. Agents representing only one company usually receive lower commissions, so their prices can be less than "independent" agents who sell insurance for several companies. Companies that don't use agents usually have the lowest rates.

Shop around! There are often surprising differences in rates among companies. Compare your rates to those charged by State Farm, the largest auto insurer in the United States and one of the lowest in cost. Amica Mutual and USAA (active or retired commissioned officers in the Armed Services only) are the best companies we know of that don't use agents. The New York and Virginia insurance departments publish buyer's guides that list company rates for auto insurance in those states.

Having trouble getting coverage? Only a few states (HI, MA, MI, NC, NH and SC) guarantee claim-free drivers the right to buy insurance from the companies they choose. If you don't live in one of these states and have the wrong statistical profile, you may be forced to seek coverage at higher rates from substandard companies like Dairyland and Progressive or from the assigned risk plan. If so, you should be aware that in some states substandard companies are allowed to charge more than the assigned risk plan.

Homeowners or Renters Insurance

Homeowners insurance provides protection for fire, lightning, wind, hail, theft and vandalism, to name a few risks. Most everything is covered except earthquakes and floods. Such policies also include liability protection in case someone sues you for damages or injuries for which you (except when driving your car) are at fault.

Renters insurance is usually inexpensive. It covers your own personal property (furniture, etc.) and most liabilities you may incur. If you own a condominium, cooperative or mobile home, similar coverage is available.

KEEP THE FOLLOWING BUYING HINTS IN MIND:

In deciding how much Homeowners coverage to buy, deduct the value of the land and foundation from the property's market value to determine the maximum policy limit. If you live in an old house whose replacement cost is greater than its market value, base your limit on the replacement cost. Some companies offer small discounts if you install smoke detectors.

To receive reimbursement for partial losses on a replacement cost basis, rather than a depreciated basis, you should buy a policy limit equal to at least 80% of the replacement cost of the house (not the land and the foundation). (If it would cost $50,000 to replace your house, get a policy for $40,000.)

Remember: the more coverage you buy, the better off your agent and company are. Premiums tend to be proportional to policy limits: a $120,000 policy costs about 20% more than a $100,000 policy, even though the extra risk for the companies (because most claims are for partial losses) is far less than 20% more. So, don't automatically go along with agent or company suggestions of higher limits.

Increased deductibles can save money. The higher the deductible, the lower the costs.

If you rent your home to others, don't assume everything is covered under your Homeowners policy; check with your agent or company.

If you have valuables, be sure they are covered; separate riders may be necessary if their value exceeds, say, $500.

Note: The Federal government will sell you flood insurance or crime insurance, if you qualify. Call 800-638-6620 for flood insurance and 800-638-8780 for crime insurance. These are toll free numbers.

Life Insurance

A recent study by the Federal Trade Commission came to the following conclusions about the life insurance business:

—Life insurance is so complex that consumers are unable to evaluate costs of different life insurance policies.

—The savings portions of cash value policies that don't pay dividends have very low rates of return.

—Prices vary widely for similar policies.

—Consumers lose lots of money when they surrender cash value policies in the first ten years or so.

To avoid problems, follow these guidelines.

Don't buy it if you don't need it. Life insurance is needed to protect a family against the loss of income due to the death of a breadwinner. Those without dependents don't need life insurance. Don't buy policies that cover your children's lives. College seniors and graduate students should be especially wary of borrow-to-buy life insurance schemes.

Buy only Annual (Yearly) Renewable Term Insurance. Don't buy any other kind of term insurance, especially deposit term insurance (a higher first year premium), no matter how good the agent makes it sound. Annual Renewable Term (ART) premiums increase each year as you get older. If you shop around, you can buy $100,000 policies for less than $200 at age 30, less than $300 at age 40 and less than $600 at age 50.

Don't buy any life insurance with cash values. It's too hard to tell good cash value policies from bad ones, and you lose too much money if you don't hold the policy for twenty years. This includes much-touted "universal life"; it isn't as good as it sounds.

Those over 55 who want life insurance in force at their deaths in their seventies or eighties will find ART won't work well. Unless you are supporting dependents, however, NICO does not recommend carrying life insurance protection beyond age 65 or 70.

Don't buy Credit Life Insurance to pay off your loan when you die. It is way over-priced in most states (New York is the major exception), and it is always too expensive if you are under age 45 because rates do not vary by age. Also, do not be coerced into buying

credit life; you do not have to buy it to get a loan approved.

Don't buy Mail Order Life Insurance, unless you compare its price to Annual Renewable Term, and find it cheaper.

Don't let an agent talk you into dropping an old policy if it pays dividends. You can make your old policy a lot more valuable if you borrow out any cash value and reinvest at higher returns.

If you are retired and feel that you don't need life insurance, consider cashing in your policy and investing the proceeds in money market funds, bank certificates of deposit, or other safe, higher yielding investments.

If you want to convert your policy to an annuity, be sure to see what other companies' annuities pay before leaving the proceeds with your own insurance company. Compre monthly incomes with those available from safe investments.

Want to learn more about life insurance? NICO offers a sixty-four page guide for $5, including postage and handling. It explains life insurance, names companies that sell low cost ART policies and the prices you should pay, and gives guidelines on whether to trade in your old policy on a new one.

Health Insurance

IF YOU'RE NOT ON MEDICARE:

Most persons are covered at work. Those not so fortunate have a major problem in getting adequate medical insurance at a reasonable price. Good coverage can cost $500-$1,000 a year for an individual, and from $1,000-$2,000 for a family; even then, the policy may have a deductible and require you to pay some portion (often 20%) of remaining expenses. If you have a policy costing much less than this, you may have poor coverage; consider dropping it and following these suggestions:

Join a Health Maintenance Organization (HMO). You'll get all the coverage you need without deductibles and coinsurance.

Blue Cross/Blue Shield is the best buy for the average person who doesn't join an HMO. These policies usually return 85%-90% of premiums paid in claims.

Comprehensive major medical policies from major life insurance companies are next best; they return about 60¢ to 65¢ per $1 of premiums. For younger people, and for those willing to take fairly large deductibles (that Blue Cross/Blue Shield may not offer), such policies may be the best choice.

If you can't afford one of these alternatives, perhaps you could qualify for Medicaid (health insurance for low-income persons); check this out with the local social service agency in your state.

In general, we think you'll do better to avoid these kinds of policies:

Mail order health insurance policies, including offers to buy "group" health insurance under some sponsorship, such as a fraternity or an auto club (commissions or other payments to the sponsor often increase your rates).

Student accident insurance offered by schools and colleges, even if sickness is covered too. Benefits often don't cover serious illnesses adequately.

Cancer insurance. A Congressional Subcommittee called it a "rip-off."

Nursing home coverage. A few policies cover such care, but none covers extended stays for older persons (custodial care). What is covered often sounds better than it is.

We hate to say so, but if you can't afford good health insurance, you may be better off not buying any policy.

IF YOU'RE ON MEDICARE:

There is great irony in the fact that although the United States has national health insurance for the aged, its older citizens are preyed upon by sellers of Medicare supplements to fill the gaps in Medicare. And Medicare's gaps are hard to understand, so elderly buyers never know how much supplementary coverage is enough.

Everyone whose coverage at work is not extended upon retirement to supplement Medicare should buy the best Blue Cross/Blue Shield Medicare supplement available. Usually, those 65 and over will be able to become Blue Cross/Blue Shield subscribers without evidence of insurability during annual "open enrollment" periods. For most people, we think this is enough coverage. You are probably better off resisting the temptation to buy

one or more other policies. Instead, take the money you would otherwise spend and bank it. If you feel you do need more insurance, try one of the senior citizen's organizations. Their policies tend to offer a reasonably good value, although not as good as Blue Cross/Blue Shield. Be warned that some of these organizations tend to offer a confusing array of policies that promote duplicate and overlapping coverage.

DISABILITY INCOME INSURANCE

We think too much attention is paid to life insurance and too little to disability income insurance, which provides a monthly income to those who are disabled for extended periods. Consider this: if you're disabled you're still a financial burden to your family, but if you're dead, you're not.

Disability income insurance is usually offered by quality companies and is quite competitive. We recommend the kind of coverage that pays benefits until age 65 and, to keep premiums low, begins to pay those benefits only after 90 days or 180 days of disability. Companies are not anxious to sell you more coverage than you need, for fear of encouraging claims, so you can usually rely on your agent for guidance on how much to buy. He or she will take into account Social Security disability benefits.

As with other kinds of insurance, you must compare rates to be sure of getting a good buy.

POLICIES YOU DON'T NEED

Don't buy travel insurance at the airport. You're not worth more dead in a statistically unlikely plane crash. Use your insurance dollars wisely by buying more ART if you're underinsured. The rates for air travel insurance represent very poor value.

Don't buy insurance at the car rental counter. It usually costs $5 a day, which is about $1,800 a year, for $500 worth of protection. Many don't realize all you get is coverage of the $500 deductible in the rental car company's policy. And, if the accident isn't your fault, you won't have to pay anything.

Don't buy mugger's insurance. This new gimmick covers you only if you die or are injured in a mugging. It probably duplicates or overlaps coverage you already have. And the rates are excessive. Buy comprehensive insurance coverage, not narrow slices designed to play on fear.

TROUBLE WITH A CLAIM?

NICO isn't set up to handle most individual claim settlement problems. If you've been patient with your agent or company, contact your state insurance department. Check directory assistance for a toll-free number. If you write, give the name of your company and your policy number; don't send your policy.

STATE INSURANCE DEPARTMENTS
Write to Insurance Commissioner:

AL, Administrative Bldg., Montgomery, AL 36104
AK, Pouch D, Juneau, AK 99811
AZ, 1601 West Jefferson, Phoenix, AZ 85007
AR, 400-18 University Tower, Little Rock, AR 72204
CA, 100 Van Ness Ave., Los Angeles, CA 94102
CO, State Office Bldg., #106, Denver, CO 80203
CT, 425 State Office Bldg., Hartford, CT 06115
DE, 21, The Green, Dover, DE 19901
DC, 614 H St., NW #512, Washington, DC 20001
FL, Capitol Bldg, Tallahassee, FL 32301
GA, State Capitol, Rm. 238, Atlanta, GA 30334
GUAM, P.O. Box 2796, Agana, Guam 96910
HI, Box 3614, Honolulu, HI 96811
ID, 700 West State St., Boise, ID 83720
IL, 160 North LaSalle St. #1600, Chicago, IL 60601
IN, State Office Bldg. #509, Indianapolis, IN 46204
IA, Lucas State Office Bldg., Des Moines, IA 50319
KS, State House, Topeka, KS 66612
KY, 151 Elkhorn Court, Frankfort, KY 40601
LA, Box 44214, Capitol Section, Baton Rouge, LA 70804
ME, Dept. of Business Regulation, Augusta, ME 04300
MD, One South Calvert St., Baltimore, MD 20201
MA, 100 Cambridge St., Boston, MA 02202
MI, P.O. Box 30220, Lansing, MI 48909
MN, Metro Square Bldg., St. Paul, MN 55101
MS, P.O. Box 79, Jackson, MS 39205
MO, P.O. Box 690, Jefferson City, MO 65101
MT, P.O. Box 4009, Helena, MT 59601
NE, 301 Centennial Mall South, Lincoln, NE 68509
NV, Nye Building, Carson City, NV 89710
NH, 169 Manchester St., Concord, NH 03301
NJ, 210 East State St., Trenton, NJ 08625
NM, State Capitol, PO 1269, Santa Fe, NM 87501
NY, 2 World Trade Center, New York, NY 10047
NC, P.O. Box 26387, Raleigh, NC 27611
ND, Capitol Bldg, 5th Floor, Bismarck, ND 58501
OH, 2100 Stella Court, Columbus, OH 43215
OK, 408 Will Rogers Bldg., Oklahoma City, OK 73105
OR, 158 12th Street, NE, Salem, OR 97310
PA, Strawberry Square, 13th Floor, Harrisburg, PA 17120
PR, Box 3508, Old San Juan Station, San Juan, PR 00904
RI, 100 North Main Street, Providence, RI 20903
SC, 2711 Middleburg Drive, Columbia, SC 29204
SD, State of South Dakota, Pierre, SD 57501
TN, State Office Bldg., Room 114, Nashville, TN 37219
TX, 1110 San Jacinto Blvd., Austin, TX 78786
UT, 326 South 5th East, Salt Lake City, UT 84102
VT, State of Vermont, Montpelier, VT 05602
VA, 700 Blanton Bldg., Richmond, VA 23209
VI, P.O. Box 450, St. Thomas, Virgin Islands 00801
WA, Insurance Bldg., Olympia, WA 98504
WV, 1800 Washington St. East, Charleston, WV 25305
WI, 123 Washington Ave., Madison, WI 53702
WY, 2424 Pioneer, Cheyenne, WY 82002

NICO'S MAJOR GOALS

—Accident-free and claim-free drivers should get all the auto insurance they need at standard rates from the companies they choose.

—Auto insurance rates ought to depend more on driving records and less on where you live. Age, sex and marital status rating variables should be abolished.

—Auto insurance rates can be lowered in most states if companies are required to account for the investment returns they derive from policyholder premiums.

—Legislation should be enacted to eliminate those gaps in Medicare that confuse the elderly. An out-patient prescription drug benefit is needed. States should do much more to regulate the sale of Medicare supplements.

—Life insurance companies should be required to tell policyholders what rates of return they pay on the savings portions of cash value policies. Industrial life insurance should be abolished.

—Consumers must be represented at insurance department rate hearings and before legislators. Insurers spend tens of millions of dollars to lobby; indeed, they are allowed to increase your premiums to get this money. The consumer side is not heard. It must be!

A tax-deductible membership in NICO is $25 yearly. New members receive our life insurance guide without charge. You are reminded that beginning in 1982, contributions to non-profit organizations are deductible from income for Federal tax purposes even if you don't itemize your deductions.

Legal Services Corporation Poverty Guidelines

establishing maximum income levels equivalent to 125 percent of the

Official Poverty Threshold: (effective July 12, 1982)

Size of family unit	Maximum income
1	$5,850
2	7,775
3	9,700
4	11,625
5	13,550
6	15,475

for family units with more than six members add $1,925 for each person

for Alaska

1	7,338
2	9,738
3	12,138
4	14,538
5	16,933
6	19,338

for family units with more than six members add $2,400 for each person

for Hawaii

1	6,738
2	8,950
3	11,163
4	13,375
5	15,588
6	17,800

for family units with more than six members add $2,213 for each person

BOSTON

States of Connecticut, Maine, Massachusetts, New Hampshire, Rhode Island, and Vermont

Paul Newman, Director
Mary Connolly, Deputy Director
Legal Services Corporation
Boston Regional Office
84 State Street, Room 520
Boston, MA 02109

Telephone: (617) 223-0230
FTS: 8-223-0230

NEW YORK

State of New York and also Puerto Rico and the Virgin Islands

Salvador Tio, Director
Harold Brooks, Deputy Director
Legal Services Corporation
New York Regional Office
120 Broadway, Suite 1034
New York, NY 10005

Telephone: (212) 264-4432
FTS: 8-264-4432

PHILADELPHIA

States of Delaware, Maryland, Pennsylvania and New Jersey and also the District of Columbia

Marttie L. Thompson, Director
Legal Services Corporation
Philadelphia Regional Office
101 North 33rd Street, Suite 404
Philadelphia, PA 19104

Telephone: (215) 596-6104
FTS: 8-596-6104

NORTHERN VIRGINIA

States of Michigan, Ohio, Virginia and West Virginia

Marjorie McDiarmid, Director
Edward McGuire, Deputy Director
Legal Services Corporation
Northern Virginia Regional Office
1730 North Lynn Street, Suite 600
Arlington, VA 22209

Telephone: (703) 235-2109
FTS: 8-235-2109

CHICAGO

States of Illinois, Indiana, Iowa, Kansas, Minnesota, Missouri, Nebraska, North Dakota, South Dakota, and Wisconsin

JoAnn Raphael, Director
Legal Services Corporation
Chicago Regional Office
6 North Michigan Avenue
Suite 900
Chicago, IL 60602

Telephone: (312) 353-0350
FTS: 8-353-0350

ATLANTA

States of Alabama, Arkansas, Florida, Georgia, Kentucky, Louisiana, Mississippi, North Carolina, South Carolina, and Tennessee

Victor Geminiani, Director
Jacquie Mitchell, Deputy Director
Legal Services Corporation
Atlanta Regional Office
615 Peachtree Street, NE, 9th Floor
Atlanta, GA 30308

Telephone: (404) 881-3049
FTS: 8-257-3049

DENVER

States of Arizona, Colorado, New Mexico, Oklahoma, Texas, Utah and Indian Programs

David Gilbert, Director
Art Lucero, Deputy Director
Legal Services Corporation
Denver Regional Office
1726 Champa Street, Suite 500
Denver, CO 80202

Telephone: (303) 837-5981
FTS: 8-327-5981

SAN FRANCISCO

John Hedges, Director
Legal Services Corporation
San Francisco Regional Office
177 Post Street, Suite 890
San Francisco, CA 94108

Telephone: (415) 556-6952
FTS: 8-556-6952

SEATTLE

States of Alaska, Hawaii, Idaho, Montana, Oregon, Washington, Wyoming and including Micronesia and Guam

William Simons, Director
Legal Services Corporation
Seattle Regional Office
506 Second Avenue
Seattle, WA 98104

Telephone: (206) 442-0593
FTS: 8-399-0593

FOOD

About Labels on Meats and Poultry Products
U.S. Department of Agriculture/
Food Safety and Quality Service
3 pages, 1979, No. FSQS-20
        USDA regulations and labels

Labeling of Fats and Oils
U.S. Depatment of Health, Education and Welfare/
Food and Drug Administration
Fact Sheet, 1978 No. 78-2078

A Consumer's Guide to Food Labels
ULSL Department of Health, Education and Welfare/
Food and Drug Administration
Fact Sheet, 1977, No. 77-2083

Nutrition Labeling--Terms You Should Know
U.S. Department of Health, Education and Welfare/
Food and Drug Administration
Fact Sheet, 1980, No. 80-2012

A New Supermarket Ripoff: Packages Without Prices
United Auto Workers Consumer Affairs Department
        Fact sheet on the new consumer price stripes,
        called Universal Product Code (UPC).

Symbols of Food Labels
U.S. Department of Health, Education and Welfare/
Food and Drug Administration
Fact sheet, 1980, No. 80-2021

How to Buy Food
U.S. Department of Agriculture
31 pages, 1971, Stock No. 0100-2512

Facts on Shopping for Food
Better Business Bureau
15 pages, 1978, No. 03235
        The Do's and Don'ts when shopping for food.

Standards for Meat and Poultry Products: A Consumer Reference List
U.S. Department of Agriculture/
Food Safety and Quality Service
8 pages, 1977

Consumers' Guide to Meat
Giant Foods
25 pages, 1979

How to Use USDA Grades in Buying Foods
U.S. Department of Agriculture
15 pages, 1977 Bulletin No. 196

Tips on Buying a Home
Better Business Bureau
13 pages, 1979, No. 24-154

Wise Home Buying
U.S. Department of Housing and Urban Development
28 pages, 1978, HUD-401

Before Buying Land...Get the Facts
U.S. Department of Housing and Urban Development
Pamphlet, 1978, HUD-183-1 (8)

What You Should Know Before You Buy a Home
U.S. League of Savings Associations
25 pages, 1971

Home Buyer's Vocabulary
U.S. Department of Housing and Urban Development
13 pages, 1978. HUD-383-H (4)
    Useful for understanding words and terms used in real estate
    transactions.

Wise Rental Practices
U.S. Department of Housing and Urban Development
24 pages, 1977, HUD-479-NYACP

Your Guide to a Savings and Loan Mortgage
ULSL League of Savings Associations
14 pages, 1978

Home Ownership Loans
ULSL Department of Agriculture/Farmers Home Administration
Pamphlet, 1976, Aid No. 977
    The FHA provides loans in rural areas to finance homes

Home Improvement Loans and Repair Loans and Grants
U.S. Department of Agriculture/Farmers Home Administration
Pamphlet, 1977, Program Aid No. 1184
    A rural homeowner whose house needs repair may be eligible
    for a loan and/or grant from the Farmers Home Administration

Self-Helf Housing Loans
U.S. Department of Agriculture/Farmers Home Administration
Pamphlet, 1975, revised in 1976

Home Improvement
COnsumer Affairs Office for the City of New York
Pamphlet, 1975

Fixing Up Your Home--What to Do and How to Finance It
U.S. Department of Housing and Urban Development
Pamphlet, 1978, HUD 52-H(8)

Tips on Home Improvement
Better Business Bureau
Pamphlet, 1978, No. 02205

How to Shop for Health Insurance
Consumer Information Center
13 pages, 1978, 582G

Your Right To Question Your Medical Insurance Payment
U.S. Department of Health, Education and Welfare/
Social Security Administration
8 pages, 1977, HEW publication #: (SSA) 77-10083

Facts About Health Insurance
Better Business Bureau
23 pages, 1972 publication #: 03238
  Facts about the different types of health insurance and
  information to help you decide which is right for your needs.

Your Right to Question the Decision on Your Hospital Insurance Claim
U.S. Department of Health, Education and Welfare/
Social Security Administration
5 pages, 1977, HEW Publication #: (SSA) 77-10085
  The steps to take when questioning your Medicare hospital
  insurance claim.

Cosmetics--We Want You to Know What we Know
U.S. Department of Health, Education and Welfare/
Food and Drug Administration
4 pages, 1974, DHEW publication #: (FDA) 74-5004

Hair Dyes--A Look at Safety and Regulation
U.S. Department of Health, Education and Welfare/
Food and Drug Administration
4 pages, 1978, HEW publication #: (FDA) 78-5010

The Hair Dye Dilemma
Environmental Defense Fund
Pamphlet, 1978

And Now a Work About Your Shampoo
U.S. Department of Health, Education and Welfare/
Food and Drug Administration
4 pages, 1978, HEW publication #: (FDA) 76-5002

Note: HEW publications now available from the U.S. Department of
   Health and Human Services (HHS).

Tips on Sales Contracts
Better Business Bureau
Pamphlet, 1977, No. 02208

Shopping for Advertised Specials
Federal Trade Commission
4 pages
>   Lists hints for wise shoppers and rights consumers have
>   when purchasing advertised goods.

Sales Tactics
California State Department of Consumer Affairs
16 pages, 1978 (also in Spanish)
>   How to heal with misleading advertising, door-to-door
>   sales and shopping by mail.

Bait and Switch
Federal Trade Commission
Pamphlet
>   How to recognize and protect against "bait and switch"
>   advertising.

Tips on Refunds and Exchanges
Better Business Bureau
Pamphlet, 1974, No. 02207

Tips on Guarantees and Warranties
Better Business Bureau
Fact sheet, 1972, No. 01248

Complaint Referral Guide
United Auto Workers Consumer Affairs Department
4 pages
>   What to do with consumer problems--a comprehensive guide.

If You Use a Credit Card
Federal Reserve System
Pamphlet, 1979
>   Information on credit card costs, unsolicited credit cards
>   and what to do if your credit card is lost or stolen.

Minimizing Mail Order Hassles
United Auto Workers Consumer Affairs Department
Fact Sheet

Tips on Life Insurance
Better Business Bureau
9 pages, 1979, No. 24-155

*You may also want to read Mimi Brien's new book, Moneywise, a guide to
financial responsibility, knowledgeable investing and survival techniques
written primarily for women. The book, published by Bantam Books (1982)
is available in paperback at your local bookstore.